Reproductive Health and Maternal Sacrifice

Pam Lowe

Reproductive Health and Maternal Sacrifice

Women, Choice and Responsibility

Pam Lowe
School of Languages and Social Sciences
Aston University
Birmingham, United Kingdom

ISBN 978-1-137-47292-2   ISBN 978-1-137-47293-9   (eBook)
DOI 10.1057/978-1-137-47293-9

Library of Congress Control Number: 2016944996

Cover illustration: © Tetra Images / Alamy Stock Photo

Printed on acid-free paper

This Palgrave Macmillan imprint is published by Springer Nature
The registered company is Macmillan Publishers Ltd. London

Acknowledgements

I am not very clear on when the idea for this book began, and hence it is difficult to acknowledge everyone who has played a part in its conception. I do know that without the numerous feminist friends and colleagues that I have debated and discussed things with over the years it would never have been written. I first began thinking and writing on reproductive health as a postgraduate student, and the many pleasurable evenings spent in Queensland Avenue with Gilma Madrid, Marianna Tortell, Shraddha Chigateri, Antje Lindenmeyer, and so many others gave me both intellectual and emotional support as a fledgling academic. Without the support of a strong feminist network at the beginning, I would not have come this far.

I have also been lucky enough to work with many other brilliant women who have also contributed to my thinking. Geraldine Brady and I met on the first day of our undergraduate degrees and our ongoing friendship has led to a number of academic collaborations. I have benefited enormously from her friendship and insight. Ellie Lee and Jan Macvarish are both inspiring to work with and excellent friends. The British Sociological Society Human Reproductive Study Group and the Centre for Parenting Culture Studies have supplied helpful opportunities over the years for me to present my work and receive excellent comments. My friends and colleagues at Aston University have also been an important source of friendship and support, especially Amanda Beattie, Chrissie Rogers, Demelza

Jones, Elaena Wells, Katie Tonkiss, Katy Pilcher, Karen West, and Sarah Page. Graeme Hayes' pedantry has inspired me to try to write better. I would also like to thank my students who over many years have taught me much and challenged me to explain things better. I hope that they will be pleased with this book. I also need to thank my friends at Coventry Feminists, who have been willing to listen and question my ideas.

I also have a debt to many people outside higher education for reminding me that there is life outside the library. Rebecca Stewart has provided me with cups of tea and glasses of wine in equal measure, and also with proofreading assistance. Andrea Wooley, Lynne Haste, and others at SWISH, THT Coventry, have become great friends and given me the privilege of volunteering with this important service. Berni Blunden, Beverley Foster, and Odette Chittem have also been there from the beginning. This book is dedicated to Chris, Tom, and Jamie. Although they are now men and no longer need me, I hope my mothering has been more of a help than a hindrance in their lives.

Contents

List of Abbreviations

BFI	Baby Friendly Initiative
BMA	British Medical Association
CMR	Caesarean by maternal request
EHC	Emergency hormonal contraception
FAS	Foetal Alcohol Syndrome
FASD	Foetal Alcohol Spectrum Disorder
HIV/AIDS	Human Immunodeficiency Virus Infection/Acquired Immune Deficiency Syndrome
HFEA	Human Fertilisation and Embryology Authority
ICSI	Intra-cytoplasmic sperm injection
IUD	Intrauterine device
IUI	Intrauterine insemination
IVF	In vitro fertilization
LARC	Long-acting reversible contraception
NHS	National Health Service
NICE	National Institute for Health and Care Excellence
NOFAS	National Organization on Fetal Alcohol Syndrome
PAS	Post-abortion syndrome
PGD	Preimplantation genetic diagnosis
PTSD	Post-traumatic stress disorder
RCOG	Royal College of Obstetricians and Gynaecologists
TRAP	Targeted Regulation of Abortion Providers

UK	United Kingdom
UNICEF	United Nations Children's Fund
US	United States
WHO	World Health Organization

1

Introduction

Advances in medical technology in conjunction with established legal rights mean that women in the 'developed' world should have an unprecedented ability to control their fertility. From reliable contraception and legal abortions to techniques such as in-vitro fertilization (IVF) and advanced health services providing safer childbirth, women are seemingly given a vast array of choices as to whether, when, and how to have children. This is often considered to be a significant contribution to gender equality, ensuring that women can fulfil their potential within the non-domestic sphere. Yet this optimistic picture often overlooks the ways in which normative ideas about women's role as mothers operate to constrain their choices. Whilst there have been significant legal and policy gains, in practice women are still expected to make the 'right' choices concerning reproduction, and discourses around 'good motherhood' produce a context in which women are nominally allowed to choose, but the 'wrong' choices can be sanctioned in different ways, from public condemnation to the removal of their children.

These issues can be illustrated by three examples that came to public attention as I was finishing this book. In Ireland, as part of a broader safe food campaign, there was a call for women at risk of pregnancy to take a

© The Editor(s) (if applicable) and The Author(s) 2016
P. Lowe, *Reproductive Health and Maternal Sacrifice*,
DOI 10.1057/978-1-137-47293-9_1

folic acid supplement in case they became pregnant (Safefood 2015). Given that no contraception is 100 % effective, this was relevant to nearly all pre-menopausal heterosexually active women. The campaign argued that this was good practice for all women as, if and when they became pregnant, they would have taken steps to reduce the risk of neural tube anomalies. The inferences in this campaign were not just that all women are likely to want children in the future but also that women should act as if they are pregnant regardless of their current conception intentions. In contrast to this call to treat all women as if they were permanently pregnant, in New Zealand, a group called for the routine prescription of long-acting contraceptives (LARCs) to young women (Radio New Zealand 2015). Arguing that teenage pregnancies are a problem, they suggest that a vaccination style programme would be the most effective policy to prevent young pregnancies. The assumption here is that (presumed heterosexual) young women are less likely to be responsible than older women regarding contraception and that there is clearly a 'right' age for pregnancy at which point the young women would no longer be routinely offered this service. Moreover, preventing pregnancy should be young women's primary responsibility regardless of the embodied implications such as any side effects even when they are not sexually active. Issues of irresponsible motherhood, in which 'bad' mothers cannot be trusted to make appropriate decisions, are illustrated further in the USA where a guardian *ad litem* was appointed to represent the foetus of a first-trimester pregnant prisoner who was seeking permission to leave the prison to access an abortion (Huffington Post 2015). Here the positioning of the woman as 'bad' meant that she lost the right to bodily autonomy. The provision by the state for legal representation for foetuses, when women are not necessarily afforded the same legal access, is a clear example of the presumption that the welfare of any foetus must come first. Regardless of the outcomes in each of these cases, it is clear that women are asked to make specific reproductive decisions and conform to particular reproductive norms regardless of their individual preferences or current position. Often these choices are about maximising foetal or child welfare. Motherhood norms dominate ideas about what women should do with their bodies and failure to comply can result in censure or sanctions.

This book will argue that the idea of maternal sacrifice is central to the ways in which normative ideas about motherhood are constructed and understood. At its heart, maternal sacrifice is the notion that 'proper' women put the welfare of children, whether born, *in utero,* or not yet conceived, over and above any choices and/or desires of their own. The idea of maternal sacrifice acts as a powerful signifier in judging women's behaviour. It is valorized in cases such as when women with cancer forgo treatment to save a risk to their developing foetus, and it is believed absent in female substance users whose 'selfish' desire for children means they are born in problematic circumstances. It is also embedded in the idea that women (not men) are both bearers *and* carers for children. Thus raising babies is still usually considered predominately a role for women.

The concept of 'good motherhood' has always been intertwined with ideas about maternal sacrifice. Although what good motherhood consists of may change over time, the existence of a standard that should be adhered to has a long history. Good motherhood is often aligned with prevailing ideas of white, heterosexual, middle-class families, particularly in family policy. Other communities or groups may have different ideas about what constitutes good mothering and these can be used to support individual reproductive practices where they are in conflict with dominant norms. However, those failing to conform to the dominant expectations may be sanctioned or even lose their children under child protection policies. As I will explore in this book, although the idea of maternal sacrifice is often embedded in ideas about good motherhood, it is not necessarily reducible to this. Good motherhood is the prevailing standard, an ideal against which both mothers and non-mothers are judged. Although it is often exacting and exhausting and clearly beyond the reach of many, the changing components of good motherhood illustrate that it can be successfully changed. So, for example, as Hays (1996) has shown, the intensification of motherhood saw a new emphasis on investing physically, emotionally, and financially in children in contrast to earlier emphasis on keeping children fed, clean, warm, and safe. Both of these models contain ideas about women making appropriate sacrifices, although what these are alters over time. Here in contrast to other analyses of motherhood, I want to foreground the idea of sacrifice and trace it though different stages of reproduction. Ideas about maternal sacrifice seem to remain constant even as other ideas about motherhood change, which suggests it is fundamentally important to the way that women are judged.

That maternal sacrifice is a constant feature of motherhood is not in doubt. It is embedded into religious texts, mythologies, and stories. For example, the biblical story of the judgement of Solomon is based on the idea that a real mother would save the life of her child even if it meant another woman would care for them. Solomon's wisdom is that he understands that he can find the real mother by threatening to divide a child in two. In Greek myths, Demeter, the harvest goddess, is willing to sacrifice the world by bringing famine and unending winter until her abducted daughter Persephone is returned. Roman mythology tells stories of the devotion of Venus, who tries to prevent her son Cupid from reuniting with his wife Psyche after she injures him. These examples illustrate the ways in which good mothers will do anything to ensure the welfare of their children, making personal sacrifices or even sacrificing others. Indeed mothers that fail in their attempts to protect their children are often depicted as revengeful, even destroying those responsible for their deaths. For example, in the legends of the Grecian/Trojan war, Hecuba kills and maims those she holds responsible for her children's deaths. Shakespeare revives this motif in *Titus Andronicus*, with the bereaved mother Tamora actually appearing as Revenge in the play (Tassi 2011). Moreover, the twin sides of motherhood, virtuous or monstrous, also play out in fairy stories such as *Cinderella and Snow White*, in the contrast between dead (and therefore presumed faultless) mothers and evil stepmothers.

This rich literary history illustrates how good mothers are those who are selfless and make sacrifices in contrast with the 'other' mother who does not. Moreover the gendering of behaviour, with women being defensive rather than offensive, emotional rather than rational, and natural rather than cultural, feeds into both passive and active forms of maternal sacrifice. Indeed, it could be argued that defending their children is potentially the only aggressive act that is culturally sanctioned for women. The naturalized assumption is that women should alter or give up all or part of their lives, even if it is to their detriment. The rights of children are clearly placed above those of women, and this is seen as natural behaviour. Despite longstanding critiques, this seems to have barely changed today.

Natural or Unnatural Mothers

The debates about women's responsibility and the choices they should make can be traced back historically. An example of this was the argument made in 1900 by Charlotte Perkins Gilman in favour of the unnatural mother. It is useful to consider this example as it illustrates the continuity in some of the discussions present today. Gilman (1900/2003) argued that although motherhood was obviously a natural state in which women offered care and protection of children, maternal instinct was not enough to ensure children would be raised to their full potential. She suggested that what was needed were unnatural mothers, women who did not rely on instinct but through education and reason could identify the best way of raising children. If they were not able to provide this care themselves, they would place their children in a 'baby-garden' during the day to ensure the children received the best of care whilst the mothers went to work. The 'baby-gardens' would be staffed by those trained and suited to the important work of raising children. Gilman suggests that:

> The "natural" mother, of course, believes that her own care of her own child is better than any one's else. She can give no proof of this (…). She simply thinks she is the best educator because she is a "mother" (…). The unnatural mother, who is possessed of enough intelligence and knowledge to recognise her own deficiencies, gladly intrusts her children to superior care for part of the time, and constantly learns by it herself. (1900/2003: 273–274)

A central thrust to Gilman's (1900/2003) argument is the idea that whilst it is clear that women have reproductive bodies and that women 'naturally' want to care for their children, successful mothering needs to go beyond instinct. Women should make sacrifices, giving up their desire to care for their child themselves and instead making the better choice in finding suitable educators. Ensuring the best outcomes for children is, she argues, a prime responsibility of mothers.

This critique illustrates both the long history of debates about motherhood and the ways in which choice and responsibility are interwoven within them. For Gilman (1900/2003), the responsibility for the care of children was firmly located with women, but that did not mean that mothers should always perform all the caring work for their children. Whilst she believed that women had a maternal instinct, she argued that this was the equivalent to other animals that raised their young, and thus should no longer be considered a significant factor for humans. In contrast, the unnatural mother was educated sufficiently to understand this, and if she did not have the right skills to give them the best upbringing, she should find an alternative that could provide the best care. In other words, mothers should make responsible, informed choices, ensuring that they select the best people and places to provide care based on their education and knowledge of raising children. The work of motherhood is thus firmly located as a cultural rather than biological function. Although at the time arguing for daycare and mothers' employment was a potentially radical stance, this position did nothing to challenge the responsibility of women to exercise choice in the best interests of children. It was not to benefit women that daycare should be provided, but to maximize children's wellbeing and education regardless of the preferences of their mothers. Indeed, she argued that women with the right skills and education to raise children should be those providing the care in the 'baby-gardens' with their own children attending as well. Gilman's writings illustrate the long-established critique that biological ability has been used to justify women's position as natural carers for children. It identified the work of motherhood as cultural and needing to be situated within current understandings of a progressive society. It also illustrates how the ideas of choice, responsibility and sacrifice are used to construct particular understandings of good motherhood, and these are still with us today.

Reproductive Bodies

Within reproductive health, ideas about choice, responsibility and sacrifice are embodied. The fact that women are the people who can grow children[1] is clearly an important element in the ways in which ideas about

---

[1] Although some transgender people who do not identify as women may become pregnant, this has little impact on the way that women and pregnancy is conceptualized.

natural motherhood and womanhood are intertwined. Yet claims made about motherhood clearly go far beyond any biological basis. Whilst the idea of the natural, maternal instinct or any other biological framing suggests that the issue under discussion is not culturally mutable, our attitudes to bearing and childraising are constructed socially. Gilman (1900/2003) pointed out that whilst our ancient forebears would have carried their children, it was natural in modern society to use a pram. Whilst this distinction is useful, she obviously did not foresee the twenty-first century arrival of advocates for 'baby-wearing', to return child transportation to its earlier natural state. This example is useful in illustrating the complexity of the issues and the ways in which nature can be drawn on to support particular ideas. As Franklin et al. (2000) argue, nature can be repeatedly reinvented in terms of understandings of the being and doing of bodies.

Even understandings or practices that use science and/or medicine as their primary frame of reference are not immune to using the rhetoric of choice to mean an embodied responsibility. In 2013, the Royal College of Obstetricians and Gynaecologists (RCOG) in the UK published an evidence summary on potential but unproven chemical risks during pregnancy. The issues that they highlighted were wide-ranging and, if adopted, would significantly restrict women's lives. They included predominately eating fresh food, avoiding plastic food containers, minimising the use of personal grooming products such as shower gel and cosmetics, not buying new household furniture and not riding in new cars (RCOG 2013). The report suggested that although it was unlikely that any of the exposures were harmful, as the risks were unknown, it was important for women to be told so they could make 'informed choices' (RCOG 2013). The emphasis on making the right choices clearly shifts the responsibility of risk from the producer of products to women as consumers. Ostensibly, the choice offered here is to more or less opt out of everyday living whilst pregnant or accept responsibility for any adverse impact on a developing foetus. Their justification, that women need to know there are unknown risks, is based on a social understanding that ideas of potential harm are more important than scientific evidence. As will be illustrated later, the ways in which precautionary principles (the elimination of known and unknown risks) use the rhetoric of choice to discipline women is a common theme in reproductive health.

Hence, the relationship between biology and cultural understandings of reproduction is complex. Often ideas about nature and maternal instinct are used to give weight to arguments, yet this does not mean they are not really social understandings. The concept of maternal sacrifice will show that whilst the cultural expectations of women often make claims to biological ideas, their use is often contradictory. As I will argue later, supporters of natural childbirth use biological claims as the basis of their understanding, yet it is clear that these are specific cultural practices rather than just a natural phenomenon. The idea of the 'biological clock' suggests that women have a natural urge to become mothers, yet this is also often linked to partnered heterosexuality. This shows how ideas are culturally based rather than just a biological imperative. I would argue that it is not possible to consider any area of reproduction in purely biological terms. Whilst women clearly have reproductive functions, all our understandings of them are constructed socially.

Outline of This Book

This book is focused on women and the ways in which the 'choices' available to them are framed around the ideas of good motherhood and maternal sacrifice. It does not consider men or fatherhood at all. Due to the differences in both biology and the cultural norms surrounding fatherhood, men are positioned very differently to women in the area of reproductive health. It would take another book to explore this in any depth. In many cases women will make reproductive decisions in conjunction with male partners, yet the implications of these decisions are clearly very different. Moreover, as I will argue later, as only women can become pregnant, in many areas of reproductive health gender equality can never be achieved. That is not to say that men should be excluded, but we need to ensure women's right to bodily autonomy is always upheld.

By problematizing the idea of maternal sacrifice, this book is not advocating that women should abandon or neglect children in ways that would seriously compromise their care. All the evidence suggests that the majority of women do care strongly about their actual or any future children. However, it will argue that women's ability to exercise choice over their fertility and childraising is compromised by normative ideas that only certain women in certain circumstances can be 'good' mothers, and that making sacrifices, regardless of any outcome, is the only way to ensure children's welfare. Moreover, it will show how the pervasiveness of this overall message seeps into all areas of reproductive health. It can be used to show why both young and older motherhood are seen as problematic as well as demonising to poorer women whose lack of financial security puts them outside this model of parenting. Whilst these ideas play out most in relation to acceptance, or critiques, of specific pregnancies, they also have a powerful hold on other areas such as ideas about respectable and unrespectable contraceptive users. It is only by understanding the complexity of the ideas of maternal sacrifice, and how it is mediated by issues such as social class, ethnicity and disability across the area of reproductive health, that the extent of its hold over women can be identified.

The literature in the field of reproductive health is vast, and it would be impossible here to cover it all comprehensively. This book seeks to weave together different examples to illustrate the links between the different areas of reproductive health and how this is a common issue in many different places. The examples chosen all come from the area often referred to as the West or developed world. I acknowledge the problematic use of these terms, and I am using them loosely to refer to nations that are generally wealthy and industrialized and have developed healthcare systems, although not necessarily universal access. Importantly, all the countries mentioned also have formal commitments to gender equality, although obviously the extent to which this is achieved will vary. To be clear, I am not arguing that the issues are the same in every place; there are important legal, policy and cultural differences that impact on the experiences of women's reproductive health in different places. Nevertheless, by looking at different places, we see some commonalities in the way that the issues are understood.

In a similar fashion, it is impossible in a book of this length to truly do justice to the complex ways in which social divisions such as social class, ethnicity, sexuality, disability and age are also implicated in ideas about good and bad motherhood. Whilst I do use examples of these throughout the book, there is not enough room to unpick their multifarious intersections. Ideas about good motherhood and maternal sacrifice are important frames that structure women's lives, however the impact that they have and the ability to accept or resist them are not universal but linked to women's social positioning. Within the dominant norms of good motherhood, there are clear ideas about who is recognized as such or encouraged to reproduce. Women outside of the dominant image of good motherhood are more likely to be seen as always or potentially bad mothers, and may be required to not have children at all.

The way that good motherhood, choice and responsibility frame women's reproductive lives is discussed in Chap. 2. It aims to develop a theoretical overview of some of the important concepts, which will be drawn on throughout the book. It will argue that these come together within a presumption of maternal sacrifice which means that women are always expected to come second to children, even if they have not actually been conceived. Drawing on and developing the concept of intensive motherhood, it will show how these ideas are influencing all areas of women's lives. It will show how, although the ability to become pregnant has always put constraints on women's lives, recent ideas about the vulnerability of the foetus/child have increased surveillance over women's bodies and behaviour. This emphasizes self-regulation as women are positioned as both producers and consumers who are solely responsible for their child's emotional and physical development. Understanding the frameworks of power relationships embedded in issues such as medicalization and heterosexuality are also important as they provide the context in which reproductive health is understood. This background chapter thus explores broad understandings of a gendered society, setting out how these issues contextualize perceptions as to who, how, and when women should make reproductive choices.

In Chap. 3, attention is shifted to contraception and abortion to illustrate how non-motherhood is also influenced by ideas of maternal sacrifice. The chapter focuses on the formal and informal regulation of contraception and abortion, and argues that ideas about good motherhood structure both the experiences of women and the attitudes of service providers within a dichotomy between 'responsible' and 'irresponsible' contraceptive users. It shows how ideas of maternal sacrifice structure understandings of when contraception should be used and the 'right' methods for different groups of women. For example, young women are encouraged to use long-acting methods that they cannot cease to use themselves. The chapter will argue that specific understandings of the 'problem' of young people's sexuality are shared among those who advocate contraception and those who promote abstinence. The emphasis on responsibility and judgements about fitness to parent structures different women's lives and also sets up the notions of abortion as a contraception failure. These ideas about responsibility can also be seen in the arguments of those who support and oppose abortion. Hence this chapter will show how ideas of maternal sacrifice, good motherhood, responsibility and choice need to be understood together in order to understand contemporary experiences of fertility control.

Chapter 4 focuses on the ways in which the presumption of maternal sacrifice within good motherhood shapes understandings of infertility, fertility treatments and pregnancy loss. It will begin by examining more deeply the association between motherhood and womanhood and the impact that it has on women without children. It will show how understandings of sacrifice can be demonstrated in experiences of infertility and fertility treatments. The emphasis on biomedical solutions not only disadvantages those without the ability to access treatment but can also impact the identity of women who become mothers through treatment. The rise of the surrogacy industry illuminates and adds complexity to the privileging of biological connectedness and women's position as natural mothers. Performing reproductive labour for others requires both sacrifice and distance to be performed properly. The chapter also explores how the development of reproductive technologies and greater emphasis on women's responsibility for the vulnerable foetus have changed experiences of reproductive loss.

This latter area is expanded on in Chap. 5. Here the focus is on how the emphasis on the welfare of the foetus means that women's status as autonomous citizens can become compromised. It will examine the experiences of being pregnant within a medicalized context in which every choice that a woman makes, from eating to prenatal testing, is taken as evidence of her willingness to perform idealized motherhood. In other words whilst nominally 'choices' can be made, there is only one 'right' option for responsible women to make. An important element within this chapter will be showing how women are expected to constrain their lives before they conceive. Moreover, given that fertility and fertility control are always uncertain, these discourses potentially constrain all heterosexually active women between puberty and menopause. Drawing on the debates around issues such as alcohol consumption, the chapter will illustrate the ways in which restrictions on women's lives can become policy despite an acknowledged lack of evidence of harm to the foetus. This focuses negative attention on visibly pregnant women who can be publically castigated for failing to comply with the increasingly tight rules. Thus, women are expected to make sacrifices even when there will be no significant outcomes to the welfare of the foetus/child.

The issue of childbirth will be explored in Chap. 6, with a focus on how specific forms of birth, whether 'natural' or 'medical', are culturally promoted within the maternal sacrifice framework. Again here, the similarities in the understanding of the issues and solutions will illustrate the ways in which women are expected to perform good motherhood and make specific sacrifices for the welfare of the developing foetus. Although as birth 'consumers' women are encouraged to exercise choice, often initially codified in a birth plan, issues of (foetal) safety are deployed by both sides to justify their position. Hence although choice is advocated by all, there is only one choice that should be made if women wish to be good mothers. The chapter will consider how women who are unable to live up to their internalized ideal of a 'good' birth may feel that they have failed, as ideas will situate how the 'right' birth contributes to or detracts from a woman's identity as a good mother. The chapter will further illustrate the issues of choice, responsibility and sacrifice through a focus on two different forms of birth, caesarean by maternal request (CMR) and unassisted birth (freebirth). Both are often condemned as examples of women failing to put the welfare of the foetus first, yet they are defended by those who choose them as the safest way to give birth. These debates illustrate how ideas about the wrong kind of sacrifice or not enough sacrifice are embedded in the different ideas about birth, and choice and responsibility are the mechanisms by which women are disciplined.

Chapter 7 turns to the issues of raising babies with a focus on the areas of infant feeding and early-years parenting policy, showing how both seek to present a normalized account of what good mothers do. It will begin by examining the ways in which breastfeeding is promoted as the only 'right' choice, regardless of the implications for women's lives. It will show how global evidence drawn from areas where women do not have access to clean water or safe formula milk is deployed to exaggerate the benefits of breastfeeding to women in developed countries. Women who choose not to breastfeed or cannot breastfeed thus appear as failing to make the 'right' choice and their position as good mothers becomes 'doubtful.' This emphasis on lactation as a moral choice illustrates how specific forms of maternal sacrifice are embedded within parenting policy. The chapter also examines the ways in which debates around early years childcare and child development, whilst nominally directed at parents, usually have more impact on women, as they predominantly position women as responsible for childrearing. In particular, the focus on brain development and emotional bonding as a key determinate for children's future lives acts to constrain women's choices over their work and social lives. Hence, whilst parenting could be gender neutral, ideas of maternal sacrifice as a normative structure dictate how and who should bring up children. This chapter also illustrates further the ways in which the socio-economic context structures women's ability to perform motherhood appropriately. It shows how even women separated from their children are affected by ideas of appropriate sacrifices to show that they are good mothers.

The final chapter looks more deeply at the concept of choice and the extent to which having a choice is an indicator of autonomy. It sets this in the context of reproductive health as an embodied-identity position and the idea of sacrifice as having both symbolic and transformative functions. It will also expand on how the idea of risk is used to affirm the positioning of the foetus/child as more important than women. It will argue that whilst the 'type' of women they need to be or the acts they need to perform to allow them to be positioned as good mothers change over time, the need to make sacrifices is a constant feature. The chapter also shows the importance of linking the different aspects of reproductive health together in order to fully understand how women are disciplined into making specific choices or having to defend their position if alternative options are chosen. It will also illustrate how the boundaries between preconception, pregnancy and postnatal periods are often blurred, despite the fact that these are obviously significantly different. Merging these in policy and practice reaffirms women's position as primarily mothers, whether or not they have children, and ensures that the naturalized assumption that women should sacrifice their lives for children continues.

That children need care, and women (and men) will want to support them as they develop, is without question. However, the disciplinary impact of the maternal sacrifice goes beyond this. It is used to discipline women into conforming to specific norms, reasserting their traditional form of womanhood. This has significant implications for women's autonomy. Women can resist or reject this disciplinary position when making reproductive decisions, but in doing so, they may be positioned as transgressing and/or need to justify their decisions. Depending on other factors, such as age, social class or ethnicity, compliance or resistance may have different implications. Making the right sacrifices can allow women who are positioned as potentially bad mothers to illustrate their worth, potentially keeping their children from being taken into state care. Options in reproductive health are often presented as natural, or as the most obvious thing to do, rather than as genuine choices. As this book will show, even in cases where there is an ideological divide, such as over abortion or birth, both sides are often using the same framing of sacrifice to support their position. This illustrates the importance of maternal sacrifice in structuring reproductive health choices and the limits that it places on women's autonomy.

References

Franklin, S., Lury, C., & Stacey, J. (2000). *Global nature, global culture.* London: Sage.

Gilman, C. P. (2003). *Concerning children—A reprint of the 1900 edition with an introduction by Michael S. Kimmel.* Oxford, England: Altamira Press.

Hays, S. (1996). *The cultural contradictions of motherhood.* New Haven, CT: Yale University Press.

Huffington Post. (2015). *Alabama moves to deny inmate parental rights so she can't have abortion.* Retrieved August 9, 2015, from http://www.huffingtonpost.com/entry/alabama-inmate-parental-rights-abortion_55b9056ee4b0224d88 34ca9b

Radio New Zealand. (2015). *Group wants contraceptive for all girls*. Retrieved May 9, 2015, from http://www.radionz.co.nz/news/national/277594/group-wants-contraceptive-for-all-girls

Royal College of Obstetricians and Gynaecologists. (2013). *Chemical exposures during pregnancy: Dealing with potential, but unproven risks to child health*. Scientific impact paper 37.

Safefood. (2015). *New safefood campaign stresses importance of women taking folic acid as a daily supplement*. Retrieved August 9, 2015, from http://www.safefood.eu/News/2015/New-safefood-campaign-stresses-importance-of-wome.aspx

Tassi, M. A. (2011). *Women and revenge in Shakespeare: Gender, genre, and ethics*. Selinsgrove, PA: Susquehanna University Press.

2

Responsible 'Choices' and Good Motherhood

Women in Western nations appear to have unprecedented control over their reproductive bodies. The development of health technologies such as effective contraceptives and IVF, together with laws and policy that support gender equality, means that women are in a better position now than they have been in history. However, at a formal level, laws, regulations and instructions from religions, the medical profession and nation states still set the parameters in which women are situated, and ideas about women's natural role and acceptable and unacceptable behaviour are reproduced through circulating discourses. As will be detailed in the later chapters, there are synergies, tensions and contradictions in the way that these play out in the different areas of reproductive health. However, taken together they all act to encourage women into making specific choices about reproduction that coalesce around the notion of maternal sacrifice.

As I briefly showed earlier, maternal sacrifice is a powerful idea that feeds from a specific understanding of the natural role of women as carers and nurturers whose only legitimate aggression is as the defenders of the young. This chapter will set out briefly how many of the structures in the organisation of Western societies allow this trope to continue. It

© The Editor(s) (if applicable) and The Author(s) 2016
P. Lowe, *Reproductive Health and Maternal Sacrifice*,
DOI 10.1057/978-1-137-47293-9_2

will begin by looking at the issue of choice and the ways in which the idea of choice promises reproductive rights yet disguises continuing constraints on women's lives. It will then look at the operation and function of notions of good motherhood and the vulnerable foetus/child and how the reproduction of these discourses operates to constrain women's lives, often through a focus on potential risks. These elements help to outline the dominant current framework in which most women are situated. In the second part of the chapter, I will look at two specific areas that often impact on women's positioning: the role of medicine and normative understandings of heterosexual relationships. As I will show, medicine has a central role to play in both constructing understandings of reproductive choices and controlling access either implicitly or explicitly, both to individual women and across social groups more broadly. Moreover, the presumption of heterosexuality often underpins reproductive health policy and practice. Hence, it is essential to consider the gendered position of women, within the norms of heterosexuality, in order to see the ways in which women's bodies and behaviour are disciplined in relation to prevailing ideas of motherhood, whether or not they have children. Moreover, through the foregrounding of choice, the structural constraints on reproductive lives are often hidden.

Choice and the Neoliberal Citizen/Consumer of Reproductive Health

The idea of choice is crucial in understanding the ideology of neoliberal economic theory. At a basic level, each individual makes their own choices and these choices collectively then move the free market in different directions. If a shop cannot attract enough individual customers for its products, it will fail and, in theory, be replaced by other shops selling 'better' products. Thus, a key element is to make and sell things that enough people want to buy to keep the business going. In other words, businesses in idealized free-market economics need to ensure consumer satisfaction, be responsive and innovative enough to encompass market change, and use resources efficiently. These ideas interrelate with rational choice theory, the assumption that in any given situation individuals weigh up the costs and benefits of an action and choose the one with fewer costs and greater benefits. The costs and benefits can be immediate or longer-term, or have a physical existence (for example money or housing) or be things such as feelings or sanctions (happiness, guilt or stigma). The freedom to make these decisions is seen as central to neoliberal societies, and having choices is usually construed as a positive issue.

The idea that free individual consumers are the basis of society ignores structural constraints, such as poverty, gender relationships and racism, and it makes people responsible for everything that happens to them. So, for example, it ignores the impact of poverty on food choices and simultaneously holds people to account for diet-related health issues. Moreover, it reduces important decisions about people's lives to an act of consumption (Salecl 2011). Salecl (2011) has argued that the emphasis on free choice within the market has meant that, increasingly, decisions about relationships and fertility are being treated in the same economic paradigm as choosing furniture or clothes. She also highlights the current prevalence of the idea that we need to 'improve' ourselves through better choices, particularly when the choices are constrained by social structures, and how this produces anxiety and guilt and undermines self-confidence. This, for Salecl (2011), is a structural shift in social life and it has had profound negative consequences for people's wellbeing. The ongoing search for 'improvement' through consumption leads to uncertainty about the range of options and hides the way that most choices are not really individual at all but influenced by wider norms and patterns in society. In reproductive health terms, we could see the 'improvement' that women should strive for is the 'best' outcome for the foetus/child. Moreover, as I will show later, the choices are not just shaped by the structures of society, but the norms of society mean that they are highly moralised.

The notion of free choice is embedded in policy making around reproductive health. For example, according to the World Health Organization (WHO), reproductive health means people have the 'capability to reproduce and the freedom to decide if, when and how often to do so' (WHO 2014, online source). They state that this includes choosing methods of fertility regulation and accessing healthcare services that enable healthy pregnancy and childbirth. For the WHO amongst others, laws enabling choice are deemed to be a central component for achieving reproductive health. In the global context, the importance of this cannot be overstated. At present, 26% of the world's population lives in countries in which abortion is either completely illegal or only permitted to save a woman's life (Centre for Reproductive Rights 2013). This is not just a problem for poorer nations: Ireland, Malta and Poland all have restrictive abortion laws despite being within Europe.

However, formal support for the granting of a right to choose does not necessarily mean that women are fully able to exercise that right. In reproductive health terms, we can divide the constraints on choice into two main areas. The first is that policy, practice and resources do not necessarily follow formal support or legal rights over aspects of reproductive health. This can be clearly evidenced in the way that a legal right to abortion does not automatically ensure that women are able to access it. For example, in the US, despite the right to abortion being confirmed in *Roe vs. Wade (1973)*, increasingly restrictive regulations constrain abortion providers' ability to practice and have led to the closing of abortion services (Boonstra and Nash 2014). In a similar way, in the UK, the National Institute of Health and Care Excellence (NICE) makes recommendations for access to IVF within the National Health Service (NHS), yet local commissioners of services are not bound to follow them (Kennedy et al. 2006).

The second constraint on choice is the one that this book focuses on: the ways that normative ideas about women, motherhood and children produce discourses of appropriate and inappropriate choices. The discourses surrounding maternal sacrifice serve to frame the context in which choices are made. Foucault (1991) argued that disciplinary power operates through the internalization of norms. He suggested that when behaviour is under constant surveillance, people discipline themselves and compliance with these norms becomes habitual. Within reproductive health, ideas about motherhood and sacrifice are thus disciplinary norms that are often embodied. They act to both produce and restrict choice by actively promoting a specific set of normative ideas. These shape policy, practice and resources, but are not reducible to this. As Foucault states:

> He [*sic*] who is subjected to a field of visibility, and who knows it, assumes
> responsibility for the constraints of power; he makes them play spontane-

ously upon himself; he inscribes in himself the power relation in which he simultaneously plays both roles; he becomes the principle of his own subjection. (1991: 202–203)

In this context, women's field of vision is the framework of good motherhood and they enact the role through making specific sacrifices. As I will argue in more detail later, maternal sacrifice goes beyond the everyday care of children and is part of the symbolic order. This can be seen in the way that sacrifices are called for even if they will lead to no substantive benefit for any foetus/child and, in some instances, may be to the detriment of women's welfare. The framework of maternal sacrifice, used by both promoters and restrictors of services, is deployed in areas that go beyond the physical needs of children for care and is often related to assumptions about the 'essential nature' of women. Reproductive health services are often presented as a 'choice', yet this overlooks the complex ways in which the normative idea of sacrifice disciplines women's lives.

Chambers (2008) argues that within liberalism, the concept of choice always invokes a just outcome; the act of being able to choose means that the decision is automatically deemed to be an indicator of freedom. She argues that this position has been challenged by many feminists who have used Foucault's writings to show how bodily compliance has been a feature of women's lives. She suggests that understanding power as it manifests in everyday actions, from beauty contests and media images to everyday conversations, can explain how gendered social norms are embodied. Moreover, it has been used to explain how, in liberal societies, choices are shaped without the need for overt commands. Yet as Chambers (2008) points out, whilst it is clear that this understanding does allow an understanding of the implicit limits to choice, it does not readily explain differentiation between competing images and an unequal impact on women. She argues that we need to understand that the decisions women (and men) make in liberal societies are 'free' choices but choices limited within the options available. This includes considering what is constructed as an appropriate option in the specific circumstances that the choice is made. The choices offered are not necessarily neutral but are an outcome of what is seen to be normative or preferable for that particular circumstance. In developed societies, it is often possible to resist or reject the discursive norms around reproductive health that are contained within the different choices. The rejection of norms may have specific adverse consequences, and a desire not to comply may not be supported by available reproductive services.

An example of how choice can be illusory in the area of reproductive health was summarized by Lippman (1999). She argues that the adoption of choice, and broader consumerist discourses, within the biomedical arena has led to a focus primarily on the individual as chooser that ignores the social, political and economic constraints of women's lives. She also argues that the co-opting of the rhetoric of choice at the level of the consumer masks the fact that the choices on offer are shaped by biomedical organisations. For example, women may be offered a choice between having or refusing a particular screening test for foetal anomalies during pregnancy, but they are unlikely to have been able to shape what technologies are available to be offered. In other words, biomedical organisations make decisions over what forms of testing will be developed and made available to women. The availability, and presentation to them, of various test options frames the decisions that women are able to make, and it also means that the ability to choose *not* to have to make a decision may be removed (Lippman 1999). She argued that the co-option of women's demands for greater reproductive freedom has led to a multitude of options but not 'the processes that determine what options will be developed and made' (Lippman 1999: 288). However, the illusion of choice that these options create often disguises social structures, such as a focus on technologies that will be useful for the more affluent rather than those which would be useful for the poor. As will be detailed in later chapters, they also hold women responsible in many different ways, even if they have not desired to have that particular choice.

These constraints on choice are clearly important, but it is not just the choices on offer that we need to be concerned about. Ideas about good motherhood mean that women are often under a moral obligation to make specific choices from the narrow range that they are offered. The idea of informed choice, which is particularly frequent in medicalized reproduction, is often morally loaded. There is a 'right' and a 'wrong' choice to be made by women, and the positioning of the options as good or bad is often linked to both changing ideas about risk and the notion that women should be prepared to make sacrifices for the welfare of any (future) child.

Risk and Responsibility

Beck (1992) argues that the idea of instrumental rational control, that we can measure and take decisions around risk, has become a central feature of modern societies. The concept of risk, and its relationship to social life, has led to a wider literature and different definitions. Here the focus is on 'risk consciousness', which, as Lee (2014) has shown, has had an increasingly important impact on family policy in the developed world. Lee (2014) summarizes risk consciousness as having four inter-related elements: risk as an untoward possibility, both individualized and generalized, as a moral concern, and as it is linked to the surveillance and policing of family life.

The first element of risk consciousness, then, is that the definition of risk has changed from the balance of probabilities to an assessment of the possibility of harm (Lee 2014). Furedi (2009) highlights how this new conceptualization of risk encourages people towards a stronger belief in the detrimental things that might happen. The encouragement to see danger also occurs when an assessment of harm is not known or is impossible to calculate (Lee 2014). A clear example of this can be seen in the move towards advocating abstinence from alcohol during pregnancy despite there being no clear evidence of harm from low levels of consumption (Lowe and Lee 2010). Lowe and Lee (2010) argue that the precautionary principle at work here equates the absence of data that proves safety with danger, and thus the need to eliminate the risk. They argue that:

> The decision on part of English health authorities to advocate abstinence constitutes an important reorientation of policy in relation to definitions of risk and uncertainty. This policy is perhaps the clearest example in the field of health to date where policy makers have opted to address scientific uncertainty by overtly associating the unknown with danger. (Lowe and Lee 2010: 309)

The second element of risk consciousness set out by Lee (2014) is the way that risk is both individualized and generalized. Risk is individualized in the threat, meaning that specific people are designated as 'at risk'. Moreover, this label 'at risk' can be attached to people regardless of any actual harm they have suffered. A belief that they may come to harm could be sufficient. Hence, there is a twin emphasis: the identification of individuals who are actually being harmed, and consideration of the more general category of people that may be harmed. This is clearly apparent in the area of children's social work in the UK. Parton (2011) has shown how in the early 1990s, the primary concern was identifying the small number of children living in 'dangerous' families. The children who needed protection by the state were then largely those where abuse was 'substantiated or highly suspected' (Parton 2011: 859). By the end of the 1990s, there had been a change to a duty to 'safeguard' children. Parton (2011) argues that this duty has a much broader remit in both identifying 'at risk' children and promoting child welfare more generally. This had the effect of bringing far more children into the realm of child protection, particularly as definitions of harm broadened to include issues such as emotional relationships. It also has consequences for women as the bearers and carers of children.

The replacement of moral judgements with ones of risk is the third element identified by Lee (2014). In many Western societies, there has been a decline in deference to institutions such as the state or religions. Hunt (2003) has argued that there has been a change from dividing acts into right and wrong towards a more complex assessment of risk and harm. Individuals are expected to minimize risks individually in opposition to the harmful 'other.' The promotion of ethical 'self conduct' for the greater good uses the language of risk but is nevertheless often about a moral judgement (Lee 2014). This can be seen in the Budds et al. (2013) study of the framing of older motherhood in the media. They found that articles usually positioned women as 'choosing' older motherhood and that this increased the risk of poorer health outcomes for both themselves and the developing foetus. Only a few articles reflected that later pregnancy could be the outcome of circumstances outside women's control. As Budds et al. (2013) point out, this moralising framework outlines that there is a correct time to become pregnant and women should adhere to it.

The final area associated with risk consciousness is that these other elements feed into a justification for increased levels of surveillance and policy for family life. Lee (2014) argues that this is particularly the case for pregnancy and childrearing. As Lowe et al. (2015a) have shown, concerns over pregnancy have recently expanded from issues related to physicality, such as diet and alcohol, into the issue of women's mental health, with an increasing focus on maternal stress as a risk to the developing foetus. In UK policy, the concern was predominately articulated as a risk to the foetus and a potential cost to future society in providing for any harm caused to the child, and concern over women's health was rarely mentioned (Lowe et al. 2015a). The articulation of this risk justified the increased surveillance of women and the promotion of particular ideas about parenting.

Individualising risk thus produces the responsibilization of women; it formulates and produces notions of choice and control, with costs and benefits that ignore wider circumstances. Ruhl (1999) has demonstrated this in relation to pregnancy. She argues that the shift in responsibility has led to a specific focus on women's behaviour that ignores the complexity of biological and social factors that affect the developing foetus. Ruhl (1999) argues that understanding the foetus as a 'product' of pregnancy ignores the many issues that are outside women's control. It is symptomatic of the shift to an actuarial society, in which economic measures (such as costs and benefits) are taken to be the only way to both account for social life and produce normative understandings.

In the area of reproductive health, the culture of risk consciousness operates by and through the ways in which choice is developed and articulated to women. Choices are presented as having different risks, and thus the decisions that women make are not morally neutral. Hence, the culture of individualized risk and responsibility is a moralising framework in which women are constrained or enabled not just by societal structures but through judgements about the choices they might consider or make. The moral positioning of different choices is linked to ideas about good motherhood.

Good Motherhood

The association between women and motherhood has been explored at length (see for example Phoenix and Woollett 1991; Letherby 1994; Lievore 2007). Put simply, the capacity to give birth is a fundamental element in the way that women, and femininity, are usually understood. Women are usually judged against the concept of motherhood, whether or not they are actually mothers (Letherby 1994). Moreover, motherhood itself is a social construction. As Smart (1996) sums up:

> Motherhood is not a natural condition. It is an institution that *presents* itself as a natural outcome of biologically given gender differences, as a natural consequence of (hetero)sexual activity, and as a natural manifestation of an innate female characteristic, namely the maternal instinct. (1996: 37, *original emphasis*)

The concept of motherhood thus acts a social structure. It is institutionalized in laws and policy, and produces normative understandings through discourses of experts, 'rules', stigma and shame. It acts as a framework from which women are judged in terms of both whether or not they are mothers and how any mothering is enacted. In contrast, mothering is the everyday practice of being a mother, the caring labour of raising children (Bortolaia Silva 1996). Mothering as a practice is of course often influenced by motherhood, and women can accept or reject, comply willingly, or be forced into enacting aspects of motherhood. Both the normative ideas about motherhood, and practices of mothering, are shaped by historical, cultural and social structures, and subjected to changes over times. However, what constitutes good motherhood in countries such as the UK and US is usually synonymous with the ideas and practices of white, middle-class women (Jones 2013).

Gatrell (2008) has argued that alongside the work of caring for children, we should understand pregnancy as a form of reproductive work. She argues that rather than understand productive and reproductive labour as separate, and in line with the divide between public and private, women's changing bodies often breach the boundaries. Moreover, Gatrell (2008) argues that the expectation that women will manage their 'leaky' reproductive bodies to resemble that of the idealized maleworker norm leaves them at a disadvantage in the workplace. The need for pregnant or breastfeeding women to continue to perform, regardless of the physical impact of reproduction, ignores the work of maternal labour. Maternal labour, she argues, is seen as 'natural' for women, and thus it is not necessarily considered work at all. Growing and feeding future humans can be exhausting and difficult, but to draw attention to this positions women as less than ideal workers and thus can negatively impact the way that they are positioned in the workforce. As Gatrell states:

> The fact that the work of reproduction goes unrecognized and unacknowledged makes it very convenient for employers to insist that such work is kept out of sight. Thus, women's hidden work is doubled as they struggle to meet the exacting standards of contemporary motherhood and the everyday needs of infants, while keeping this maternal labour out of the employment arena. (2008: 181)

Raising children has long been seen as women's work. Yet what this work consists of has been subject to change. In the late twentieth century, Hays (1996) argues that, in the US, the expectations changed towards intensive motherhood. Hays (1996) sees intensive motherhood as a project in which women 'invest' in children physically, emotionally and financially, following expert guidance within a child-centred framework to try to ensure their children reach an (imagined) full potential. For Hays (1996) this organising framework involves extensive work, time and money, and whilst not all women will want or be able to practise this form of motherhood, she argues that it has become the normative framework of motherhood. Lareau (2003) has described part of this trend as the 'concerted cultivation' of children. Middle-class parents in particular try to identify and develop children's talents through organized leisure pursuits and learning activities. As Smyth's (2012) more recent study of the US and Northern Ireland has shown, whilst mothering practices can follow or reject normative models, the concept of maximising child development through following a rational plan often now dominates understandings (Smyth 2012). This also highlights the importance of socio-economic positioning, as the ability to 'invest' in concerted cultivation is not available to all (Gillies 2007; Nelson 2010).

Wolf (2011) argues that the requirements made of women now go beyond intensive motherhood. She argues that the current emphasis around risk, which deploys science and 'expert knowledge' to support minimising risk, rather than considering the balance of probabilities, has led to an ideology of 'total motherhood.' Wolf argues that:

> total motherhood stipulates that mothers' primary occupation is to predict and prevent all less-than-optimal social, emotional, cognitive, and physical outcomes; that mothers are responsible for anticipating and eradicating every imaginable risk to their children, regardless of the degree or severity of the risk or what the trade-offs might be. (2011: 71–72)

As the requirements for women to assess and minimize risk increase, inevitably this comes at a cost for women. During pregnancy eradicating risk means constraining women's lives, but the requirements of maternal sacrifice in line with total motherhood extend into breastfeeding and early childcare. Total motherhood, as a new form of good motherhood, is thus still dependent on women's obligations to put the needs of others first.

Thus the norms of good motherhood require that women make sacrifices to maximise the welfare of the foetus/child. The particular sacrifices that need to be made are often communicated within the framework of risk consciousness. Although in most cases women are not compelled to make specific choices, the presentation of options is shaped by understandings of good motherhood and the minimization of reproductive work. The dominant frameworks of individualization and the responsibilization of women give weight to the expectation that women should make sacrifices, regardless of the implications for their own lives.

Vulnerable Foetus/Child

Concerns about the body and behaviour of women in relation to reproduction are, as Yuval-Davis (1980, 1997) has shown, linked to their position as bearers of the collective. It is only through women's bodies that collectives, such as social class, ethnicity or nation can continue. This has resonances with the ways in which children are often understood in public imagination and policy as 'future' citizens, rather than as individuals in their own right (Lowe et al. 2015b). Taken together, concerns over the ongoing reproduction of social groups and children as developing rather than fully formed help feed into the construction of childhood vulnerability. More recently, with the development of image technologies, this notion has been extended backwards to include the developing foetus. Indeed, as Lupton (2012) has argued, the division between foetus and child has become increasingly eroded as ideas of 'rights' and 'citizenship' come to be associated with the foetus. The notion that women and the foetus are separate beings is perpetuated by the widespread use of foetal images in which the woman's body is either obscured or completely absent (Lupton 2013). This is the context that justifies surveillance and sanctions on women's behaviour. As women are increasingly constructed as foetal carriers, the pregnant body is divided and women are potentially positioned as a risk to the foetus. For example, in legal cases in the US, pregnant women, particularly those from poor or marginalized communities, have been incarcerated in order to 'protect' the foetus (Paltrow and Flavin 2013).

The conceptualization of the pregnant body as divided, with women as potential abusers, is often conceptualized as maternal/foetal conflict. The appointment of legal representation of the foetus mentioned earlier is a clear example of this. As Jackson (2001) has shown the law has been used in two different forms of maternal/foetal conflict. The first is one in which a woman's behaviour is believed to put the foetus' development 'at risk', and the second is when women's refusal to follow medical advice is believed be potentially harmful or put the foetus' survival in doubt. In both cases, the law may be used to restrict women's behaviour or force them to undergo particular medical treatments. In different legal jurisdictions, the specific legal status of the foetus will vary. For example, currently in the Irish Constitution, the foetus and the women currently have equal rights to life (Lentin 2013). In contrast, whilst in UK law a foetus is not yet considered a person, as Jackson (2001) has shown, there is little doubt that they are treated as patients by healthcare professionals.

Of course, what the term maternal/foetal conflict masks is that legal cases that arise in this area are predominately disputes between women and health or other professionals. The medicalization of pregnancy led to health professionals having authority over childbirth and the ability to proscribe 'appropriate' health behaviours during pregnancy. It is when women fail to comply with health advice or agree to specific medical interventions, such as caesarean sections, that the law can be turned to enforce compliance. The discursive construction of the vulnerable foetus as being at risk from the behaviour or choices of pregnant women carrying them is significant. It is seen as a major failure in responsibility, which goes beyond the immediate issue of pregnancy. It points to women's failure in a primary role within femininity, the protector of their young, thus positioning them as non-women. Indeed as Young (1997) amongst others have pointed out, a mother who harms her child is positioned as monstrous. She is an aberration from women's 'natural' position as nurturers. The choices that women make in the area of reproductive health are thus not just about a moral responsibility to a foetus/child but also a statement about their identity. Making appropriate sacrifices through making the 'right' choice enables women to maintain their status as good women as well as good mothers.

Medicalization and Reproductive Health

As the issue of maternal/foetal conflict illustrates, the medicalization of reproduction provides opportunities for the surveillance and sanctions of women by health professionals. Its powerful position also gives it the ability to impact laws and regulations governing reproductive health and to define what is and is not 'risky' behaviour. The process of medicalization is usually seen to occur when an area of social life comes to be seen as a legitimate concern of health professionals. Crucially, health professionals are able to define what is and is not within their remit, as well as decide how to consider and treat the issue once it has been brought into the medical domain. As many writers such as Ehrenreich and English (1979) have documented, for centuries reproduction was typically seen as the preserve of women. As part of the development of the medical profession, different aspects of reproduction started to be medicalized. This process happened at different points of time.

For example, in relation to childbirth, the beginnings of medicalization have been associated with the growth of the use of obstetric forceps in the eighteenth century. As Rothman (2007) argues, this technology meant that male barber-surgeons were increasingly given control over births when women had difficulties. As over time more births were defined as risky, this began to shift control despite any evidence that medical involvement produced any better outcomes for women (Rothman 2007; Oakley 1980). At this time, the developing profession of medicine excluded women from medical training because of wider beliefs about women's lack of abilities (see for example Cahill 2000; Ehrenreich and English 1979; or Rothman 2007). Whilst the balance between midwives and obstetric medicine varies cross-culturally, over time biomedical understandings of childbirth came to dominate the discourse (Cahill 2000). This remains the case today, despite the rhetoric of natural or normal childbirth in many healthcare services (Phipps 2014).

From the 1970s, a growing movement of birth activists began to challenge the medical control of childbirth. As Henley-Einion (2009) has shown, by this point women were often not necessarily treated as central to birth. Instead health professionals were interested in the birthing process, within which birth was expected to follow a specific order and timeframe. Whilst ostensibly promoting women's safety, the emphasis was on medical control and efficiency for health professionals, which often made it harder for women to give birth. Activists from a range of Western countries, such as Wendy Savage (UK), Ina May Gaskin (US) and Frederick Leboyer (France), all sought to promote a less technological approach to birth within the broad natural childbirth movement.

This movement was successful in challenging many of the unnecessary routine practices; however, as Phipps (2014) has shown, this has replaced one set of hegemonic ideas about birth with another. Rather than a radical shift, we need to see this campaign as reaffirming women's position in relation to motherhood and having close links to specific biological understandings about the 'natural' role of women (Phipps 2014). Moreover, as will be explored later in greater depth, in many areas of reproductive health, the same concepts of risk consciousness and responsible choices can be used to support ostensibly different positions. Often both sides suggest specific sacrifices that women should make in line with the responsible choices of good motherhood.

Phipps (2014) argues that the natural childbirth movement that sought to empower women and take back control from medicine has been misappropriated to further support ideas about women's natural position. Phipps (2014) suggests that this misappropriation is linked to the ways in which neoconservatism is currently linked to neoliberalism. In relation to the family, neoconservatism as an ideology argues for the gendered division of labour and is often linked to right-wing Christian understandings of the family and home. Phipps (2014) argues that alongside the individualization within neoliberalism, neoconservatism has played an important role in justifying the disciplining of women's bodies. Although rooted in ideas about traditional gender roles linked to essentialism, neoconservatism often adopts proto-feminist discourses to support its position on women (Phipps 2014). This is linked to morality discourses within risk consciousness. Women's 'natural' place means that they should eliminate all possible risks to the foetus/child. By utilising neoliberal ideas about choice in areas such as childbirth, Phipps (2014) argues that neoconservatism can support traditional gender roles and appropriate motherhood. The shift to choice, such as women 'choosing' natural childbirth, clearly shows a neoliberal emphasis on making the responsible 'choices', and the embodied experiences of pregnancy and birth are utilized to reaffirm women's 'natural' roles through the positioning of some choices as better than others.

Using the rhetoric of choice to promote a specific form of birth is not confined to the natural childbirth movement. Moreover, the idea of maternal sacrifice is a central mechanism within this and other positions related to motherhood and reproductive health. As I will detail later, in each area of reproductive health women are expected to comply with health regimes in the name of a foetus/child, whether or not they are pregnant or a mother. For example, the idea that women must take steps to promote their foetus's health supports both calls for natural childbirth and medically advised caesarean sections. It is within the power of the medical profession to decide which is the 'best' course of action and to promote compliance through ideas of 'informed choice'. To reject or question medical advice positions women as a risk to their foetus. To use or not use particular forms of birth control in line with health professionals' expectations of women when preventing conception should be a priority. The idea of maternal sacrifice is built into specific health discourses and the institutional authority of medicine allows them to be promoted often without question.

Indeed, as Howson (1998) has argued, acceptance of the medical gaze on women's bodies is often seen as a normative aspect of femininity. This can be linked to the idea of women's bodies as irregular, temperamental and in need of regulation, as Martin (1987) has shown. Howson (1998) suggests that women have an 'embodied obligation' to be compliant, and whilst some may resist or question this, this notion has not yet been challenged. Regulatory regimes in reproductive health are thus one aspect of this disciplinary technique. Moreover, as Phipps (2014) argues, by promoting the rhetoric of choice they give an illusion of women's agency whilst sustaining control through the denial of structural factors and discursive regimes of truth. The normative power of the idea of maternal sacrifice, I would argue, is the central thread to the disciplinary gaze within reproductive health. It helps to assert the right 'choices' for normative women's behaviour.

Production and Consumption

Within the medical discipline, it has long been argued that reproduction has been treated as industrial production. The idea that bodies are like machines has a long history, and it is argued that biomedicine structures understandings of women's reproductive health within a dominant narrative of production. Martin (1987), for example, outlined the ways in which medical textbooks use metaphors of factory lines to describe labour. She suggested that the uterus was positioned as the machine that makes the baby, the woman as a worker operating the machine, and the (male) health professionals as the supervisors responsible for efficient production. This technocratic model of birth led to standardized 'operating procedures' and the routinization of specific interventions to assist the 'birthing machine' in its production (Davis-Floyd 2003). The introduction and widespread usage of monitoring equipment in both pregnancy and childbirth is seen as assisting in the quality assurance of the product under construction (Davis-Floyd 2003; Martin 1987; Rothman 2007).

Many of the accounts of reproduction as production draw attention to the way in which the attention is shifted away from women's experiences and towards the 'product' of the pregnancy. This is through a concern that women's inefficient labouring bodies pose a potential 'threat' to the wellbeing of the foetus (Davis-Floyd 2003). Alternatively, it could be through prenatal screening in which the foetus is measured and tested against standardized criteria for growth or foetal anomalies (Rothman 1988). Rothman (1988) argued that the rise of prenatal screening, with an assumption that 'products' not meeting the criteria could be aborted, have made pregnancy tentative. Women cannot emotionally invest in the foetus until they are given positive messages about appropriate development. Yet as Taylor (2008) has shown, within ultrasound screenings, the meanings are more complex than this model of production indicates.

Taylor (2008) argues that alongside a model of reproduction as production, we also need to understand it as a model of consumption. As outlined earlier, within neoliberal societies, consumption and choice are an important structure of society, and as Taylor (2008) argues, within a model of production, it makes sense to ask who the consumer is. In her study of ultrasound screening, Taylor (2008) argues that there a number of ways that women are positioned as consumers. First, there is a huge market around pregnancy and baby products that women need to purchase on behalf of the foetus/child. Indeed, the revealing of the sex of the developing foetus during prenatal screening is increasingly important as the gendering of baby products becomes ubiquitous. As I have argued elsewhere, although many in the West believe that investment in the sex of the foetus is a problem of the developing world, in Europe, some still express preferences and/or take steps to select the sex of future children based on naturalized assumptions of gendered behaviour (Lowe 2015). Taylor (2008) further argues that reproduction is rooted in consumption in the way that pregnancy is marked by a need to consume, and abstain, from particular substances. The recommendations for women to abstain from alcohol, watch their diet and to take folic acid supplements are examples of this. Indeed, as Taylor (2008) has shown, increasing pregnancy itself 'begins' with an act of consumption with pregnancy testing kits. Prior to any embodied signs, a positive result from 'peeing on a stick' has become the boundary from the non-pregnant to pregnant state for many women in the developed world.

The idea of choice is built into understandings of reproductive health, positioning women as potential consumers enabled to choose between the appropriate options, such as pregnancy or abortion, screening or non-screening during pregnancy, home or hospital birth. Yet despite this rhetoric of choice, the options available to women are clearly constrained. Women may be positioned as potential consumers in the reproductive marketplace, but some choices are clearly identified as 'better' than others. The need to ensure the welfare of the foetus means women have to operate with risk consciousness shaped by normative understandings of what is 'best.' The efficient and effective production of future citizens, rather than the desires of women, shapes this discourse. Moreover, not all women are in a position to choose, and those positioned as 'others' may have limited options and/or increased sanctions for non-compliance. Certain women are more likely to be positioned as 'superior' producers and have a better 'market' position as consumers than others.

Gendered Understandings and Normative Heterosexuality

In order to understand the normative positioning of women in relation to reproductive health, it is important to remember that it is fundamentally different to many other aspects of social life. All Western societies formally support the principle of gender equality. Many areas have a long way to go to achieve this, and what it might look like is still debated, but the principle is still upheld. Yet in reproductive health, gender equality can never be achieved as long as, generally speaking, only women can get pregnant. Whilst in many heterosexual relationships partners will agree on issues of fertility, if they do not, then one person's decision has to take precedence. For me, there is no question that it should be the woman's sole decision. Pregnancy is an embodied state for women, so all decisions that relate to being or not being pregnant have to remain with women. Whilst this does not mean that partners should necessarily be excluded, involving them should always stop short of giving them the right of decision-making over women's bodies.

So reproductive health is, and will likely remain, an issue in which gender differences can never be eliminated due to the inherent biological divide. However, understandings of these different biological positions are constructed socially in line with gendered expectations. Having a womb and ovaries does not mean that women are biologically programmed with a desire to grow a child. As I have already shown, the idea of motherhood has long been associated with femininity, but these gendered constructions arise from social expectations. In normative expectations of femininity, women are often positioned as nurturers and carers (Skeggs 1997, 2001), and they are expected to always consider the needs of others (Jaggar 1989). Good motherhood epitomizes the performance of these values (DiQuinzio 1999). Ideas about femininity and motherhood will also be affected by other issues of identity. For example, Siraj's (2012) study of Muslim women in Glasgow revealed that the Qur'an was an important reference point for understanding their identity as women and mothers. Nevertheless, the gendered expectations of women are often the basis for normative understandings within reproductive health.

As Jackson (1999) pointed out, it is important to retain a distinction between gender and heterosexuality, even though the frameworks are interwoven. The term heterosexuality has been used to describe sexual practices, sexual identities and aspects of social structures, and its position as 'normal or 'natural' meant that previously it was not necessarily examined or questioned (Jackson 1999; Jackson and Scott 2010). As Carrera et al. (2012) have shown, heteronormative scripts still dominate understandings even if there are challenges to heterosexuality's dominate status. Whilst, like gender, heterosexuality is always constructed in relation to other aspects of identity, it retains a binary construction within differing expectations of women and men (Jackson and Scott 2010). The automatic link between heterosex/heterosexuality and reproduction has been challenged through the development of many reproductive technologies and changes in legal practices in which same-sex couples and single people can become parents. Nordqvist (2008) has shown how the increasing use of assistive conception techniques undermines heterosexual presumptions about conception and parenthood. However, as Mamo (2007) has argued, heteronormativity still retains a dominate framework and shapes the experiences of reproduction whether or not they are heterosexual. Her study of lesbian mothers found that their practices of motherhood both challenged and reinforced dominant understandings in complex ways. For example, whilst assisted reproduction allows the possibility of conception beyond heterosexuality, as Mamo (2007) argues, it can also reaffirm the fertility industry's presumption that pregnancy is desirable for all women.

Maternal Sacrifice

As Ehrenreich (1998) points out although sacrifice is often thought of in terms of selflessness and self-denial, its origins come from a different position. Sacrifice was first and foremost a religious ritual in which there was often bloodshed, the slaughter of an animal or human as an offering made to a god or gods (Ehrenreich 1998). Through this act of violence, there was a route to deliverance, salvation, an appeasement or the building of a relationship between humans and those that they worship. In this sense, we can understand sacrifice as both symbolic and transformative, a sacred act to ward off or control the profane. The slaughter was symbolic as an offering, and through the act of sacrifice those involved in the ritual or the wider community were transformed either in relation to each other or to their deity. Although in many cases the body to be sacrificed was an animal or an enemy, rather than part of the group seeking salvation, the ritual itself was important to reinforce the community's borders, building relationships with each other as well as the deity they sought to please or appease.

In this sense, ritual sacrifice was important because of the relationship it built within the social order. It was a symbolic act that created and recreated specific social relationships. Whilst over time, offerings or gifts made in religious rituals changed so slaughter was ended or transformed, the symbolic position of suffering as a transcendent or potentially godly act has remained. Those who endure suffering without complaint, especially those who suffer on behalf of others, have a high moral position. Indeed the willing acquisition of potential or actual suffering - for example, taking on an endurance challenge for charity - is seen as a sacrifice of self-interest for the greater good. It is not necessarily enough to just give money to a worthy cause: there needs to be a physical trial in which a person can demonstrate their commitment through embodied (painful) actions.

Thus, the idea of sacrifice goes beyond acts of selflessness or suffering and needs to be seen as having an important symbolic role in the social order. Sacrifice is a way of creating and maintaining relationships and binding the community together. Moreover, as Yuval-Davis (1980, 1997) pointed out so succinctly, women literally give birth to the nation. Hence the important positioning of maternal sacrifice in the understanding of both motherhood and gendered relationships.

As I have briefly outlined already, the idea of maternal sacrifice arises from the historical ideas about the 'essential nature' of women as nurturers based on presumptions about reproductive bodies of women. If women grow children, then this defines them as natural carers for the young, and, as natural carers, they will naturally place the needs of their children (and others) before their own. Women who do not may be seen as unnatural, and thus cannot be good mothers. This normative framework suggests that the needs and desires of women must be suppressed, sacrificed for the potential wellbeing of any developing foetus or child. What good motherhood consists of changes over time, and women are expected to comply with whatever the prevailing norms are. The idea of sacrifice remains constant. In Western societies today, this predominately means making the 'right' informed choices in line with dominant medical and/or policy understandings of responsibility for minimizing any risks to the developing foetus.

Whilst the exact requirements may change, good motherhood is an embodied expectation of women. It prescribes the age, bodily disposition and behaviour that women should conform to during the expectation or practice of motherhood. Like many normative concepts, good motherhood is often most visible in the stigma and sanctions against 'bad mothers' (Ladd-Taylor and Umansky 1998). Disapproval of young mothers (Arai 2009), older mothers (Budds et al. 2013), obese mothers (McNaughton 2011) and substance-using mothers (Benoit et al. 2014), for example, all help to define the parameters of who or what good motherhood is. Moreover, groups of women such as these are defined within the prevailing discourse as presenting too much risk to the vulnerable foetus/child. Moralisation is reconstructed as an actuarial risk but nevertheless stigmatizes specific women's choices. The logical assumption is that those who do not meet the required standard should refrain from motherhood until they fit, despite the normative assumption that it is a requirement of womanhood. Hence, as I will argue in more detail later, maternal sacrifice is also called for through the forgoing of motherhood. Women should give up ideas about becoming or being a mother if they cannot meet the normative standard set.

The responsibilization of women in the area of reproductive health ignores wider structural concerns and promotes risk consciousness as a dominant narrative. Hence eliminating risks becomes the responsible choice, and this can often mean trying to modify women's behaviour in the name of protecting the vulnerable foetus/child. Communications to women are couched in the biomedical discourse of 'informed choice', but this is not a neutral exercise. The emphasis is on self-regulation within the context of a society in which women are both producers and consumers who have the sole or main responsibility for the welfare for their child's development. Good mothers will 'naturally' make responsible choices that will include minimizing any potential risks to the developing foetus/child.

Moreover, if certain groups of women cannot be trusted to make the right choice, then more coercive means, including in extreme cases criminalization, could be promoted. These explicit measures, combined with pressure that is more implicit, are used to try to ensure women's compliance with required sacrifices. For example, the construction of conflicts as maternal/foetal rather than, for example, women/health professional is further evidence of the way that maternal sacrifice is the important element underpinning the debates. By hiding the central feature of women disagreeing with health professionals, and instead focusing on the (vulnerable) foetus, it positions women as potentially rejecting their nurturer role.

Conclusion

Despite living in societies in which choice, as a neoliberal consumer, often appears to be part of the framework of reproductive health, normative ideas about women, motherhood and children shape dominant narratives. This disciplines and constrains women's reproductive bodies. The disciplinary impact is shaped by the socio-economic context of individual women's lives. The prevailing norms have an unequal impact on women, and the implicit and explicit range of 'choices' depend on where women are positioned in relation to issues such as social class, ethnicity, disability and sexuality. Moreover, the areas where choice may be championed are an outcome of a broader framework of norms and values that discipline women into specific choices. The structural framework, including laws, policy and biomedicine, also shapes the limits of the choices available to women. Moreover, women are often held accountable for choices, regardless of whether or not the options available are necessarily the ones they would have wanted.

Risk consciousness is one of the dominant frames that currently shapes the choices that women are offered and can make, with the need to eliminate any risk to the foetus/child a central idea framing women's reproductive lives. The individualization of risk has led to the responsibilization of women and this operates through the idea of the good mother. What constitutes good motherhood may change over time and between places; however, the need for women to make sacrifices in order to be good mothers is a constant. Today, one of the prevailing dominant discourses is that of intensive motherhood. Intensive motherhood requires that women invest time and resources into a child-centred model of mothering in order to ensure that their children reach their full potential. The requirement to eliminate risks and invest in their children positions women as more or less solely responsible for their future lives and ignores both children's role in shaping their own futures and the constraints that society places around women. Moreover, by discursively positioning options within a moral hierarchy, choice has now become a mechanism for the disciplining of women.

The idea of maternal sacrifice is built on the positioning of women as natural nurturers, the bearers and carers of children. This is the underpinning of good motherhood, an essentializing discourse that fits with neoconservative ideas about gender and family life. The idea that children come first, regardless of the costs to women's lives, is used to justify ideas about who should have children and in what circumstances women should have children, as well as how they should care for them. Clearly children do need appropriate love and care, but the framing of maternal sacrifice goes beyond what is necessarily needed, and it is used to promote dominant understandings of appropriate reproduction. The understanding of maternal sacrifice as natural means that women who challenge this position are clearly 'unnatural' mothers who potentially pose a risk to the vulnerable foetus/child. In the next chapters, I will illustrate how these ideas play out in different areas of women's reproductive lives. This begins with the questions surrounding those who should be allowed to conceive, as some women are required to sacrifice their desire to be mothers if they do not live up to the prevailing standards of good motherhood.

References

Arai, L. (2009). *Teenage pregnancy: The making and unmaking of a problem.* Bristol, England: The Policy Press.

Beck, U. (1992). *Risk society: Towards a new modernity.* London: Sage.

Benoit, C., Stengel, C., Marcellus, L., Hallgrimsdottir, H., Anderson, J., MacKinnon, K., et al. (2014). Providers' constructions of pregnant and early parenting women who use substances. *Sociology of Health and Illness, 36*(2), 252–263.

Boonstra, H. D., & Nash, E. (2014). A surge of state abortion restrictions puts providers—and the women they serve—in the crosshairs. *Guttmacher Policy Review, 17*(1), 9–15.

Bortolaia Silva, E. (1996). The transformation of mothering. In E. Bortolaia Silva (Ed.), *Good enough mothering? Feminist perspectives on lone motherhood* (pp. 10–36). London: Routledge.

Budds, K., Locke, A., & Burr, V. (2013). "Risky business" constructing the "choice" to "delay" motherhood in the British Press. *Feminist Media Studies, 13*(1), 132–147.

Cahill, H. (2000). Male appropriation and medicalization of childbirth: An historical analysis. *Journal of Advanced Nursing, 33*(3), 334–342.

Carrera, M. V., DePalma, R., & Lameiras, M. (2012). Sex/gender identity: Moving beyond fixed and 'natural' categories. *Sexualities, 15*(8), 995–1016.

Center for Reproductive Rights. (2013). *The world's abortion laws map 2013 update.* New York: CRR.

Chambers, C. (2008). *Sex, culture, and justice: The limits of choice.* University Park, PA: Pennsylvania State University Press.

Davis-Floyd, R. E. (2003). *Birth as an American rite of passage* (2nd ed.). London: University of California Press.

DiQuinzio, P. (1999). *The impossibility of motherhood: Feminism, individualism and the problem of mothering*. New York: Routledge.

Ehrenreich, B. (1998). *Blood rites: Origins and history of the passions of war*. London: Virago Press.

Ehrenreich, B., & English, D. (1979). *For her own good: 150 years of the experts' advice to women*. New York: Anchor Press/Doubleday.

Foucault, M. (1991). *Discipline and punish: The birth of the prison*. London: Penguin Books.

Furedi, F. (2009). Precautionary culture and the rise of possibilistic risk assessment. *Erasmus Law Review, 2*(2), 197–220.

Gatrell, C. (2008). *Embodying women's work*. Maidenhead, England: Open University Press.

Gillies, V. (2007). *Marginalised mothers: Exploring working class experiences of parenting*. London: Routledge.

Hays, S. (1996). *The cultural contradictions of motherhood*. New Haven, CT: Yale University Press.

Henley-Einion, A. (2009). The medicalization of childbirth. In C. Squire (Ed.), *The social context of birth* (pp. 180–190). Abingdon, England: Radcliffe Publishing.

Howson, A. (1998). Embodied obligation: The female body and health surveillance. In S. Netterton & J. Watson (Eds.), *The body in everyday life* (pp. 218–240). London: Routledge.

Hunt, A. (2003). Risk and moralization in everyday life. In R. V. Ericson & A. Doyle (Eds.), *Risk and morality*. Toronto, Ontario, Canada: University of Toronto Press.

Jackson, S. (1999). *Heterosexuality in question?* London: Sage.

Jackson, E. (2001). *Regulating reproduction: Law, technology and autonomy*. Oxford, England: Hart Publishing.

Jackson, S., & Scott, S. (2010). *Theorising sexuality*. Maidenhead, England: Open University Press.

Jaggar, A. (1989). Love and knowledge: Emotion in feminist epistemology. In A. Jaggar & S. Bordo (Eds.), *Gender/body/knowledge: Feminist reconstructions of being and knowing* (pp. 145–171). New Brunswick, NJ: Rutgers University Press.

Jones, C. (2013). Human weeds, not fit to breed? African Caribbean women and reproductive disparities in Britain. *Critical Public Health, 23*(1), 49–61.

Kennedy, R., Kingsland, C., Rutherford, A., Hamilton, M., & Ledger, W. (2006). Implementation of the NICE guideline—Recommendations from the British Fertility Society for national criteria for NHS funding of assisted conception. *Human Fertility, 9*(3), 181–189.

Ladd-Taylor, M., & Umansky, L. (1998). *'Bad' mothers: The politics of blame in twentieth-century America*. London: New York University Press.

Lareau, A. (2003). *Unequal childhoods: Class, race, and family life*. London: University of California Press.

Lee, E. (2014). Introduction. In E. Lee, J. Bristow, C. Faircloth, & J. Macvarish (Eds.), *Parenting culture studies* (pp. 1–24). Basingstoke, England: Palgrave Macmillan.

Lentin, R. (2013). A woman died: Abortion and the politics of birth in Ireland. *Feminist Review, 105*, 130–136.

Letherby, G. (1994). Mother or not, mother or what? Problems of definitions and identity? *Women's Studies International Forum, 17*(5), 525–532.

Lievore, D. (2007). Reproductive refusal: Not all choices are equal. *Women Against Violence: An Australian Feminist Journal, 19*, 37–45.

Lippman, A. (1999). Choice as a risk to women's health. *Health, Risk & Society, 1*(3), 281–291.

Lowe, P. (2015). Milk for a girl and bananas for a boy: Recipes and reasons for sex-preference practices in a British Internet forum. *Women's Reproductive Health, 2*(2), 111–123.

Lowe, P., & Lee, E. (2010). Advocating alcohol abstinence to pregnant women: Some observations about British policy. *Health Risk & Society, 12*(4), 301–311.

Lowe, P., Lee, E., & Macvarish, J. (2015a). Growing better brains? Pregnancy and neuroscience discourses in English social and welfare policies. *Health, Risk & Society, 17*(1), 15–29.

Lowe, P., Lee, E., & Macvarish, J. (2015b). Biologising parenting: Neuroscience discourse, English social and public health policy and understandings of the child. *Sociology of Health & Illness, 37*(2), 198–211.

Lupton, D. (2012). 'Precious cargo': Foetal subjects, risk and reproductive citizenship. *Critical Public Health, 22*(3), 329–340.

Lupton, D. (2013). *The social worlds of the unborn*. Basingstoke, England: Palgrave.

Mamo, L. (2007). *Queering reproduction*. London: Duke University Press.

Martin, E. (1987). *The woman in the body*. Buckingham, England: Open University Press.

McNaughton, D. (2011). From the womb to the tomb: Obesity and maternal responsibility. *Critical Public Health, 21*(2), 179–190.

Nelson, M. K. (2010). *Parenting out of control: Anxious parents in uncertain times.* London: New York University Press.

Nordqvist, P. (2008). Feminist heterosexual imaginaries of reproduction: Lesbian conception in feminist studies of reproductive technologies. *Feminist Theory, 9*(3), 273–292.

Oakley, A. (1980). *Women confined: Towards a sociology of childbirth.* Oxford, England: Martin Robertson.

Paltrow, L. M., & Flavin, J. (2013). Arrests of and forced interventions on pregnant women in the United States, 1973–2005: Implications for women's legal status and public health. *Journal of Health Politics, Policy and Law, 38*(2), 299–343.

Parton, N. (2011). Child protection and safeguarding in England: Changing and competing conceptions of risk and their implications for social work. *British Journal of Social Work, 41*(5), 854–875.

Phipps, A. (2014). *The politics of the body.* Cambridge, England: Polity Press.

Phoenix, A., & Woollett, A. (1991). *Motherhood, meanings, practices and ideologies.* London: Sage.

Rothman, B. K. (1988). *The tentative pregnancy: How amniocentesis changes the experience of motherhood.* London: Pandora.

Rothman, B. K. (2007). Laboring then: The political history of maternity care in the United States. In W. Simonds, B. K. Rothman, & B. M. Norman (Eds.), *Laboring on: Birth in transition in the United States* (pp. 3–28). Abingdon, England: Taylor & Francis.

Ruhl, L. (1999). Liberal governance and prenatal care: Risk and regulation in pregnancy. *Economy and Society, 28*(1), 95–117.

Salecl, R. (2011). *The tyranny of choice.* London: Profile Books.

Siraj, A. (2012). 'Smoothing down ruffled feathers': The construction of Muslim women's feminine identities. *Journal of Gender Studies, 21*(2), 185–199.

Skeggs, B. (1997). *Formations of class and gender.* London: Sage Publications.

Skeggs, B. (2001). The toilet paper: Femininity, class and mis-recognition. *Women's Studies International Forum, 24*(3), 295–307.

Smart, C. (1996). Deconstructing motherhood. In E. Bortolaia Silva (Ed.), *Good enough mothering? Feminist perspectives on lone motherhood* (pp. 37–57). London: Routledge.

Smyth, L. (2012). *The demands of motherhood: Agents roles and recognition.* Basingstoke, England: Palgrave.

Taylor, J. S. (2008). *The public life of the fetal sonogram: Technology, consumption, and the politics of reproduction.* New Brunswick, NJ: Rutgers University Press.

WHO. (2014). *Reproductive health.* Retrieved August 25, 2014, from http://www.who.int/topics/reproductive_health/en/

Wolf, J. B. (2011). *Is breast best: Taking on the breastfeeding experts and the new high stakes of motherhood.* London: New York University Press.

Young, I. M. (1997). *Intersecting voices: Dilemmas of gender, political philosophy and policy.* Chichester, England: Princeton University Press.

Yuval-Davis, N. (1980). The bearers of the collective: Women and religious legislation in Israel. *Feminist Review, 4*(1), 15–27.

Yuval-Davis, N. (1997). *Gender and nation.* London: Sage.

3

Regulating Contraception and Abortion

As set out in Chap. 2, maternal sacrifice is the trope that can weave together complex ideas about reproduction and define when and which women should become mothers. As contraception and abortion are ways to prevent motherhood, this chapter will show how ideas about good motherhood define who should refrain from considering childbearing for the good of imagined children or to reduce a possible cost to future society. The idea of maternal sacrifice means that women who are culturally expected to 'fail' at motherhood should prevent pregnancy, even if they desire to be mothers. For some women, this sacrifice may not be life-long. If they later move into the category of potentially good mothers, perhaps by becoming older or wealthier, then their sacrifice might only be temporary. Others, however, may never fit the criteria for good motherhood, and thus should always forgo becoming pregnant.

As this chapter will detail, this picture is fairly straightforward in relation to contraception but can be more complex in regards to abortion. Whilst attitudes and access to both contraception and abortion in different social, cultural and national settings vary considerably, it is often the case that the former is considered more acceptable than the latter. As I will demonstrate, for those who oppose abortion, concerns about the developing foetus can

© The Editor(s) (if applicable) and The Author(s) 2016
P. Lowe, *Reproductive Health and Maternal Sacrifice*,
DOI 10.1057/978-1-137-47293-9_3

overtake the undesirability of some pregnant bodies. Yet here too we can see how sacrifice is utilized, as anti-abortion activists insist that women continue with pregnancies regardless of any cost to themselves. However, before these issues are explored in depth, it is necessary to consider further the meaning of contraception and abortion more generally. The divide between contraception and abortion is often taken for granted, yet is constructed socially by and through particular understandings.

The Problematic Distinction?

In popular understanding, there is often a clear distinction between contraception and abortion. Usually contraception is deemed a device, or act, that prevents a pregnancy from starting, whereas an abortion is the termination of an existing pregnancy. Indeed, as Beynon-Jones (2013) has shown, abortion is often conceptualized by health professionals as contraceptive failure. Delving deeper into the difference, the crucial element is the point at which pregnancy begins, and this is the area that is contested. For some, pregnancy begins at the point at which an egg is fertilized, and thus an act or medication that prevents the fertilized egg from developing into a foetus is considered to be an abortion. For others, it is only when a fertilized egg embeds in the womb and begins to develop into an embryo that the pregnancy has started, and thus abortion only occurs when a developing embryo is deliberately disrupted. However, the fertilization and/or embedding of a fertilized egg is usually an invisible process, so at an individual basis the beginning of pregnancy is largely unknowable.

An example of the complexity of the situation can be seen in the UK. As in many other nations, the law in the UK treats abortion and contraception differently (Jackson 2001). Abortion is still a criminal offence in the UK (although, as will be explained later, there is a statutory defence in certain circumstances), and it is defined under the *Offences Against the Person Act 1861* as 'procuring a miscarriage.' Yet 'miscarriage' is not clearly defined in the Act (Jackson 2001). However, within the *Human Fertilisation and Embryology Act 1990*, pregnancy was defined as beginning when an embryo is implanted (Jackson 2001). Jackson (2001) argues that whilst this Act states that the definition is limited to this piece of legislation, it could be taken as a broader endorsement to exclude particularly post-coital methods such as emergency contraceptive pills (EHC) or intrauterine device (IUD) insertion from being considered as causing a miscarriage. Whilst it is generally agreed that post-coital methods of contraception prevent pregnancy (through preventing fertilization and/or implantation of a fertilized egg), this is disputed by some anti-abortion organizations who claim that these are a method of abortion.

Indeed, the social construction of a divide between contraception and abortion can be further illustrated in changes over time. In today's Western societies, pregnancy is often demonstrated by a positive response on a home testing kit, in contrast to earlier dependence on embodied changes or foetal movement. In earlier centuries, the detection of foetal movement in the second trimester, quickening, was widely believed to be the 'start' of pregnancy; before then, women had just failed to menstruate (Duden 1993; Riddle 1997). Duden's (1993) historical analysis has shown that women who had not had menstruation for several months did not necessarily consider pregnancy as a potential option. Instead, they sought a diagnosis from physicians to understand their condition and remedies to restore menstruation. Moreover, in earlier periods herbal remedies used to prevent conception were also often used to induce abortions, again negating a clear distinction between the two (Riddle 1997).

McLaren (1990) argues that separating contraception and abortion was a strategy of early twentieth century birth control campaigners in order to encourage medical professionals to support the contraceptive devices that they were promoting. Cook (2004) suggests that the divide was earlier than this. She shows how Francis Place, who produced the first birth control handbills (leaflets) in the UK in 1820, was aware of abortions but deemed them unrespectable in contrast to his support for contraceptive methods. Whatever the origins of this separation, the divide still dominates normative understandings today and explains the difficulties some people have with post-coital methods such as the EHC. Within this chapter, I use both terms in their conventional sense. However, it can also be useful to consider whether, rather than a straightforward dichotomy, fertility control can be conceptualized as a continuum, with different methods and acts placed along it that are deployed for different reasons at different times.

Sexual Consequences

As Cook's (2004) history of contraception has shown, whilst fertility control methods may have been widely utilized, it is only since the early nineteenth century that widespread information about effective practice began to be known in England. She argues that the birth control campaigners were often motivated by a belief that it would improve women's lives through female sexual autonomy, whereas opponents felt that this would lead women into inappropriate sexual relationships. These debates about women's appropriate sexual conduct have continued to surround contraception, although the target of 'unrespectable users' has changed. For example, the first birth control clinic in the UK, opened by Marie Stopes in 1921, was specifically aimed at existing married mothers. In other words, women who had already performed their natural role were seen as respectable. The medical preference for only supplying married women with contraception continued beyond the introduction of the contraceptive pill in the 1960s (Cook 2004).

Within heterosexual imaginaries, traditionally men have been positioned as active and women as passive, and whilst there is now an increased emphasis on women's sexual pleasure, the meaning of orgasm is still gendered (Jackson and Scott 2010). Prevailing sexual scripts are still important in defining 'real' heterosex and this impacts sexual practices (Braun 2013; Jackson and Scott 2010; Lowe 2005a). Another crucial element within the definition of 'real' heterosex is the naturalization of penile/vaginal penetration. The construction of heterosex as penile/vaginal penetration ending with male orgasm as the dominant sexual script has implications for understandings of contraception and contraceptive practice (Braun 2013; Lowe 2005a). For example, much of the emphasis in safer heterosex literature following the Human Immunodeficiency Virus Infection/Acquired Immune Deficiency Syndrome (HIV/AIDS) pandemic equated women's empowerment as the ability to carry condoms, rather than promoting non-penetrative sexual activity (see for example Griffin 1998). This put an emphasis on women's potential responsibility, due to the risk of pregnancy and in contrast to 'uncontrollable' male sexuality. Yet, paradoxically within medical discourse, women's sexuality is also potentially 'chaotic' and 'uncontrollable', and, as I will illustrate later, this can lead to the promotion of birth control methods that are outside of women's control.

Yet as (hetero)sex outside of marriage has become more openly practised, and understandings of marriage itself have arguably shifted as part of broader social changes, new issues have been debated regarding the practice of contraception. Here I want to focus on two interrelated issues: the rise of sexual abstinence movements for young people and the construction of teenage pregnancy as a problem. Both issues are inherently gendered, with a greater emphasis on young women's sexual behaviour than young men's. Moreover, both are clearly embedded in understandings of appropriate femininity in relation to motherhood and expect women to sacrifice their desires for the greater good of society. It is important to point out that although the initial focus of policy concerns was specifically teenagers, concerns over young motherhood are no longer confined to this age group. For example, a poster campaign that ran in New York City in 2013 suggested that becoming a parent under the age of 22 posed a risk to children (Taylor 2013).

The idea of abstinence is not new either as a method of contraception or a required role for women outside of marriage; however, the rise of the Christian evangelical chastity movements in the USA such as *True Love Waits* and *Silver Ring Thing* place a new emphasis on preserving virginity until marriage. This is constructed through the rhetoric of choice rather than prohibition (Gardner 2011). Gardner (2011) writes that these carefully designed campaigns argue that whilst mainstream culture only situates young people at the mercy of uncontrollable adolescent hormones, abstinence movements promote the idea that young people have a 'choice' to decline sexual activity, and that this is in their best interests. This message is clearly gendered and built on traditional ideas of heterosexual partnerships. As Gardner (2011) states, the movements often use fairy-tale narratives of threatened princesses waiting for their prince to arrive to ensure their happily-ever-after.

Whilst nominally aimed at both women and men, the reliance of abstinence movements on traditional heterosexual relationships means that they are clearly promoting women's dependence on men. Indeed, as Ehrlich (2006) argues, it was the image of unmarried pregnant teenagers, and increased emphasis on providing them contraception, that pre-empted the rise of today's chastity movements. Moreover, by basing their campaigns on an essentialist view of gender, they reaffirm attention on female purity. Magnusson's (2014) photographic study of purity balls clearly illustrates this. He documents how young women, often wearing quasi-wedding dresses, attend the balls with their fathers and often pledge to remain pure until marriage. Their fathers can reaffirm this sentiment by committing to protect their daughter's purity. In other words, young women are positioned as dependent on their fathers until marriage, when presumably they become dependent on their husbands. The possibilities of alternative futures are thus discursively rejected.

Chastity movements thus go beyond the promotion of early sexual abstinence and attempt to assert essentialist heteronormative dependence for women. It is clear from the campaigns and literature that whilst they are nominally aimed at both men and women, the requirements for women include behaving modestly to ensure that their behaviour does not tempt men (Gardner 2011). In the USA, state funding for abstinence-only education included school programmes as well as some other activities of chastity movements (Ehrlich 2006; Williams 2011). Whilst often justified on the basis of concerns about reducing the numbers of teenage mothers, the movement needs to be contextualized within a wider stance of traditional family values advocated by the US Christian right (Williams 2011). The abstinence movement has clear links to the neoconservative agenda and its concern for family values and traditional gender roles. Although purity balls themselves remain largely a US phenomenon, the underlying concepts about women's sexual and fertile lives can be clearly linked to trends in other places.

Young Women, Teenage Motherhood and Long-Acting Reversible Contraceptives (LARCs)

In the UK, concerns over teenage pregnancy began to rise in the 1980s and 1990s, and it is still often seen as a problematic issue today. As many authors such as Arai (2009) have documented, the amount of concern was unrelated to the numbers of births, which peaked in the 1970s and were in decline at the time that concerns started to grow. Arai (2009) points out that over time there was a shift in policy concerns from the marital status of women to the age of the mother, and this led to a focus on teenage mothers. Visibly pregnant young women or young mothers are a physical representation of young women's sexual behaviour which disrupts ideas about childhood innocence, particularly for the minority who are under the age of sexual consent, which is 16 in the UK. This also needs to be situated in the context of broader changes in the transition to adulthood (such as increasing emphasis on post-compulsory education) and the presumption of a need for welfare payments that often accompany discussions of young mothers (Arai 2009).

In the UK, following the election of the New Labour government in 1997, a less overtly moralistic approach was adopted as the discourse of risks and social exclusion was used in place of the earlier moral framework (Hoggart 2003). Many of the initiatives aimed at increasing knowledge of contraception and attempted to 'raise aspirations.' This latter element demonstrates the continuing association between young motherhood and the pathologization of working class cultures that ignore the impact of social structures (Arai 2009). The logic in many of the strategies is based on the premise that if the 'costs' of early motherhood are explained properly and young women have knowledge and access to contraception, then they will logically choose to delay pregnancy. Moreover, once the premise of delayed motherhood as inevitably the 'right' choice is accepted, the discussion moves on to the effectiveness of education and the suitability of particular methods. For supporters of birth control, this can mean the promotion of LARCs.

Promoting LARCs enables birth control advocates to support young women who are heterosexually active without being seen to condone early motherhood. Discussion is often couched in the discourse of ensuring proper counselling and the 'benefits' of a lack of user control in an 'unreliable' population. For example, in the US context, Boonstra (2013) discusses LARCs in the context of high teenage pregnancy rates that are presumptively assumed to be something to be avoided. She argues that LARCs offer a solution:

Adolescents—like all women seeking reproductive health services—should be able to pick a contraceptive method that is right for them (…) Fewer cost barriers for long-acting methods, increased provider training and greater awareness of these options among adolescents themselves are currently in the works and may well translate to more young women choosing LARCs. That would enable more of them to have greater control over their own reproductive lives—a win for them and for society at large. (Boonstra 2013: 17)

In this example, we can see an acknowledgment that women have a right to choose contraception, but young women will most likely choose LARCs if it is explained properly and there are no barriers such as cost. Boonstra's (2013) central argument is that the lack of user control benefits women individually and society more generally by removing risk of early motherhood through contraceptive non-use or failure. There is no question as to whether or not delaying motherhood is universally desirable; instead, later conception is deemed to be equated with greater control over reproductive lives. This is clearly similar to the support given in New Zealand for a vaccination style programme for young women mentioned earlier.

This prevailing discourse also has an impact on young women themselves. Fallon's (2013) study of women seeking EHC found that shame was a significant issue. They had concerns about how healthcare professionals would perceive them and worried about negative judgements from family or peers. Fallon (2013) points out that the negative feelings about accessing EHC were in many ways similar to concerns about being seen to be prepared for sex by using other methods of contraception. The worries about negative judgements about their sexual reputation that are part of the wider discourse structured the specific request for EHC. Indeed many women report they took the contraceptive pill primarily for gynaecological reasons when young, even if they were sexually active, suggesting the need to have a 'respectable' reason (Lowe 2003; Mills and Barclay 2006).

The presumption that contraception, or abstinence, is the only rational choice for young women illustrates how young women are expected to sacrifice any desire to become mothers until later. The meaning of 'later' will vary. It could be until after marriage, following successful post-compulsory education, or after a career has been established, depending on other prevailing cultural and structural ideas in which women are situated. Both abstinence advocates and birth control advocates use the discourse of choice for young women; they disagree on whether the right choice is chastity or contraception. For the chastity campaigners, young women should sacrifice sexual desires until marriage and dependency on a husband have been established. Whereas for birth control advocates young women should sacrifice any desires for motherhood until they are older and preferably financially independent, or at least a reduced risk of cost to the state. However, neither accepts that young women could legitimately choose early motherhood (although for the Christian right, this is still preferable to abortion). Consequently, although their particular positions are different, ideas of good motherhood and the desirability of sacrificing individual desires until specific conditions have been achieved underpin the logic of both of their positions. As well as the shared rhetoric of choice, they also both reaffirm the responsibilization of women in promoting their particular position on preventing births.

'Undesirable' Mothers

The promotion of contraception, particularly LARCs, needs to be contextualized within the history of coercion of marginalized women to reduce childbearing (Gomez et al. 2014). Young women are unusual in that their position as potentially 'undesirable' mothers is almost universal, crossing social divisions such as social class, ethnicity and disability. In most other cases of 'undesirable' motherhood, the specific social positioning of women is often the reason that contraception should be used. This is not a new emphasis; historically, many birth control advocates were interested in their use to reduce births amongst 'problematic' populations. For example, both Stopes and Sanger (an early 20th Century US campaigner) were known to be supportive of some eugenic ideas and felt that widening access to birth control was a good way of ensuring that improvement in births of the unfit could be prevented, although the extent to which this influenced their practice is debatable (Berkman 2011; Cook 2004).

Moreover, the widespread adoption of enforced sterilization in the early twentieth century in places such as the USA, Sweden and Japan illustrates how nations placed ideas of 'racial improvement' above the interests of women (Jütte 2008).

As Flavin (2009) has documented, at the heart of the eugenics movement was the notion that some women should be prevented and others encouraged to have children in order to avoid 'race suicide.' In the USA, it was white middle-class Protestant women who had too few children, whilst African Americans, immigrants and poor women were having too many (Flavin 2009). At the beginning of the twentieth century, sterilization was court ordered in many states for 'feeblemindedness' and 'delinquency' (Flavin 2009). Flavin (2009) shows that, although the rates of institutional sterilization declined after the Second World War, a new emphasis on 'welfare mums' emerged, and coercive sterilization, particularly of poor Black and Hispanic women, continued to take place. Jones (2013) illustrates how, in the UK in the 1980s, the injectable contraceptive Depo Provera was trialled on Black women and poor white women who had not been fully informed of the risks. This was also at a time when the Conservative government demonized single mothers and named the 'breakdown' of the family as a symptom of moral decline (Fox Harding 1999).

A more recent example of the persistence of the pressure applied to 'undesirable' women to prevent conception is Project Prevention. Project Prevention was set up in the USA to target users of alcohol or drugs and pay them to agree to accept LARCs or be sterilized (Project Prevention undated). Their website states that the project's objectives are to raise awareness and that:

> Project Prevention seeks to reduce the burden of this social problem on taxpayers, trim down social worker caseloads, and alleviate from our clients the burden of having children that will potentially be taken away. (Project Prevention undated)

Although on other parts of their website they refer to the welfare of women and children, it is clear that their primary motivation is to reduce the perceived potential costs, both social and financial, of children born to women who use substances. Whilst they do admit that not all children born to substance-using mothers will have health problems, they suggest that, as it is likely that they will be taken into foster care, this will inevitably lead to significant lifelong costs. They argue that, because foster care often fails to provide proper support, this will cause the children long-term issues (Project Prevention undated). With established links to the criminal justice system, the scheme links punishment and rehabilitation to reproductive coercion (Flavin 2009). Project Prevention expanded into the UK in 2010, although its website states that it is unable to offer sterilization in the UK due to the stance taken by the British Medical Association. The website claims that in total, 31 women in the UK (November 2014) have been paid to accept LARCs, although it does not give details of any previous contraceptive use. LARCs, like all other prescribed contraception, is free from the NHS, so clearly these women could have received money for something they were intending to do anyway.

Whilst the ethics of paying women to renounce their fertility in the style of Project Prevention might be debated, the idea that substance use is incompatible with good motherhood is more widely accepted. As Boyd (2004) has shown, good motherhood is often deemed to be irreconcilable with substance use, as the immature desire for drugs will allegedly lead to neglected children in chaotic homes. Yet as Boyd (2004) amongst others has shown, substance-using women are not homogeneous and many share the same parental values as non-using women. Indeed, it is often criminalization and the lack of policy emphasis on reducing harm that compound any difficulties with mothering that substance-using women encounter. Moreover, as Olsen et al. (2014) found in their study of women who inject drugs, the motivations and ability expressed towards contraceptive use are similar to those who are not substance-users. The construction of substance-users as unreliable and irresponsible contraceptive users who need to have their choices removed or reduced is thus debatable.

Women outside the framework of 'good motherhood' have long been the target of coercive strategies to reduce or remove their ability to have children. In some cases, this is done forcibly, whilst in others, choices have been offered, although it is clear what the 'right' choice should often be. So just like the concerns expressed about young women, ideas of good motherhood infuse the debates over when and which women should use birth control. Women who choose to reject these normative positions are thus constructed as selfish, immature or having a lack of regard for any (future) children. In other words, it positions their desire to be mothers above the perception of negative impacts on children's welfare. Hence, the absence of maternal sacrifice, choosing to give birth when non-motherhood is the cultural preference, undermines any claim to good motherhood. The medicalization of contraception allows the surveillance and policing of women's bodies, making it difficult to avoid these moral-ising frameworks.

Medical Power and Contraception

Modern contraceptives are more effective than historical methods, but the widespread involvement of the medical profession has increased sur-veillance over women's lives (Oakley 1993; Lowe 2005b). It also needs to be situated within the wider medicalization of women's reproductive bodies (Martin 1987; Lupton 1994). This situation was not inevitable. Burns (2005) suggests that Sanger actively targeted medical acceptance in the USA in order to give birth control legitimacy. Thomas's (1985) his-torical review of attitudes of UK doctors in the 1950s and 1960s showed a marked divide as to whether contraception should be seen as a medical matter. It was only after the development of the contraceptive pill and separate NHS payments to General Practitioners (GP) that contraceptive prescriptions began to be a routine part of their workload (Foster 1995).

Yet although contraception may have been placed under the remit of medicine, women may not support the idea that health professionals have a legitimate right to limit their decisions over which method to use (Lowe 2005b). As I have argued elsewhere, female users see contracep-tion as different from 'medical matters' and they do not expect health professionals to challenge or refuse them access to their method of choice (Lowe 2005b). Whilst they recognized that many forms of contraception had health implications, for the women in this study, women's bodily experiences rather than medical training were the foundation of 'expert' knowledge. They often trusted female health professionals' advice as they assumed that they were speaking from personal experience. When they were denied their method of choice, this was usually seen as an illegitimate use of medical power. This was especially true when they were able to access their chosen method through a different healthcare provider.

Studies of healthcare providers have illustrated how women are often judged on the basis of their 'respectability' and/or 'responsibility' when accessing contraception (Beynon-Jones 2013; Foster 1995; Hawkes 1995). This is particularly the case in discussions of EHC. Barrett and Harper (2000) found that health professionals in the UK believed that changing the status of EHC to an over-the-counter medicine would encourage the 'sexual irresponsibility' of young women and that consumption was not considered to be a rational decision to prevent pregnancy. These views have persisted in the UK following deregulation, and a study of advanced provision of EHC found that some health professionals were reluctant to promote the service to young or deprived women (Fairhurst et al. 2005). The study found that:

> Even when unintended pregnancy rates were perceived to be high, and the need for EC great, distribution was stifled by perceptions of the practice population as too chaotic to use advance supplies appropriately. (Fairhurst et al. 2005: 285)

This example illustrates the complexity of judgements made about women's access to contraception. Whilst health professionals can be in broad agreement about the 'right' and 'wrong' sort of women to reproduce, that does not mean that they are refraining from restricting access to contraceptive methods. Clearly of course, LARCs solve this problem by ensuring certain women do not become pregnant while keeping the control of contraception among medical professionals rather than in women's hands.

Cultural Limits to Choice

Social and cultural constraints over choices in contraception methods are not just limited to those deemed the 'wrong' sort of mothers. Studies have shown how other cultural imperatives influence the ability of women to exercise agency. Whilst women readily accept their embodied responsibility for preventing pregnancy, they do so within the context of medicalized implications of different contraceptive methods and within normative heterosexuality (Lowe 2005a, b). In her study of birth control pill use, Granzow (2007) found that whilst all the women interviewed discussed the context of contraceptive decision-making as one of choice, in their own cases, there were no viable alternatives. This finding is similar to Mills and Barclay (2006) who found that the women often used the contraceptive pill because they could not find anything better. Central to both these studies is women's recognition that, in order to achieve broader control over their lives, they need to be in a position to be able to restrain the limits of their fertility, but the means to be able to do this are currently imperfect.

Mills and Barclay (2006) found the side effects of contraception were a significant issue for women and shaped their quest to find the least worst option. All contraception has a potentially negative impact on women's bodies, and many women encounter difficulties with different methods (Lowe 2005b; Mills and Barclay 2006). Side effects are a major reason for the discontinuation of contraceptive methods (for example see Hoggart et al. 2013; Moreau et al. 2007). Yet there is a prevailing attitude by some healthcare professionals that these side effects need not be fully disclosed to women to avoid causing unnecessary alarm (Hoggart and Newton 2013). This reluctance could also be linked to the idea that women may not make the 'right' or 'rational' decisions over contraception. These ideas are part of the structures of the power relationships between female contraceptive users and healthcare providers (Fairhurst et al. 2005; Foster 1995; Hawkes 1995).

In addition to the embodied implications of different contraceptive technologies, normative understandings of heterosexuality also impact on women's contraceptive use. As my previous research has shown, whilst women believe that they have the right to control fertility decision making as they will be the ones becoming pregnant, this contrasts sharply with ideas about gender equality within heterosexual relationships (Lowe 2009). Moreover, accounts of how women negotiate decisions within heterosexual relationships have shown that many women choose from the narrower range of contraception that they feel their partners will be comfortable with (Lowe 2005a). Moreover, methods such as condoms can be constructed as anti-sex if they are perceived to interfere with normative ideas of intimacy and sexual activity (Braun 2013; Lowe 2005a). Wider issues of power and control within heterosexual encounters and relationships also mean that women may not be able to use contraception even if they desired to do so.

The general widespread availability of contraception in countries such as the UK and USA means that women are generally expected to use it if they wish to prevent pregnancy. In popular understandings, women are expected to take responsibility for pregnancy, and thus contraceptive failure is usually deemed to be their error. For example, in their study of contraceptive advertising in the USA, Medley-Rath and Simonds (2010) found that companies usually reinforced this message, emphasising that women rather than imperfect technologies were usually responsible for any pregnancies. In addition, the idea that women have complex interpersonal lives, which can act as a barrier to contraceptive use, is rarely considered. This is despite substantial research that has examined the issues involved. For example, Luker's (1975) study, which used a similar rational choice approach, outlined how contraception risk-taking was often a logical step in women's lives. She considered factors such as side effects and the impact of different heterosexual relationships and argued that the risk of pregnancy was often considered as less important than using contraception. Decades later Edin and Kefalas (2007) came to a fairly similar conclusion and argued that for women in poorer neighbourhoods, children brought meaning to women's lives even if they had not set out to conceive them. This further illustrates the need to consider how discourses of normative practices are influenced by social positioning. Whilst wider judgements may position women as unsuitable for motherhood, local cultural norms can offer some support for different life trajectories.

Taken together the cultural discourses construct women as wholly or mainly responsible for contraceptive use and failure, and yet at the same time women are not necessarily trusted with this responsibility. Normative ideas about heterosex and heterosexual relationships also structure the context within which women access and use contraception. These discourses arise from and reinforce understandings of women's sexual and reproductive bodies. Ideas about motherhood also affect these areas.

Women who should avoid motherhood, either due to their social positioning, behaviour or lack of a committed (male) partner, are expected to use the most effective methods of contraception, even if the side effects are difficult to manage. This could be seen as part of the embodied sacrifice that structures all aspects of women's reproductive lives.

Legal and Social Framing of Abortion

As I have outlined earlier, abortion is often considered in opposition to abstinence or contraception, and, for many, a less desirable way to manage women's fertility. Whilst undesirability is often a constant element, understandings of abortion are subjected to other particular frames of reference. The framing of abortion is related to, but not necessarily dependent on, either the legal status of abortion or popular understandings. The complexity of the interplay between the law, policy and practice will be explored using a few specific examples.

In the UK, abortion is still currently a crime, yet despite this, the vast majority of female residents of mainland Britain can access free abortions on the NHS. The *Offences Against the Person Act* (1861),[1] which is still in place, sets out severe punishment of women who try or allow an action with the intention of 'procuring a miscarriage.' However, the *Infant Life (Preservation Act)* (1929) stated that 'intentional destruction' of infants capable of being born alive was illegal unless it was done to save the life of the mother. This latter element allowed women to seek legal terminations, and this was confirmed in the *R vs. Bourne* case (1938) in which the law upheld the view that a severe risk to women's mental health was a justifiable reason. The 1967 *Abortion Act* in the UK did not revoke the earlier laws but instead created a legal defence to the crime of procuring an abortion (Jackson 2001). The *Abortion Act*, which only applies to England, Scotland and Wales, states that if two doctors believe that one of the conditions set out in the law are met, then there is a statutory defence against the law (Jackson 2001). The 1967 Act did not apply to

---

[1] The *Offences Against the Person Act* (1861) did not apply to Scotland, but abortion is an offence under common law. See Sheldon (2015) for more details about the legal position.

Northern Ireland, and abortion there remains more restricted than in the rest of the UK. Hence in the UK, the law still does not give a woman any legal right to an abortion, and legal control is with the medical profession. This is a similar picture to other countries such as New Zealand (Leask 2013).

In the USA, prior to the beginning of the nineteenth century, there was minimum legal regulation, and abortion before quickening (foetal movement) was largely unregulated (Luker 1984). Luker (1984) points out that, as the most obvious person to be able to detect foetal movements was the mother, it is likely that many terminations after quickening could not be reliably prosecuted. By the end of the nineteenth century, laws against abortion at any stage of pregnancy were enacted across the USA, and this campaign was led by the medical profession (Luker 1984). In a similar way to the UK, the legal ability to carry out abortions to save the life of the woman was used in a variety of situations during the early twentieth century (Luker 1984). Challenges to abortion laws emerged during the 1950s and some states had already changed their laws before the 1973 *Roe vs. Wade* decision of the Supreme Court. The Court found that in the earlier stages of pregnancy, women's right to privacy was more significant than the state's interest in the foetus. Hence the right to abortion was qualified by time rather than by being an absolute right. Within both UK and US legal histories, there are a number of different frames of reference. First is the extent to which abortion is a health or medical issue, second is whether or not women should have control over their reproductive bodies, and last is the status of the foetus.

In relation to the law in the UK, Sheldon (1997) has argued that rather than seeing the 1967 Abortion Act as a permissive move in legislation, the Act was actually about extending medical control over women's reproductive bodies. The Act does not give women the right to decide whether or not to have an abortion even if they meet the criteria: it is only if two doctors give a supportive opinion that termination is legally possible. This medical framing, alongside the quite vague wording of the specific conditions in the Act, means that doctors have the power to veto women's preferences yet also have extensive discretion as to what meets the legal position. For example, one of the grounds for permissible termination is:

that the pregnancy has not exceeded its twenty-fourth week and that continuance of the pregnancy would involve risk, greater than if the pregnancy were terminated, of injury to the physical or mental health of the pregnant woman or any existing children of her family. (Abortion Act 1967, as amended).

In practice, this clause is usually interpreted quite liberally. However, the law requires doctors to make formal judgements over women's health in order to meet the criteria for abortion (Jackson 2001; Sheldon 1997). Jackson (2001) argues that although this means that women had to present themselves to doctors as potentially desperate or at risk of harm, it did make abortion a medical rather than a moral question, and it may have helped stop attempts by men to intervene in their partners' decisions.

However, the medicalization of abortion has led to medical challenges to termination. Lee (2003) has documented the ways that anti-abortion groups began to promote the notion that abortion was a traumatic event that has a detrimental impact on women's health. The term postabortion syndrome (PAS) appeared in the 1980s in both Britain and the USA as groups claimed that abortion was a risk to women's mental health (Lee 2003). As Lee (2003) has documented, the claims about PAS emerged outside of the medical and scientific community, and although strong medical evidence has discredited PAS, it has reaffirmed the issue of abortion as a medicalized issue. More recently, other concerns about the 'health' risks of abortion have been used in different parts of the USA to increase regulation of abortion clinics. These regulations are promoted by anti-abortion activists as a way to close abortion clinics without having to directly challenge the legal status of abortion. Known as targeted regulations of abortion providers (TRAP) laws, the legislation is introduced requiring connections to local hospitals or reaching the standard of surgical centres even if they are only offering medical abortions (Gold and Nash 2013). The legislation is often pushed through in the name of protecting women from harm, although it is usually clear that restricting access to abortion is the main rationale, given that it has led to a reduction in the availability of abortion (Gold and Nash 2013).

This new emphasis on women's health is closer to a reproductive rights frame in which women are deemed to have the right to decide whether or not to continue with the pregnancy. As Burns (2005) has shown, the medical framing of abortion has often been present yet moves in and out of dominance over time. He argues that the *Roe vs. Wade* case occurred at a time when medical support for legal abortion was high, and whilst privacy was the significant rationale, it was clear that the Court used medical reasoning in their decision. Moreover, Petchesky (1986) argues this 'right' to abortion was upheld in the US because it was not possible to uphold prohibition given both the widespread practice of abortion and broader changes in women's lives, which were increasingly publicaly acknowledged to be about more than marriage and motherhood. Thus, the status of women in general can be linked to the framing of abortion.

Sweden is an example of a place where legal abortion has usually been framed in relation to the rights of women. In 1974, abortion on request was legalized, enabling women to request abortion without any medical reason up to the 18th week of pregnancy. Eduards (1991) argues that this was part of the broader political project of gender-neutral welfare policies in which the concept of parents-as-workers was established. Yet despite this apparent emphasis on women as decision-makers, it does not necessarily mean that their abortion decisions were not subject to social pressure. For example, Ekstrand et al. (2009) found that young women in particular felt pressure from partners, parents and peers to go ahead with terminations due to the stigmatization of teenage pregnancy. In addition, there is growing emphasis on a need to reduce the number of women having repeat abortions, which also indicates that the concept of abortion on request is still discursively limited and abortions are still viewed within a framework of right and wrong decisions.

Ideas about right and wrong reasons for abortion can be associated with the rise of the public foetus. As Lupton (2013) amongst others has illustrated, the use of foetal images has been crucial to anti-abortion campaigns in trying to assert that life begins at conception. Often depicting the foetus as a free-floating entity separate from women's bodies, the images are often assigned human characteristics, such as waving, in an attempt to ascribe them personhood (Lupton 2013). Moreover, within medicine, the availability of scanning technologies has led to the construction of the foetus as a patient who requires intervention and is almost separate from women's bodies. For example, Lupton (2013) has shown how research on foetal surgery omits or discounts any impact on the maternal body in its descriptions.

This concept of the foetus as citizen/patient divides the pregnant body and undermines understanding of abortion as either an issue of health or of women's rights. It helps to frame abortion as an extreme action which therefore can only be justified in certain circumstances. In other words, it can be used to suggest that women need a 'good' reason to terminate a pregnancy, one that goes beyond the fact that they just do not want to be pregnant. 'Good' reasons for abortion could include issues such as poverty, sexual violence or maternal age. In contrast, 'bad' reasons for termination might be failing to use contraception, especially if this was a repeated occurrence, or sex selection purposes. Regardless of the specific reasons, judging or restricting women's access to abortion on the basis of a moral judgement inevitably means limiting women's control over their bodies and encourages the stigmatization of abortion. It is within this frame that the discourse of the 'selfish' woman emerges.

O'Neil's (2013) study of abortion on Turkish television details the ways in which the 'selfish' woman is constructed. She found that characters undergoing abortion tend to be those who have rejected aspects of acceptable womanhood, often through putting their own lives ahead of others. In a similar way, in Poland, abortion has been depicted by the Polish Catholic Church as women's rejection of motherhood (Mishtal 2012). Purcell et al. (2014) examined abortion stories in UK newspapers and found that the motive for abortion was often depicted as a 'lifestyle' choice, or in other words as a superficial reason rather than a reasoned and reasonable option. Purcell et al. (2014) argue that this is a central element in the stigmatization of abortion. The concept of the 'selfish' woman who undergoes abortion for frivolous reasons is not a new idea. Leask (2013) has shown how, in New Zealand, this was common in the 1930s and was embedded in the McMillan Report published in 1939. This was a Parliamentary Inquiry which set out to explore the issue of illegal abortions, which were viewed as potentially threatening the future of the (white) population at the time.

All three frames of reference surrounding abortion can be related to ideas about motherhood in which maternal sacrifice is the organising principle. The health frame of abortion suggests that pregnant women need to have their position assessed by qualified medical professionals who can judge whether or not they are fit to be mothers. Particularly when this judgement rests on the mental health of women, it suggests that women who are 'approved' to undergo termination fail to reach the required standard. Whilst the women's rights framing should position women as beyond judgement, in practice, fitness to be a mother still seems to be a key criteria. The final frame, foetus as potential citizen, is the one in which women are often judged the most. Within this discourse, the construction of the selfish woman clearly illustrates the way that maternal sacrifice is deemed to be normative for 'good' womanhood. Women who choose terminations for 'bad' reasons are putting their own lives above that of the foetus and thus failing to act as appropriate women.

Rationing Abortion

Within many of the frames of reference, there is an element of abortion being a regrettable decision. In the anti-abortionist rhetoric, the only circumstances in which abortion could possibly be considered would be when refusing to terminate the pregnancy would result in the death of both the woman and the foetus. Yet within the pro-choice position, all too often abortion is still seen as a regrettable if necessary decision. Weingarten (2012) has pointed out that the framing of abortion as a regrettable choice is bound up with the individualization and responsibilization of women in the area of reproductive health. For Weingarten (2012), it necessitates women to confirm to self-regulation as a disciplined subject. Hence, whilst 'choice' is positioned as an option for women, the good chooser will not need to access abortion as they have planned appropriately so as not to experience a pregnancy out of place.

Weitz (2010) has argued that, in the US context, the pro-choice mantra that abortion should be legal but 'rare' emerged as an attempt to bridge the pro-choice and anti-abortion divide. She suggests that whilst this move was seeking to reduce conflict over abortion, it undermines women's position and reinforces negative opinions. As Weitz suggests:

"rare" suggests that abortion is happening more than it should, and that there are some conditions for which abortion should and should not occur. It separates good abortions from bad abortions (…) Abortion is currently one of the most stigmatized events in a woman's life and the widespread endorsement of "rare" both produces and reproduces this stigma. (Weitz 2010: 164)

Hence, for Weitz (2010), this discursive shift adopted by pro-choice advocates, in which abortion is constructed as necessary but not desirable, undermines an understanding of abortion as an essential element for women's health. It also potentially supports making access difficult or suggests restrictions to its use, 'rare' occurrences should not need large amounts of resources.

As both Weitz (2010) and Weingarten (2012) have shown, the idea of the responsible chooser who would only need to access abortion in 'rare' circumstances is predicated on notions of rational family planning, in which preventing conception is more desirable than terminating an existing pregnancy. Moreover, these ideas feed into the construction of repeat abortions as a social problem. For example, in their review of 'determinate factors', McCall et al. (2014) state that repeat abortion is a 'significant' health problem. This is similar to the views of health professionals in which repeat abortion is conceptualized as a failure of women rather than a failure of contraceptive technology (Beynon-Jones 2013). As Beynon-Jones (2013) argues, policy requirements that may mandate contraceptive counselling for women requesting abortion build on this particular understanding. Hence, women who request abortions are often positioned as having failed at responsible choosing rather than active decision-makers.

The understanding of women as failed choosers, and as such, irrational rather than active agents, reflects broader understandings of women as potentially unstable. Moreover, if irrationality is a central feature of abortion requests, calls for abortion counselling thus become a potential solution. It is clear that anti-abortion activists see abortion counselling as a mechanism to dissuade women from having terminations (Lee 2003; Joffe 2009), but they do so by building on the notion of women's inherent instability, and this notion has been supported in the US legal system (Manian 2009). In the UK, there have been attempts to restrict those who can provide abortion counselling and to prevent abortion providers from providing it, and supporters have claimed that this would reduce the number of abortions taking place (Jackson 2011). In other words, the proponents of 'independent' counselling are assuming that some women do not really want an abortion but are being persuaded by abortion providers. They have not provided any evidence to support this claim (Jackson 2011). Indeed, whilst some women may take longer to decide than others, most are sure about their decision before approaching an abortion provider (Brown 2013).

The idea that counselling is always necessary feeds into the hierarchy of 'good' and 'bad' abortions. This is entwined with ideas of desirable and undesirable motherhood. Cockrill and Nack's (2013) study revealed some women seeking abortion had previously associated abortion with negative positionings, such as being uneducated, irresponsible, promiscuous or selfish. Once they were considering an abortion, many of the women judged themselves or had concerns about being judged by others in relation to these stereotypes and sought to either conceal or distance themselves from negative perceptions. Kumar et al. (2009) have suggested that the stigmatization of abortion is related to the idea that it challenges the 'essential nature' of women as mothers and caregivers. In different social contexts, the stigma present will vary depending on culturally-dependant ideas of idealized family life (Kumar et al. 2009).

As the construction of 'good' and 'bad' abortions is intrinsically linked to broader ideas about responsible motherhood, ideas of maternal sacrifice are also present. Whilst less obvious than in the area of contraception, they nevertheless still help to frame the debates. The idea that women seeking abortion are potentially irrational, impoverished choosers suggests to those who support abortion that motherhood should be prevented/delayed until such time that they are better placed to put any child's interest first. This position can be clearly symbolized by the image of the potentially benefit-dependent teenage mother, which often surrounds debates on abortion. For the anti-abortionists, the sacrifice that should be made is for women to proceed with pregnancy when they do not wish to do so.

Pregnancy as Penance

The stated position of many anti-abortionists is that abortion is not permissible under any circumstances, although they accept that some life-saving treatments needed by pregnant women will cause the death of the foetus (for example see Society for the Protection of Unborn Children undated). They thus require women to continue with pregnancy regardless of the circumstances of conception. Whilst they claim that this is because of a belief in the personhood of the foetus, many of those involved in the anti-abortion movement are also critical of women's sexual behaviour. The insistence that pregnancy should continue regardless of whether or not women want to be mothers is also partly about the presumed 'failure' of women to keep their sexual activity within the narrow confines of heterosexual marriage. Women who become pregnant when they should not be can therefore be 'punished' by not being able to absolve themselves of their responsibility for growing a foetus.

As Begun and Walls (2015) have shown, anti-abortion stances are associated with sexist ideas about women's position in society. Their study showed that both hostile misogynistic ideas and more benevolent notions of complementary gender differentiation were likely to influence the extent to which their participants were anti-abortion. In this respect, women are not equal citizens and thus decisions about bodily integrity should be made by others. As Flavin (2009) has argued, the law often positions women as wives and mothers, as this reaffirms gendered citizenship. She also points out that the positioning of adoption as an alternative to abortion is an extension of these ideas. It is only if the embodied state of pregnancy is disregarded that they can be seen as potential equivalents, and this is legitimated through the position that motherhood, and thus pregnancy, is synonymous with womanhood.

Lee (2003) argues that the claims-making around PAS often made connections to Post-Traumatic Stress Disorder (PTSD), particularly in relation to rape. The promotion of the idea that abortion is 'medical-rape' by anti-abortion organizations allows them to claim that a termination would double the trauma for rape victims. This claim that abortion is as bad as, or even worse, than being raped allows the anti-abortion movement a defence in one of the few areas where most agree there might be a 'good' abortion. As Luker (1984) pointed out, if the anti-abortion movement accepted some reasons for abortion, it would be difficult to justify their position more broadly. Moreover, this needs to be situated within a broader social context where women are often disbelieved about rape and women can be held responsible for assaults against them (see for example Suarez and Gadalla 2010). If accounts of rape are doubted, and positioned as a way of explaining 'bad' sex, then women who seek abortions on the basis of rape can be associated with 'illicit' sexual activity.

A classic example of the way that 'illicit' sexual activity was punished was in the Irish Magdalene Laundries. As Titley (2006) has shown, the Magdalene Laundries, which operated until the 1990s, were places where women who were deemed to have violated the norms of Irish Catholic life were sent to be reformed. These often ran in tandem with Catholic Mother and Baby Homes. Both types of institution sought to redeem the women through hard work and prayer, and the babies born within the system were often taken for adoption. In the 1950s and 1960s, the Catholic Church was involved in a transnational adoption process in which the children of unmarried Irish women were shipped to families in the USA. Garrett (2000) suggests that this trade was popular with American potential parents for racist reasons, as they felt it was less likely that the children would have Black relatives. Hence in a hierarchy of desirable motherhood, the offspring from children from 'immoral' white mothers were considered preferable. Moreover, given the illegal status of abortion in Ireland, and the public condemnation of unmarried mothers, many women had little choice but to agree with this regime.

Whilst few would now agree with the incarceration of women on the basis of sex outside of marriage, the idea that women who seek abortions are selfish and immature also feeds into the notion that women should 'live with' any consequences of sexual activity. This view is not solely held by anti-abortion groups but can also be seen in particular communities. In Edin and Kefalas' (2007) study of poorer women, their participants felt that people who do not use contraception should accept the consequences of any sexual activity, and that the responsible action is to continue with the pregnancy. Whilst some may still choose to terminate pregnancies, this was seen as a last resort and it was preferable to continue with the pregnancy if at all possible. Motherhood was a valued position

for women, and as such successfully raising a child in difficult circumstances could give women status in their community. Edin and Kefalas
(2007) point out how this contrasts to life expectations of middle-class
women, who often have other ways to gain esteem. Hence, the ways in
which abortion is conceptualized as a choice can only be understood
within the specific context of women's lives.

Clearly not all who hold an anti-abortion position have traditional
views on the role of women. However, people who believe that women
should continue with a pregnancy regardless of personal cost position
women as mothers above all other potential identity positions. The anti-
abortion position is thus built on the notion that women should sacrifice other aspects of their lives in the name of protecting the foetus. The
extreme end of this position can be vividly seen in the stories of pregnant
women who refuse terminations and delay or reduce medical treatments
for life-threatening conditions that are often posted on anti-abortion
organization websites (for example, Lifezone undated). However, the UK
and Ireland Confidential Enquiries into Maternal Deaths and Morbidity
2009–2012 (Knight et al. 2014) notes the significant risk to women's
health posed by non-compliance with medical treatment during pregnancy. Abstaining from or reducing medical treatments can ultimately
mean that women sacrifice their lives in the name of preserving the foetus
if the penance of pregnancy is taken to the extremes.

Conclusion

As this chapter has shown, the idea of maternal sacrifice can be seen
to underpin different understandings of fertility control. Members of
the sexual abstinence movement and advocates for young people having
access to contraception both agree that young women should not become
pregnant, and thus any desire for early motherhood is not acceptable.
More generally, the targeting of particular women for contraception,
such as substance users, on the basis of a presumption of irresponsible
motherhood indicates how some women are expected to sacrifice any
desire to be a mother until they are deemed suitable. The medicalization
of contraception is a central way of disciplining women, with the ongoing

preference for giving LARCs to women deemed unsuitable for mother-hood. Women are thus responsible for any pregnancy but not necessarily trusted to be able to make the 'right' decisions over contraception.

In a similar way, the three frameworks for positioning abortion also use the notion of maternal sacrifice to underpin their position. Within the health position, medical professionals have the right of judgement over the health and/or mental state of women. Health professionals are thus formally seeking to assess women's fitness to parent as part of the decision-making rationale. Whilst the women's rights frame should not in theory take this into consideration, the evidence shows that normative values of acceptable and unacceptable motherhood are still an important consideration. Both of these positions often place abortion as ideally rare and/or a regrettable decision which sets up the notions of 'good' and 'bad' abortions within which women's suitability can be judged. In the foetal rights frame, the sacrifice called for is for women to continue with a pregnancy when they do not wish to do so. In this sacrifice, pregnancy can be seen as a penance. Historically, women could be punished for illicit sexual activity through incarceration, and whilst this has declined, some stigma, particularly for young women, remains. The responsibilization of women can also mean that some women feel the only course of action is to continue with pregnancy even in difficult circumstances, building on the notion of motherhood as a positive identity in which others' desires and wellbeing are always put first. The complex ways in which ideas of motherhood intertwine with women's identities can also be seen in the difficult journey that some women face when trying to conceive.

References

Arai, L. (2009). *Teenage pregnancy: The making and unmaking of a problem.* Bristol, England: The Policy Press.

Barrett, G., & Harper, R. (2000). Health professionals' attitudes to the deregulation of emergency contraception (or the problem of female sexuality). *Sociology of Health and Illness, 22*(2), 197–216.

Begun, S., & Walls, N. E. (2015). Pedestal or gutter exploring ambivalent sexism's relationship with abortion attitudes. *Affilia, 30*(2), 200–215.

Berkman, J. (2011). The question of Margaret Sanger. *History Compass, 9*(6), 474–484.

Beynon-Jones, S. M. (2013). 'We view that as contraceptive failure': Containing the 'multiplicity' of contraception and abortion within Scottish reproductive healthcare. *Social Science & Medicine, 80*, 105–112.

Boonstra, H. D. (2013). Leveling the playing field: The promise of long-acting reversible contraceptives for adolescents. *Guttmacher Policy Review, 16*(4), 13–18.

Boyd, S. C. (2004). *Mothers and illicit drugs: Transcending the myths.* London: University of Toronto Press.

Braun, V. (2013). 'Proper sex without annoying things': Anti-condom discourse and the 'nature' of (hetero)sex. *Sexualities, 16*(3/4), 361–382.

Brown, S. (2013). Is counselling necessary? Making the decision to have an abortion. A qualitative interview study. *European Journal of Contraception and Reproductive Health Care, 18*(1), 44–48.

Burns, G. (2005). *The moral veto: Framing contraception, abortion, and cultural pluralism in the United States.* Cambridge, England: Cambridge University Press.

Cockrill, K., & Nack, A. (2013). "I'm not that type of person": Managing the stigma of having an abortion. *Deviant Behavior, 34*(12), 973–990.

Cook, H. (2004). *The long sexual revolution: English women, sex, and contraceptives 1800-1975.* Oxford, England: Oxford University Press.

Duden, B. (1993). *Disembodying women: Perspectives on pregnancy and the unborn.* Cambridge, MA: Harvard University Press.

Edin, K., & Kefalas, M. (2007). *Promises I can keep: Why poor women put motherhood before marriage.* London: University of California Press.

Eduards, M. (1991). Toward a third way: Women's politics and welfare policies in Sweden. *Social Research, 58*(3), 677–705.

Ehrlich, J. S. (2006). From age of consent laws to the silver ring thing: The regulation of adolescent female sexuality. *Health Matrix, 16*(1), 151–181.

Ekstrand, M., Tydén, T., Darj, E., & Larsson, M. (2009). An illusion of power: Qualitative perspectives on abortion decision-making among teenage women in Sweden. *Perspectives on Sexual and Reproductive Health, 41*(3), 173–180.

Fairhurst, K., Wyke, S., Ziebland, S., Seaman, P., & Glasier, A. (2005). "Not that sort of practice": The views and behaviour of primary care practitioners in a study of advance provision of emergency contraception. *Family Practice, 22*(3), 280–286.

Fallon, D. (2013). 'They're gonna think it now': Narratives of shame in the sexual health experiences of young people. *Sociology, 47*(2), 318–332.

Flavin, J. (2009). *Our bodies, our crimes: The policing of women's reproduction in America*. London: New York University Press.

Foster, P. (1995). *Women and the health care industry: An unhealthy relationship*. Buckingham, England: Open University Press.

Fox Harding, L. (1999). 'Family values' and conservative government policy: 1979–97. In J. Jagger & C. Wright (Eds.), *Changing family values* (pp. 119–135). London: Routledge.

Gardner, C. (2011). *Making chastity sexy: The rhetoric of evangelical abstinence campaigns*. London: University of California Press.

Garrett, P. M. (2000). The abnormal flight: The migration and repatriation of Irish unmarried mothers. *Social History, 25*(3), 330–343.

Gold, R. B., & Nash, E. (2013). TRAP laws gain political traction while abortion clinics—and the women they serve—pay the price. *Guttmacher Policy Review, 16*(2), 7–12.

Gomez, A. M., Fuentes, L., & Allina, A. (2014). Women or LARC first? Reproductive autonomy and the promotion of long-acting reversible contraceptive methods. *Perspectives on Sexual and Reproductive Health, 46*(3), 171–175.

Granzow, K. (2007). De-constructing 'choice': The social imperative and women's use of the birth control pill. *Culture, Health & Sexuality, 9*(1), 43–54.

Griffin, K. (1998). Beyond empowerment: Heterosexualities and the prevention of AIDS. *Social Science and Medicine, 46*(2), 151–156.

Hawkes, G. (1995). Responsibility and irresponsibility: Young women and family planning. *Sociology, 29*(2), 257–273.

Hoggart, L. (2003). Teenage pregnancy: The government's dilemma. *Capital and Class, 27*(1), 145–165.

Hoggart, L., & Newton, V. L. (2013). Young women's experiences of side-effects from contraceptive implants: A challenge to bodily control. *Reproductive Health Matters, 21*(41), 196–204.

Hoggart, L., Newton, V. L., & Dickson, J. (2013). "I think it depends on the body, with mine it didn't work": Explaining young women's contraceptive implant removal. *Contraception, 88*(5), 636–640.

Jackson, E. (2001). *Regulating reproduction: Law, technology and autonomy*. Oxford, England: Hart Publishing.

Jackson, E. (2011). *A new amendment on abortion guidance will instead institute delays for women seeking medical help*. British Politics and Policy at LSE (31 Aug 2011) Blog Entry.

Jackson, S., & Scott, S. (2010). *Theorising sexuality*. Maidenhead, England: Open University Press.

Joffe, C. (2009). *Dispatches from the abortion wars: The costs of fanaticism to doctors, patients and the rest of the US*. Boston: Beacon Press.
Jones, C. (2013). Human weeds, not fit to breed? African Caribbean women and reproductive disparities in Britain. *Critical Public Health, 23*(1), 49–61.
Jütte, R. (2008). *Contraception: A history*. Cambridge, England: Polity Press.
Knight, M., Kenyon, S., Brocklehurst, P., Neilson, J., Shakespeare, J., & Kurinczuk, J. J. (Eds.) on behalf of MBRRACEUK. (2014). *Saving lives, improving mothers' care—Lessons learned to inform future maternity care from the UK and Ireland confidential enquiries into maternal deaths and morbidity 2009–12*. Oxford, England: University of Oxford, National Perinatal Epidemiology Unit.
Kumar, A., Hessinia, L., & Mitchell, E. M. H. (2009). Conceptualising abortion stigma. *Culture, Health & Sexuality, 11*(6), 625–639.
Leask, M. (2013). From bad women to mad women: A genealogical analysis of abortion discourses in aotearoa New Zealand. *New Zealand Sociology, 28*(2), 104–119.
Lee, E. (2003). *Abortion, motherhood and mental health: Medicalizing reproduction in the United States and Great Britain*. New York: Aldine de Gruyter.
Lifezone. (n.d.). *Personal stories: The mothers who had a medical emergency when pregnant*. Retrieved December 20, 2014, from http://www.prolifeinfo.ie/women/medical-matters/personal-stories--medical/
Lowe, P. (2003). *Power and the pill: Midlife women negotiating contraception*. Unpublished PhD thesis, University of Warwick, Coventry, England.
Lowe, P. (2005a). Contraception and heterosex: An intimate relationship. *Sexualities, 8*(1), 75–92.
Lowe, P. (2005b). Embodied expertise: Women's perceptions of the contraception consultation. *Health: An Interdisciplinary Journal for the Social Study of Health, Illness and Medicine., 9*(3), 361–378.
Lowe, P. (2009). A 'snip' in the right direction? Vasectomy and gender equality. In C. Kevin (Ed.), *Feminism and the body interdisciplinary perspectives* (pp. 68–79). Newcastle upon Tyne, England: Cambridge Scholars.
Luker, K. (1975). *Taking chances: Abortion and the decision not to contracept*. London: University of California Press.
Luker, K. (1984). *Abortion and the politics of motherhood*. London: University of California Press.
Lupton, D. (1994). *Medicine as culture: Illness, disease and the body in western societies*. London: Sage.
Lupton, D. (2013). *The social worlds of the unborn*. Basingstoke, England: Palgrave.

Magnusson, D. (2014). *Purity*. Stockholm, Sweden: Bokforlaget Max Strom.

Manian, M. (2009). The irrational woman: Informed consent and abortion. *Duke Journal of Gender Law and Policy, 16*(2), 223–292.

Martin, E. (1987). *The woman in the body*. Buckingham, England: Open University Press.

McCall, S. J., Nur Ibrahim, U., Imamura, M., Okpo, E., Flett, G., & Bhattacharya, S. (2014). Exploring the determinant factors for repeat abortion: A systematic review. *Journal of Epidemiology and Community Health, 68*(Suppl 1), A57.

McLaren, A. (1990). *A history of contraception*. Oxford, England: Basil Blackwell.

Medley-Rath, S. R., & Simonds, W. (2010). Consuming contraceptive control: Gendered distinctions in web-based contraceptive advertising. *Culture, Health and Sexuality, 12*(7), 783–795.

Mills, A., & Barclay, L. (2006). None of them were satisfactory: Women's experiences with contraception. *Health Care for Women International, 27*(5), 379–398.

Mishtal, J. (2012). Irrational non-reproduction? The 'dying nation' and the postsocialist logics of declining motherhood in Poland. *Anthropology & Medicine, 19*(2), 153–169.

Moreau, C., Cleland, K., & Trussell, J. (2007). Contraceptive discontinuation attributed to method dissatisfaction in the United States. *Contraception, 76*(2), 267–272.

O'Neil, M. L. (2013). Selfish, vengeful, and full of spite: The representations of women who have abortions on Turkish television. *Feminist Media Studies, 13*(5), 810–818.

Oakley, A. (1993). *Essays on women, medicine and health*. Edinburgh, Scotland: Edinburgh University Press.

Olsen, A., Banwell, C., & Madden, A. (2014). Contraception, punishment and women who do drugs. *BMC Women's Health, 14*(5). Retrieved from http://www.biomedcentral.com/1472-6874/14/5

Petchesky, R. (1986). *Abortion and women's choice*. London: Verso.

Project Prevention. (n.d.). Retrieved November 10, 2014, from http://www.projectprevention.org/

Purcell, C., Hilton, S., & McDaid, L. (2014). The stigmatisation of abortion: A qualitative analysis of print media in Great Britain in 2010. *Culture, Health & Sexuality: An International Journal for Research, Intervention and Care, 16*(9), 1141–1155.

Riddle, J. M. (1997). *Eve's herbs: A history of contraception and abortion in the west*. London: Harvard University Press.

Sheldon, S. (1997). *Beyond control: Medical power and abortion law.* London: Pluto Press.

Sheldon, S. (2015). The decriminalisation of abortion: An argument for modernisation. *Oxford Journal of Legal Studies.* doi:10.1093/ojls/gqv026

Society for the Protection of Unborn Children. (n.d.). Abortion briefi ng. Retrieved December 20, 2014, from https://www.spuc.org.uk/education/abortion/briefi ng

Suarez, E., & Gadalla, T. M. (2010). Stop blaming the victim: A meta-analysis on rape myths. *Journal of Interpersonal Violence, 25*(11), 2010–2035.

Taylor, K. (2013, March 6). Posters on teenage pregnancy draw fire. *New York Times.* Retrieved September 8, 2015, from http://www.nytimes.com/2013/03/07/nyregion/city-campaign-targeting-teenage-pregnancy-draws-criticism.html?_r=0

Thomas, H. (1985). The medical construction of the contraceptive career. In H. Homans (Ed.), *The sexual politics of reproduction* (pp. 45–63). Aldershot, England: Gower.

Titley, B. (2006). Heil Mary: Magdalen asylums and moral regulation in Ireland. *History of Education Review, 35*(2), 1–15.

Weingarten, K. (2012). Impossible decisions: Abortion, reproductive technologies, and the rhetoric of choice. *Women's Studies: An Inter-disciplinary Journal, 41*(3), 263–281.

Weitz, T. (2010). Rethinking the mantra that abortion should be 'safe, legal, and rare'. *Journal of Women's History, 22*(3), 161–168.

Williams, J. C. (2011). Battling a 'sex-saturated society': The abstinence movement and the politics of sex education. *Sexualities, 14*(4), 416–443.

4

Conceiving Motherhood

As the previous chapter has shown, concerns about who is and who is not suitable for motherhood structure approaches to fertility regulation, and at the centre of these ideas is the notion that 'good mothers' should always put (potential) children first. These views about acceptable and unacceptable motherhood also have a strong influence over some women's journeys towards motherhood, particularly if they encounter problems conceiving. This chapter will look at how ideas about motherhood as a 'natural' role for women affect conception issues. It will begin by building on the issues raised in Chap. 2 about the association between womanhood and motherhood and how this can lead to a division among women on the basis of motherhood/non-motherhood, a division which may overlook the complexity of fertility issues in women's lives. These ideas have a strong influence on women's experiences of infertility and the idea of the biological clock; fertility is thus positioned as an embodied finite resource that women should not ignore. The chapter will then examine the ways in which motherhood as a natural role and ideas about fitness to parent are embedded in medicalized infertility treatments. This will include a consideration of gamete transactions and understandings of surrogacy that indicate how these are also built around notions

© The Editor(s) (if applicable) and The Author(s) 2016
P. Lowe, *Reproductive Health and Maternal Sacrifice*,
DOI 10.1057/978-1-137-47293-9_4

of maternal sacrifice, albeit in different ways to the 'intended' parents. Finally, the issue of reproductive loss will be explored, in particular in relation to how motherhood without children further adds to our understanding of broader conceptions of motherhood.

Mothers and 'Others'

As Letherby (1994, 1999) has argued, the long history of associating womanhood with motherhood can place women without children in a problematic position. Women without children (who are socially positioned as potential good mothers) are often asked to explain or justify their position in a way that women with children are usually not (Bute 2009). Hence, whilst conception at the 'wrong' time or for the 'wrong' person should be prevented, for women positioned as potentially good mothers, non-conception can be seen as a discrediting identity. Meyers (2001) defines pronatalist discourse as one in which motherhood is not just seen as destiny for women but is supported through other structures such as heterosexual norms. Whilst there are cultural variations to how and the extent to which pronatalism operates, arguably it is still a feature of many contemporary societies (Allison 2013; Letherby 1999; Remennick 2000).

Women without children are often divided into the 'childless' and 'childfree.' The childless are those who would like to have children, either at that time or at some point in the future, whereas the childfree are those who do not intend to be mothers. This divide is problematic, as it is better understood as a continuum on which women may be positioned differently at different points in their lives (Letherby 1999; Maher and Saugeres 2007; Wilson 2014). Wilson (2014) found that her attempts to recruit 'infertile' women to her research were difficult in that many rejected this label even if they had had problems conceiving. She argues that the different possible parameters (such as timing, suitable partners, and decisions about fertility treatments) all interact in complex ways and that women who do not conceive may not actually 'test' their fertility to any great extent. Tonkin (2010) uses the term 'contingently childless' to describe women who thought they would become mothers but did not have children before menopause. She argues that whilst this is often conceptualized as a 'choice', in practice it is not perceived as such, and this disguises the sense of loss that some women feel about not becoming mothers.

Not all women feel a sense of loss, however: some have never considered themselves as potential mothers, and others who postpone motherhood until (if ever) it seems a viable option do not necessarily have any undue concerns (Meyers 2001). Indeed, women who never considered motherhood may not necessarily articulate non-motherhood as a conscious decision but rather as something they had always known (Meyers 2001). In Maher and Saugeres's (2007) study this was seen as a natural decision, and whilst they needed to articulate their position against the dominate narrative of pronatalism, their non-motherhood was as predestined as motherhood was for those with children. Maher and Saugeres (2007) found that the fertility decisions of their interviewees were closely tied to their ideas of motherhood as selfless and dedicated to their children, regardless of whether they were postponing or had never intended to conceive.

In her study of infertility, many of Wilson's (2014) participants also commented on motherhood primarily as work and sacrifice. These accounts were contrasted with the descriptions given by women of the bad, neglectful 'nominal' mothers who were often perceived as conceiving easily yet failed to meet the standards of 'good motherhood.' Moreover, as Wilson (2014) argues, within the cultural lens of motherhood as a 'compulsory' status, women without children can be seen as also deviant alongside the image of 'bad mothers.' Indeed, if motherhood is synonymous with womanhood, 'bad mothers' are closer to the ideal woman. She states:

> Infertile and childless women of all backgrounds grapple with this concept of the nominal mother, who represents an inferior kind of woman who, despite her immorality, is still assigned higher status in terms of womanhood than they are thanks to a technicality. (Wilson 2014: 58–59)

As I outlined in Chap. 2, failing to put children first is part of the cultural construction of 'bad' mothers. Hence pursuing the dream of having children, regardless of cost, can thus be positioned as an indicator of potential 'good motherhood.'

These accounts indicate that ideas about the necessity of maternal sacrifice are also present in the lives of some women who are not or do not want to be mothers. The idealization of what good motherhood consists of may form part of their ambivalence or decision not to have children. Indeed the negative discourse which is sometimes applied to childfree women as 'selfish' (Gillespie 2000; Letherby 2002; Throsby 2004; Wilson 2014) illustrates the extent to which being 'selfless' is seen as a necessary quality of women/mothers. Rich et al. (2011) revealed how, in the Australian context, women without children felt that they were systematically undervalued in comparison to having a status as mothers, and their childless state undermined their position as adult women. Hence women without children, whether intentional or not, are still measured within and against the broad narratives of motherhood both by others and often themselves.

The pressure on women who are considered potential 'good mothers' often increases as they age, and messages about preventing pregnancy can change into an obligation to reproduce, with this becoming particularly intensive as women move through their 30s. The growing trend for women to have children later than in previous generations has led to anxiety, and this can be illustrated in the notion of the 'biological clock' which often pervades media accounts. Whilst there is still some debate as to the rate and pace of age-related fertility decline in women (Eijkemans et al. 2014), media coverage tends to covey it as a significant risk (Budds et al. 2013; Graham and Rich 2014; Harter et al. 2005; Shaw and Giles 2009). Budds' et al. (2013) found that stories of later conception oversimplified the issues and likened delaying motherhood to 'gambling' with the chances of becoming pregnant. Media articles also focused on delay always being women's 'choice', overlooking the social factors, such as the formation of partnerships, which structure their lives. Graham and Rich (2014) found similar trends in the Australian media. They found many articles reprimanding women with alarmist accounts. They report:

> With the use of such emotive language such as "urgent," "profound," "fears," and "consequences," the tone of these newspaper items is threatening

and alarming. Rather than merely cautionary, these newspaper items appear to be intended to alarm ageing childless women into paying attention to their declining fertility. (Graham and Rich 2014: 512)

The narrative of negative consequences of women ignoring the 'biological clock' can be portrayed as a personal tragedy and/or a failure to perform women's 'natural' role in society (Graham and Rich 2014). Yet simultaneously there is a strong cultural message to not have children until materially and socially ready (Allison 2013). Locke and Budds (2013) investigated how some women tried to reconcile these messages. They found that some women felt obliged to try to conceive once they reached the age when they thought their fertility would be declining. Their expectation that it would be difficult meant that they chose this path even if they did not feel ready. In their study, women were then surprised that they did not experience any difficulties getting pregnant. The complex web of cultural scripts around fertility and motherhood also affects the ways in which women who are finding it difficult to conceive experience their condition.

Infertility Experiences

As Greil et al. (2010) amongst others have argued, infertility is often now understood in relation to the standard medical definition: the inability to conceive after a year of regular unprotected heterosexual intercourse. Yet that definition overlooks the socially constructed nature of the condition. Greil et al. (2010) suggest that infertility is better understood as a process whereby individuals come to define their inability to have children as a problem. This definition encompasses how it is the desire for a particular way to become parents, rather than just biological functioning, that is the central element to being infertile (Greil et al. 2010). In addition, Hampshire et al. (2012) suggest that seeing infertility in individual terms overlooks the importance of wider social and kinship expectations. They suggest that infertility needs to be considered as a relational concept, as individual aspirations for family life are made in the context of broader family networks and cultural norms. Moreover, as Remennick (2000) has shown, in some pronatalist state policies, infertility treatments are constructed as almost obligatory, and this will also impact how infertility is understood. Thus, the ways in which infertility is constructed as a problem need to be considered at individual, kinship, cultural and national levels.

The medical definition is clearly based on the normative assumption of heterosexual sex as leading to parenthood. Indeed, given the cultural emphasis often placed on women preventing pregnancy, it can be a significant shock to women to find they have difficulties conceiving (Allison 2013). It is also important to remember that the fertility or otherwise of those not having regular heterosexual penetrative sex cannot be assessed in this way. As Mamo (2007) has argued, because infertility treatments were developed to assist heterosexual reproduction, lesbian and single women are thus outside the biomedical 'problem.' Mamo (2007) argues that, in the USA, to 'qualify' for treatment lesbian and single women may need to be labelled within the biomedical definition of infertility, regardless of whether or not they have problems conceiving. Donovan (2008) points out that the accounts of lesbian women who experience problems conceiving when they access fertility services are often hidden. The dominance of biomedical and heteronormative understandings only positions heterosexual women with partners as potentially infertile. Yet given the additional challenges faced by non-heterosexual women seeking motherhood (Peel 2009), this is also likely to impact their experiences of infertility.

Infertility has been experienced in many different and often negative ways. Recent accounts have identified that despite often larger numbers of women choosing not to have children, many of the issues associated with infertility in the past are still present. Allison (2013) identified that emotions such as a sense of grief, sorrow and loss were still prevalent amongst the women she interviewed, and that these were shaped by the particular status of motherhood within Ireland. Loftus and Andriot's (2012) research in the USA showed that infertility was still understood as a failed life course transition. The women reported that they were often seen as 'girls' rather than women, regardless of age, and that they felt excluded from communities of women. Hampshire et al. (2012) found similar issues of grief and exclusion amongst British-Pakistani Muslim

women, and they argue that this is compounded by specific understandings of extended family networks. For their interviewees, childlessness
was not just unacceptable but was unthinkable. In all these accounts, the
failure of the female body to conform to normative expectations of reproduction led to a sense of gendered identity failure. The close association
between womanhood and motherhood means that for these women the
performance of gender usually requires growing children. Yet it is important to remember that not all infertile women will consider themselves
in this way. Many of the women in Wilson's (2014) study stressed that
although they had desired children the lack of desired conception was not
viewed as a matter of crisis but just an outcome of a particular life journey.
Seeking treatment is not the only decision that is made, and given that
in initial stages the reasons for infertility can be unclear within couples,
it must be understood as a complex process (Sol Olafsdottir et al. 2012).

If women are experiencing the inability to conceive as a threat to their
identity, fertility treatments such as IVF can become seen as technologies
of hope (Franklin 1997; Throsby 2004; Whiteford and Gonzalez 1995).
As Franklin (1997) identified, for some women, opting for IVF is not
necessarily conceptualized as a choice but 'having to try' was seen as part
of their gendered role. The women she interviewed were determined to
pursue the extensive reproductive work involved in the IVF process in
order that everything had been attempted. Hence for women seeking to
overcome infertility through treatment, maternal sacrifice can be seen in
willingness to seek assisted conception. By choosing to endure hardship,
whether physical, emotional and/or financial, women can show their suitability for motherhood (Franklin 1997; Throsby 2004). Indeed, one of
Throsby's (2004) participants argued that people who decided not to pay
for IVF showed a lack of commitment to the ideals of motherhood. The
quest for children needs to be pursued as a way of overcoming the limbo
position of infertility and notions of failed gendered identity. Whilst not
all infertile women will seek out treatment, the existence of the technologies has reshaped fertility understandings. Indeed, for those with the ability to access treatment, a decision about pursuing IVF could now be seen
to be the divide between the childless and childfree. Moreover, if sacrifice
is at the heart of motherhood, then pursuing arduous infertility treatment can be seen to be demonstrating the right qualities of motherhood.

Fertility Treatments

Just like the long history of birth control, actions to encourage fertility are not a recent occurrence. Fraser (1999) gives details of advice to women written in seventeenth century books, and donor insemination can be dated back to 1790 (Farquhar 1996). Yet it could be argued that the birth of the first 'test-tube' baby in the UK in 1978 radically changed the experience and treatment for infertility. New clinics and services began to be established across the world. In the early years, some of these were highly questionable, using experimental techniques or disguising extremely low success rates with misleading statistics (Thompson 2005). Over time, this has becomes less of an issue with the standardization of many aspects of treatment and, in some places, tighter regulation (Thompson 2005). It is, however, still the case that the majority of IVF cycles fail and the chances of live birth are closely related to women's age. For example, in the UK, the Human Fertilisation and Embryology Authority (HFEA) give national rates of live birth per cycle as ranging from 32 % for women under 35 to 2 % for women over 45 (HFEA 2010).

Although it is clear that infertility has now been highly medicalized, many of the techniques are not necessarily used to 'cure' the infertility but to bypass the effects of a difficulty (social or medical) within the usual route of conception. In many popular understandings, IVF is seen to restore the 'natural' (heterosexual) order of things, assisting the conception that should have occurred anyway (Throsby 2004). It is this particular framing of IVF that has contributed to being seen as the normative option, an expected 'choice' that must be undertaken (Allison 2013; Throsby 2004; Remennick 2000). The public image of IVF as usually a benign technology producing 'miracle babies' obscures two important issues: first, the amount of reproductive work involved in undergoing fertility treatment, and second, disappointment as a common outcome. Both of these issues are related to understandings of women as potential self-sacrificing mothers.

Fertility treatment usually begins with investigations into women who have not yet conceived. These vary in nature and invasiveness and may include blood tests, ultrasound scans or a laparoscopy. Depending on the outcome of the investigations, different treatments could be suggested. For example, specific drugs could be prescribed to encourage ovulation, or surgery could be offered for blocked fallopian tubes. If these are unsuitable or unsuccessful then assisted conception techniques such as IVF are likely to be recommended. Whilst IVF is often seen as the most common practice, other procedures such as intrauterine insemination (IUI) could also be used. For many, the exact reason that conception has not taken place may not be known, even after numerous tests. Pandian et al. (2012) suggest that up to a third of couples seeking treatment have unexplained infertility, which is when no clear biological reason can be identified that would explain the lack of conception.

A cycle of IVF starts with drugs being given to women to suppress ovulation. These can be given by injection or a nasal spray, and they need to be taken for a couple of weeks. After this, drugs are given to stimulate egg production, and this also includes a daily drug regime for usually one to two weeks. During this time, women need to attend a clinic frequently for monitoring by both blood tests and ultrasound scans. When the follicles are judged to be nearly ready, a further injection is given to assist with this process. The operation to collect the eggs takes place about 36 hours after this injection. After women are sedated, a needle is inserted through the vagina to reach each ovary. The eggs are then mixed with the sperm in the laboratory. Women begin to take other medications to prepare the lining of the womb. If embryos have developed, they are inserted into women's bodies a few days later. It is not until one to two weeks after this that a pregnancy can be confirmed. Within this broad technique there are a number of variables, from particular drug combinations to the use of donor gametes, thus the term IVF is more of a broad process than an exact medical technology.

This basic description barely portrays the extensive reproductive work involved in IVF. The daily drug regimes, frequent visits to the clinic, and invasive bodily procedures mean that undergoing IVF is a serious endeavour that often needs to be fitted into a woman's daily life such as her employment (Franklin 1997; Throsby 2004). In Throsby's (2004) research in the UK with heterosexual couples, the majority of this work was women's responsibility. Not only were they the ones undergoing the treatment, but the gendered responsibility for reproduction meant that they often needed to take responsibility for informing or organising things for male partners as well. Sol Olafsdottir et al. (2012) found a similar pattern in Nordic countries. Indeed, if it is the male partner that is infertile, women can elect to undergo IVF with intra-cytoplasmic sperm injection (ICSI) rather than having less invasive insemination with donor sperm. Allison (2013) suggests this gendered practice is related to women's responsibility for infertility, no matter what the cause; a cultural association between male infertility and sexual impotence is highly stigmatized. Moreover, as Allison (2013) points out, throughout the process of infertility treatment, women's bodies are evaluated and graded as to the extent they measure up to the goal of motherhood, and regardless of sperm quality, it is their bodies that 'fail' should an embryo not implant. Silva and Machado (2010) found similar ideas in Portugal. They argue that women felt responsible for IVF failures and did not necessarily see IVF as a potentially unreliable medical technology. In contrast, in Remennick's (2000) study in Israel, women felt that doctors had given them unrealistic expectations of the chances of success. Differing experiences and outcomes of IVF will clearly shape the extent to which women feel responsible for any success or failure.

The potential to adjust the IVF process in each cycle means that there are endless possibilities, and the unsuccessful have to decide when to cease treatment rather than exhausting the possibilities (Franklin 1997; Remennick 2000; Thompson 2005; Throsby 2004). For Throsby's interviewees, it was important that they 'tried their best', although this did not necessarily mean that they exhausted all possibilities (2004: 164). Moreover each cycle 'adds' to the knowledge of the particular embodied issues, and can suggest a way to overcome that particular barrier in future (Throsby 2004). Yet at the same time, each failed cycle is a step closer to the end of fertility possibilities measured by the 'biological clock' (Thompson 2005). It can also exhaust the resources of women, financially and/or emotionally (Franklin 1997; Thompson 2005; Throsby 2004), which can add to the complexity of deciding if and when treatment options have really been exhausted. As Franklin (1997) argued, the popular conceptualization of IVF as a 'helping hand' overlooks the significant reproductive work involved in technologically assisted conception.

Cultural emphasis on fertility technologies as a potential solution to infertility also overlooks the ways in which access is limited for many disadvantaged groups. Access to fertility treatments will vary depending on how healthcare is provided, but even in publicaly funded healthcare systems access can still be stratified. Many health insurance plans in the USA do not cover IVF, as it is not deemed to be a medical necessity (Mladovsky and Sorenson 2010). In Sol Olafsdottir's et al. (2012) study of Nordic countries, they found waiting lists for some public clinics could be up to two years. In the UK, it is recommended that women under 40 have three cycles of IVF publically funded through the NHS, but this is not enforced (NICE 2014). Many local NHS healthcare commissioners have declined to pay for this level of treatment (Kennedy et al. 2006; NICE 2014).

Bell (2009) argues that the common cultural positioning of poorer women as 'hyperfertile' is significant in a lack of understanding of the infertility issues of disadvantaged women. As they are not necessarily positioned as 'good' potential mothers, their infertility is not positioned as problematic (Bell 2009; Wilson 2014). This raises a question as to the extent to which this narrative is structuring the widening access to fertility treatments. As Wilson (2014) points out, in the USA, the lack of access to fertility treatments is in direct contrast to the widespread availability of free sterilization. Moreover, poorer women's lack of options means that their experiences of infertility are different from those who have the resources to opt for treatment, and they often pursued options for social mothering instead (Bell 2009). It is important to note that the barriers for poorer women are not just financial, as they may also experience the 'language' of biomedical treatment as alienating (Bell 2009; Wilson 2014).

The impact of stratification means that private medicine often dominates fertility treatments even in countries where publically funded healthcare is the norm. Electing for fertility services is thus an act of reproductive consumption (Spar 2006; Throsby 2004). In countries like the UK, where healthcare services are not usually something that you buy, this can be uncomfortable for prospective patients (Throsby 2004). Throsby (2004) found that some of her participants were suspicious that financial transactions might corrupt the services of the clinics and, potentially, those seeking treatment. As Throsby (2004) argues, the idea of motherhood as a selfless act could be seen as the opposite to an individual as consumer, and although they wish to be seen as getting the best treatment, women may resist being fully positioned as a 'savvy customer'. The spectre of the motif of the 'designer baby' (chosen wholly or partially to order or as a lifestyle accessory) is commonly used in media coverage to criticise less 'natural' forms of motherhood (Throsby 2004). Moreover, within the cultural script of natural motherhood, biological motherhood tends to be seen as preferable to other forms (Loftus and Andriot 2012). Indeed, as Letherby (1999) found, women who became mothers though assistance, such as IVF treatment or adoption, felt that they had not achieved the same status as mothers who are more 'natural.' Hence the means by which women achieve motherhood also needs to be considered as part of the hierarchy of motherhood (Letherby 1999).

The importance of biological connectedness, combined with fears about age-related fertility decline, can be clearly seen in the emergence of egg freezing. Indeed egg freezing can be conceptualized as the expansion of infertility treatment to the fertile (Martin 2010; van de Wiel 2014). Egg freezing involves the same egg collection processes as an IVF cycle but the collected eggs are frozen rather than being fertilized. Historically, the success rates for live birth after egg freezing were extremely low, but more recent techniques have improved these rates (Mertes and Pennings 2011). As Mertes and Pennings (2011) point out, even if they were equivalent to the success rates of IVF, this still means that many women will not become pregnant. Van de Wiel (2014) argues that part of the appeal of egg freezing is that it is seen as a rational act of neoliberal consumers, who recalibrate their biological clock through extending their reproductive time. Similarly, Waldby (2015) found that some women struggled to reconcile the idea of ageing eggs with their understanding of their bodies and lives as still youthful, and thus egg freezing allowed a realignment of their biological and social clocks. This motive is not necessarily culturally accepted. Martin (2010) found that media reports distinguished between 'worthy' patients such as women with cancer and 'selfish' social postponers. As Martin states:

The selfish/altruistic dichotomy represents two sides of the same gender ideology of motherhood as role fulfilment. In the first instance freezing eggs is selfish because it delays motherhood, whereas in the second, freezing eggs is altruistic because it enables it. (2010: 537)

Moreover, as Martin (2010) clearly argues, whilst egg freezing is sold as fertility preservation, it is really about preserving genetic connection. If the issue was just ageing eggs, then egg donation could be used if women experienced difficulties conceiving. Waldby (2015) found a similar rejection of the idea of using donor gametes amongst the women she interviewed, giving further evidence of a potential hierarchy in motherhood.

Biological Connections

At the current time, biological parenthood is usually seen as preferable to social parenthood, and thus for heterosexually partnered women, using donor gametes is often seen as less desirable than their own eggs and partners' sperm. The national context of laws and regulation makes a significant contribution to the ways in which egg donation is understood and practised. There is variation in different parts of the world in as to whether the donor is paid a fee, just expenses or not paid at all. In addition, there are variations as to if donors can be known or remain anonymous, or if details can be released when a child reaches maturity. This variation has led to reproductive tourism in which women cross borders to seek egg donor procedures that are unavailable or illegal in their home countries (Lundin 2012). For women who have had difficulty conceiving and have then undergone IVF with donor eggs, pregnancy can be experienced as a significant success at mothering (Nordqvist and Smart 2014). Moreover, doing the work of mothering after a child is born is also significant in claiming proper kinship ties (Nordqvist and Smart 2014). As Kirkman (2008) found, the social 'failure' of infertile women and the acceptance of donor eggs challenges ideas about natural motherhood, yet simultaneously her participants' pursuit and eventual success in becoming mothers via egg donation realigns them with cultural norms.

Sol Olafsdottir et al. (2013) found that whilst many of the heterosexual couples they interviewed initially rejected the idea of using donor gametes, gradually this became more acceptable. They argue that over time the desire to become pregnant becomes more significant than having their 'own' child and there is a re-emphasis on social rather than biological parenting. This is in contrast to the accounts of women seeking to freeze their eggs, as discussed earlier; being able to use their own eggs, rather than a donor's, is often a motive for engagement with the process (Waldby 2015). The experience of lesbian women is clearly very different. Most will have not previously perceived themselves as infertile, and they have always known that parenthood would involve donor sperm. Nordqvist and Smart (2014) suggest that for lesbian women the decision of whether or not to have a known or unknown sperm donor is likely to be one of the most significant issues. The potential for known donors to claim more kinship than the mother(s) consider reasonable is one of the reasons that unknown donors may be chosen. Here it could be argued that the concern that the donors might interfere with the business of mothering is part of the risk posed. As heteronormativity is still usually culturally significant, and lesbian mothers are still potentially seen as deviant, it is not surprising that there can be a wariness towards men positioned as potential fathers, as others might perceive them as having a significant claim over their children.

Both sides in the gamete transaction can be seen to have concerns about the suitability of the other. For example, Boulos et al. (2014) found that, in Australia, many egg donors had clear ideas about who would and would not qualify as suitable recipients. Issues such as being 'deserving' and fitting cultural norms of good parenting were significant. In Australia, profiting from egg donation is illegal, but donors can be compensated for their expenses. Boulos et al. (2014) state that intended parents usually have to find their own donors either from their own social network or through advertising. Almeling (2011) found that commercial egg brokers in the USA were also looking for specific traits in their donors. Despite the commercial nature, clinics wanted donors motivated by altruism rather than money and expected them to fulfil specific requirements of femininity such as attractiveness, having a caring nature and being motherly. She argues that the clear differences in the ways in which egg donors and sperm donors (who are rarely questioned about motive) are perceived go beyond the reproductive work of donation and are linked to broader views of motherhood and fatherhood.

In many studies of gamete donation, motherhood is separated into different components: genetic, gestational and childrearing. Depending on how women are positioned, the emphasis is put on some aspects rather than others. Boulos et al. (2014) found that for women donating eggs the important elements of motherhood were perceived to be pregnancy and childrearing. They did not consider the issue of genetic material to be significant in conferring a relationship with a child. The women in Almeling's (2011) study also described a lack of significant concerns about the kinship connectedness inscribed in egg donation. She points out that the contradiction of egg donation being conceptualized as a significant gift and any downplaying of the genetic significance in the idea that it is only an egg. In contrast, Nordqvist and Smart (2014) found that whilst the gestational element was seen as the most significant, there was still some sense of genetic 'loss.' Their study of donor-conceived families in the UK revealed that some families needed to find ways of claiming connectedness. They suggest that the knowledge that the children were not their genetic offspring led families to focus more on proving that kinship existed.

Just as there are concerns raised by some over the commercialization of IVF, women's involvement in egg donation has the potential to be seen as constructing them as bad mothers. This is a significant reason why, even in commercial egg transactions, the dominant discourses are around altruism and gifts (Almeling 2011). As Almeling has argued:

> If egg donors were categorised as mothers, then, culturally speaking, they would be the worst kind of mothers. Not only are they not nurturing their children, they are selling them for $5,000 and never looking back. (2011: 163)

Almeling (2011) suggests that whilst egg donors undertake the same technical process as infertile women undergoing IVF, it is experienced very differently. In her study, she did not find the same descriptions of intensive reproductive work that took over women's lives. Almeling

(2011) suggests that, because they are not as emotionally invested in the outcome and are receiving money for their time, this gives a different meaning to the daily regimes and frequent clinic appointments. Even when they described painful or discomforting side effects, they still gave more straightforward descriptions than those found in other studies (such as Franklin 1997). The lack of struggle found in the donor accounts could also be related to differences in cultural understandings about the levels of sacrifice needed by the women. As I have outlined above, the accounts of infertile women enduring hardship are a way of proving themselves worthy of motherhood in the face of a lack of conception. In contrast, there is a need for egg donors to exhibit enough care that financial motives are deemed to be secondary, but to be distanced from motherhood as an outcome means that the labour of donation needs to be downplayed. This position of limited rather than unlimited selflessness is also seen in accounts of surrogacy.

Surrogate Motherhood

In surrogacy, the relative importance of gestation in defining motherhood cannot be relied on, and others ways need to be found to produce connections between intended mothers and their children. Surrogacy has often been seen as a controversial issue since it came to widespread public attention with the Baby M case in the USA in the 1980s. This case involved traditional surrogacy; it used artificial insemination to create a pregnancy with the carrier mother's egg and intended father's sperm. Since then surrogacy has grown into a transnational industry, not least because of the emergence of the practice of gestational surrogacy, which more easily distinguished between mothering roles (Spar 2006). Gestational surrogacy uses IVF techniques to implant fertilized eggs from the intended mother or egg donor into a carrier mother. Whilst the success rates are much lower than in traditional surrogacy, the genetic separation is seen as significant and, Spar (2006) argues, led to the significant expansion of the industry. Thus the 'market for wombs' runs alongside egg donation, providing for up to three potential claims for motherhood: egg donor, pregnant carrier and intended mother. Gestational surrogacy is also used by single men and gay couples, but here I am focusing on issues of motherhood constructed within the transactions.

There has been a great deal of research that has examined the competing claims to motherhood that have played out in different legal arenas. Hartouni (1997) has shown how, in the Baby M case, Mary Beth Whitehead, the birth and biological mother, was initially positioned as an inadequate mother in the New Jersey Superior Court of because she had entered into a surrogacy contract. It was entering into the contract in the first place that undermined her position as a potential mother. She argued that when this judgement was overturned on appeal, the New Jersey Supreme Court reasserted the notion of pregnancy and birth as asserting natural motherhood, but it still upheld that Whitehead was an inadequate mother through awarding primary custody to the Sterns, the biological father and his wife. Markens (2007) suggests that this case was primarily framed in the US media as one of 'baby-selling' that positioned Whitehead in particular as outside the norms of society. A few years later, a case involving the Caverts, a white biological father and a Filipino biological mother, and Anna Johnson, a Black woman acting as a gestational surrogate, similarly became a custody dispute. In this case, it is clear that ideas about racialized reproduction were a central element of both the court decisions and the media coverage (Hartouni 1997; Markens 2007). Here, gestational surrogacy was framed as primarily a story of the needs of infertile couples to reproduce and Johnson was deemed to be an 'inadequate' mother because of her position as a poor Black woman (Hartouni 1997; Markens 2007). Moreover, the lack of biological connection was deemed to be the significant issue within gestation surrogacy, with the birth mothers being positioned as akin to foster mothers (Markens 2007). Moreover, as Markens (2007) argues, the result in this case prioritized the concerns of the white parents and (re) positioned Black women as temporary carers of white women's children.

This positioning as temporary carers is one that many women acting as gestational surrogates use to describe their situation. Kroløkke et al. (2010) examined surrogate mothers' websites and found that the metaphor of extended babysitting was common to describe gestational surrogacy. Many of the websites presented claims about the ideals of mother-love and, for the surrogates, success in motherly duties. Previous successful pregnancies and performances as mothers were used as a selling point to attract potential intended parents and to construct their understanding of the longing of intended parents. Good surrogates would enact a form of mother-love during pregnancy as temporary time-limited care. Indeed Ragoné (1998) found that having no biological connection was of fundamental importance to women acting as gestational surrogates in the USA. It was through this that they could relinquish any claims to motherhood. In contrast, for women involved in traditional surrogacy, social motherhood was the significant element (Ragoné 1998). However, in both forms of surrogacy, the carrier mothers' success in biological reproduction meant that women could overlook social class differences between 'buyers' and 'sellers.' For the surrogate mothers, infertility was deemed to negate the privilege and success of women needing their services. Hence, both the surrogate mothers and the status of the female intended parents are measured by motherhood successes.

However, as Teman (2010) has found, women acting as gestational surrogates in Israel need to undertake specific forms of reproductive labour on themselves in order to be able to affirm this temporary-carer position. She highlights the 'body-mapping' of the pregnant women in which they disembody their pregnant bellies from the rest of themselves. Teman (2010) argues that this practice involves both emotional management and physical actions such as turning away from images during ultrasound scans. They may also choose specific birth plans, such as caesarean sections or no skin-to-skin contact, and aim to deliver straight to the intended mother. These are chosen in the belief that they will avoid bonding during or after birth. (The social construction of bonding during and after childbirth will be discussed later.) Teman (2010) found that intended mothers also enacted specific reproductive work in order to validate their mothering claims. They emphasized biological connections or constructed symbolic links to the donor eggs. They organized the appointments and paperwork, bonded through scans, and studied pregnancy texts. Both sets of practices illustrate the importance of validating or repudiating potential claims to motherhood, and the necessity of emotional management in ensuring their positions.

The importance of cultural differences in the understanding of surrogacy arrangements can be seen when contrasting the experiences of women in Israel with those acting as gestational surrogates in India. In Israel, surrogacy is controlled by the state and surrogacy committees screen couples and surrogates and oversee the contracts that they sign. This leads to individualized and usually frequent contact between gestation surrogates and intended mothers (Teman 2010). In contrast, the global framework of reproductive tourism in India has resulted in a very different experience. There women acting as surrogates often live in hostels or dormitories and may have infrequent contact with intended parents (Pande 2014). The organization, including high levels of surveillance and control, is primarily handled by the commercial clinics (Rudrappa 2012; Pande 2014). Pande (2014) argues that in India, women acting as gestational surrogates are positioned as mother-workers, and as such they intersect the traditional boundary of production and reproduction. She has shown that they need to be good workers in terms of fulfilling the surrogacy contracts and submitting themselves to the disciplinary regime of the clinic. They also need to be good mothers, enacting care over the developing foetus, and as part of the selfless role of motherhood they should refrain from negotiating or showing explicit interest in their earnings as surrogates. This balance is achieved through the organization of the clinics and through the way that the clinic staff treat the female residents. Pande (2014) argues that during pregnancy the women-as-mothers are expected to care for the foetus as if it were theirs, whilst after birth the worker-identity should be enacted ensuring that the baby was handed over willingly. As she states:

> At various stages of the disciplinary process, the clinic employs the rhetoric of "good motherhood" to restrain the surrogates as workers, and the rhetoric of "good workerhood" to contain them as mothers. (…) Ultimately, through a strategic use of the dual mother-worker identity, the clinic constructs the perfect mother-worker of the clients' dream. (Pande 2014: 167)

Rudrappa (2012) has shown how the option of surrogacy can be preferable to the other work available locally in India. Moreover, reproductive work for others can reinforce women's position in their own families as the money earned can be used to support them. (Rudrappa 2012; Pande 2014). When women are positioned primarily as mothers, assisting other women to be mothers has more meaning than other work (Rudrappa 2012). As Rudrappa (2012) explains, this does not mean that women are uncritical of the work, but given their limited options this be seen as a good option.

Whilst commercial surrogacy is a recent practice, there is of course a longer history of using poorer women's labour to care for the children of the more wealthy. From wet-nursing to nannying, poorer women have often been expected to care for the children of others, even if this meant that they could not necessarily look after their own. Moreover, in some contexts, such as slavery in the USA and apartheid in South Africa, issues of racism were often a central feature of this. Thus, the mother-worker roles within transnational surrogacy can be seen as new forms within the existing stratification of reproduction in which the relative wealth position of the buyers and sellers within the reproductive marketplace is implicated in the ways in which the different parties are positioned.

The positioning of motherhood is seen as natural, and a lack of children for those who want them is seen as an obstacle that should be overcome. This has led to the commercialization of eggs and wombs internationally, as clinics compete to offer services and women travel over national borders seeking the services that they feel they need. Whether through commercial or altruistic concerns, the rise of fertility services has led to new ways of enacting motherhood. Whilst it was always possible to divide biological and social mothering, this division has been reconstructed and further divided through the development of specific reproductive technologies and services. Yet at the same time, ideas about what constitutes a 'real' mother have had a remarkable consistency. Women acting as surrogates are disciplined to display selflessness during pregnancy and sacrifice any claims to motherhood for the benefit of the intended parents. In contrast, the quest for motherhood undertaken by infertile women is understood as facing challenges and overcoming barriers. Moreover, the levels of fluidity in whether it is intent, eggs or pregnancy that constructs motherhood indicate that this is not necessarily the whole story. Indeed the trials undergone by people involved—infertile women, intended mothers and women acting as surrogates—to gain a wanted child are seen as both proving their success and reaffirming the idea of sacrifice as the heart of good motherhood. The importance of this status can also be seen in accounts of those who experience reproductive loss.

Reproductive Loss

As Layne (2003) has argued, the development of reproductive technologies has also had a profound impact on the experience of reproductive loss. The diagnosis of pregnancy, and pregnancy loss, is determined through blood tests and scans rather than women's embodied experience. This has led to new categories of reproductive states such as the 'chemical pregnancy' in which hormones are detected that may or may not lead to physical development of an embryo. Moreover the development of home pregnancy testing kits, particularly those designed to be used before menstruation is due, has meant that many more women will experience a pregnancy loss, whereas in previous years they may have understood themselves as having a late or heavy period. Some women undergoing fertility treatments conceptualize pregnancy as beginning at implantation, and failed attempts are perceived as a reproductive loss (Layne 2003; Allison 2013). Moreover, pregnancy loss may be experienced even when ultrasound has revealed that there was no embryo present, such as in the case of blighted ovum (Layne 2003). These examples illustrate the ways in which reproductive loss is more complex than understanding it simply in biological terms.

Allison's (2013) study of infertility in Ireland is a good example of this. She found that for her participants the loss some of the women felt when they were unable to conceive was similar to grief expressed over reproductive loss. She argues that grieving for children who were never conceived was complicated, as they did not have a 'death' on which to rest their claims. One of the women asked her parish priest to say a mass for her children 'in her heart' in order for her to be able to move on with her life. Allison argues that for women in this position, 'motherhood lingers as a presence of absence in their identities' (2013: 74). Tonkin (2012) found similar issues in the lives of the unintentionally childless women in New Zealand. She suggests that imagined children are often the first form of a maternal subjectivity, and whilst these are 'replaced' by actual children in the lives of some women, the fantasies take on new meanings for those who do not conceive. This means that whilst some of the women might be childless, they maintain an identity as mothers alongside women who have experienced loss through miscarriage, stillbirth or the death of a child (Allison 2013). Indeed, for some of Allison's (2013) interviewees, constructing unsuccessful IVF treatment as miscarriage allowed them to understand the process as loss rather than failure.

Miscarriage is a common experience for women, and it is estimated that 15–20 % of recognized pregnancies will end in this way (Brier 2008). Many women will have subsequent successful pregnancies and so it is fairly common, particularly after early miscarriages, for a medical response to be 'just try again' (Layne 2003). Like other reproductive issues, not all women will experience miscarriage in the same way. Whilst many women do experience miscarriage as a significant loss, much of the research on grief recruits women from support services, so it is currently unclear how widespread acute feelings of loss actually are (Brier 2008). Moreover, the extent of the loss is likely to be related to the issues surrounding conception and the numbers of previous pregnancy losses. Experiencing a miscarriage after feeling ambivalent about continuing with a pregnancy is likely to be very different from experiencing a repeat miscarriage following arduous fertility treatment.

Gerber-Epstein et al. (2008) found that the sense of loss in a first pregnancy in Israel was related to the level of anticipation that women had developed about their future lives as mothers. The grief that they encountered was often about this loss of future and the fear of infertility alongside the loss of the developing embryo itself. These findings are similar to those found by Abboud and Liamputtong (2002) in Australia, and they suggest that women who took on a maternal role early in pregnancy often felt more loss than those who had not made as many adaptations to their identity. In many cases, women wanted to understand the reason for their loss, and some blamed themselves or felt blamed by others. It is common for no medical reason to be known for miscarriage and this can increase anxiety over the issue (Layne 2003). The attitude of healthcare professionals also has a significant impact on women's experiences.

As Peel's (2009) study of lesbian and bisexual women experiencing pregnancy loss has shown, the heteronormative structures of reproductive services can exacerbate distress. She argues that the necessity for assisted conception means that there is a greater chance that the loss will be amplified. Part of the reason for this is the level of heterosexism and/or homophobia that is experienced or feared during encounters in health-care settings. Craven and Peel (2014) also identified the lack of research around the loss of 'social' mothers, with most research focusing on the biological mother. Their review suggests that 'social' mothers are also likely to find the experience distressing. The lack of attention given to the position of non-heterosexual mothers arises because of the normative understandings of conception as a heterosexual practice by which women are transformed into mothers. Women who do not meet these normative understandings because they do not wish to conceive or are experiencing infertility or reproductive loss are potentially seen to be failing to achieve the 'natural' destiny of women.

Allison (2013) suggests that for some women the absence of children does not prevent them from constructing themselves as mothers. Layne (2012) has found similar trends in the USA and notes in particular the rise of mourning rituals for 'angel babies', a collective term increasingly used for reproductive losses during pregnancy or the neonatal period. Layne (2003) suggests a number of reasons that have combined to shift the cultural meaning of reproductive loss. She suggests that the rise of medical technologies, the general understanding of medicine as authoritative, and media images of 'miracle babies' have obscured the frequency of reproductive loss. Moreover, modern contraceptives and changes to women's social roles have meant that motherhood is considered to be something chosen, which has altered the landscape for those whose choice does not materialize. In addition, the responsibilization of women for conception and fertility within an era of intensive motherhood means that losses are a female failure (Layne 2003). Moreover, as the following chapter will detail, these choices are often linked to the embodied sacrifices demanded during a 'good mothers' pregnancy. Hence a sense of failure and/or guilt can be linked to the idea that their bodies failed to produce, and this moral failing could be because they did not make the right decisions over timing, lifestyle or other factors. As Layne suggests:

While women are assured after the fact that there was nothing that they could have done to have caused the loss, this message contradicts all the messages they received from their doctors and popular culture through the pregnancy on the importance of their agency in "producing" a healthy baby through self-discipline and submitting to the authority of experts. (2003: 149)

Hence, whilst reproductive losses are rarely women's fault, the cultural message is that they somehow did not make the right decisions and this was a contributing factor.

Conclusion

Normative ideas about motherhood have a significant impact on the conception journeys of many women. Whilst there are cultural and national differences about the extent to which motherhood is synonymous with womanhood, as well as the level of pronatalism present, it is clear that ideas about 'good motherhood' structure the lives of women who both have, and do not have, children. Thinking of this divide as a continuum in which women can be placed differently over the course of their lives helps to illustrate the ways in which individual positions and broader social circumstances shape the level of choice that women are able to exercise over fertility. The stereotype of women who have chosen not to have children as 'selfish' is an important reminder of the necessity of 'good mothers' to be selfless; cultural norms about always putting children first are a way of normalising the sacrifice required of women when conceiving children.

Women who have experienced infertility may understand this as a failure of gender and/or a normative life course. They may see themselves as less of a woman, particularly when compared to the image of a hyperfertile 'bad mother.' Taking on the responsibility for fertility treatment and undergoing numerous procedures can be seen as a way of proving that they are willing to make any sacrifice necessary and thus meet the criteria for good motherhood. Not all women will seek fertility treatment, and their ability to do so is likely to be related to their socio-economic position. For those who do, unsuccessful cycles can heighten a sense of failure. Whilst each unsuccessful cycle adds to the knowledge of what may work, it is also situated within the discursive construction of the biological clock measuring out the end of reproductive time. The development of egg freezing may 'stop the clock', but the division between 'worthy' and 'unworthy' users of the technology reinforces the notion that women need 'good' reasons to justify postponing motherhood.

Within the market for donor gametes, a biological connection is seen as preferable to social motherhood. The different ways in which women acting as egg donors or surrogate mothers are positioned further illustrates the importance of understanding how cultural norms construct the ways in which women are positioned in relation to any developing foetus. Baby selling is the antithesis of 'good motherhood' and thus it is important for those in the baby 'market' to be able to distance themselves from this image. A focus on altruism, body mapping and 'intent' as a marker of 'real' motherhood all help to construct a distance between egg donors, women pregnant as surrogates, and intended mothers. Moreover, the lack of struggle described by those undergoing fertility treatment as egg donors or surrogates, in comparison with accounts of infertile women, further illustrates how ideas about sacrifice structure experience. In the area of infertility, the meaning of the reproductive work involved depends on the specific positioning of women in the reproductive marketplace. Comparing these accounts to those who have experienced reproductive loss further illustrates the ways in which it is social desire and investment, rather than biological experiences, that frame understandings of conception and loss. Moreover, as I will detail in the next chapter, women are held responsible for pregnancy outcomes and making appropriate sacrifices, regardless of a lack of evidence that their actions are or were harmful to a developing foetus.

References

Abboud, L. N., & Liamputtong, P. (2002). Pregnancy loss: What it means to women who miscarry and their partners. *Social Work in Health Care, 36*(3), 37–62.

Allison, J. (2013). *Motherhood and infertility in Ireland: Understanding the presence of absence*. Cork, Ireland: Cork University Press.

Almeling, R. (2011). *Sex cells: The medical market for eggs and sperm.* London: University of California Press.

Bell, A. V. (2009). "It's way out of my league": Low-income women's experiences of medicalized infertility. *Gender & Society, 23*(5), 688–709.

Boulos, M., Kerridge, I., & Waldby, C. (2014). Reciprocity in the donation of reproductive oöcytes. In M. Nash (Ed.), *Reframing reproduction: Conceiving gendered experiences* (pp. 203–220). Basingstoke, England: Palgrave Macmillan.

Brier, N. (2008). Grief following miscarriage: A comprehensive review of the literature. *Journal of Women's Health, 17*(3), 451–464.

Budds, K., Locke, A., & Burr, V. (2013). "Risky business" constructing the "choice" to "delay" motherhood in the British Press. *Feminist Media Studies, 13*(1), 132–147.

Bute, J. J. (2009). "Nobody thinks twice about asking": Women with a fertility problem and requests for information. *Health Communication, 24*(8), 752–763.

Craven, C., & Peel, E. (2014). Stories of grief and hope: Queer experiences of reproductive loss. In M. F. Gibson (Ed.), *Queering motherhood: Narrative and theoretical perspectives* (pp. 97–110). Toronto, Ontario, Canada: Demeter Press.

Donovan, C. (2008). It's not really seen as an issue, you know, lesbian infertility it's kind of what's that?: Lesbians' unsuccessful experiences of medicalised donor insemination. *Medical Sociology Online, 3*(1), 15–24.

Eijkemans, M., van Poppel, F., Habbema, D. F., Smith, K. R., Leridon, H., & te Velde, E. R. (2014). Too old to have children? Lessons from natural fertility populations. *Human Reproduction, 29*(6), 1304–1312.

Farquhar, D. (1996). *The other machine: Discourse and reproductive technologies.* London: Routledge.

Franklin, S. (1997). *Embodied progress: A cultural account of assisted conception.* London: Routledge.

Fraser, A. (1999). *The weaker vessel: Women's lot in seventeenth-century England.* London: Arrow Books.

Gerber-Epstein, P., Leichtentritt, R. D., & Benyamini, Y. (2008). The experience of miscarriage in first pregnancy: The women's voices. *Death Studies, 33*(1), 1–29.

Gillespie, R. (2000). When no means no: Disbelief, disregard and deviance as discourses of voluntary childlessness. *Women's Studies International Forum, 23*(2), 223–234.

Graham, M., & Rich, S. (2014). Representations of childless women in the Australian print media. *Feminist Media Studies, 14*(3), 500–518.

Greil, A. L., Slauson-Blevins, K., & McQuillan, J. (2010). The experience of infertility: A review of recent literature. *Sociology of Health & Illness, 32*(1), 140–162.

Hampshire, K. R., Blell, M. T., & Simpson, B. (2012). 'Everybody is moving on': Infertility, relationality and the aesthetics of family among British-Pakistani Muslims. *Social Science & Medicine, 74*(7), 1045–1052.

Harter, L. M., Kirby, E. L., Edwards, A., & McClanahan, A. (2005). Time, technology, and meritocracy: The disciplining of women's bodies in narrative constructions of age-related infertility. In L. M. Harter, P. M. Japp, & C. S. Beck (Eds.), *Narratives, health, and healing: Communication theory, research, and practice* (pp. 83–105). Mahwah, NJ: Erlbaum.

Hartouni, V. (1997). *Cultural conceptions: On reproductive technologies and the remaking of life*. London: University of Minnesota Press.

Human Fertility and Embryology Authority. (2010). *IVF—Chance of success*. Retrieved February 12, 2015, from http://www.hfea.gov.uk/ivf-success-rate.html

Kennedy, R., Kingsland, C., Rutherford, A., Hamilton, M., & Ledger, W. (2006). Implementation of the NICE guideline—Recommendations from the British Fertility Society for national criteria for NHS funding of assisted conception. *Human Fertility, 9*(3), 181–189.

Kirkman, M. (2008). Being a 'real' mum: Motherhood through donated eggs and embryos. *Women's Studies International Forum, 31*(4), 241–248.

Kroløkke, C., Foss, K. A., & Sandoval, J. (2010). The commodification of motherhood: Surrogacy as a matter of choice. In S. Hayden & D. L. O'Brien Hallstein (Eds.), *Contemplating maternity in an era of choice: Explorations into discourses of reproduction*. Plymouth, England: Lexington Books.

Layne, L. L. (2003). *Motherhood lost: A feminist account of pregnancy loss in America*. London: Routledge.

Layne, L. (2012). 'Troubling the normal': Angel babies and the canny/uncanny nexus. In S. Earle, C. Komaromy, & L. Layne (Eds.), *Understanding reproductive loss: Perspectives on life, death and fertility* (pp. 129–141). Farnham, England: Ashgate.

Letherby, G. (1994). Mother or not, mother or what? Problems of definitions and identity? *Women's Studies International Forum, 17*(5), 525–532.

Letherby, G. (1999). Other than mother and mothers as others: The experience of motherhood and non-motherhood in relation to 'infertility' and 'involuntary childlessness'. *Women's Studies International Forum, 22*(3), 359–372.

Letherby, G. (2002). Childless and bereft? Stereotypes and realities in relation to 'voluntary' and 'involuntary' childlessness and womanhood. *Sociological Inquiry, 72*(1), 7–20.

Locke, A., & Budds, K. (2013). 'We thought if it's going to take two years then we need to start that now': Age, infertility risk and the timing of pregnancy in older first-time mothers. *Health, Risk & Society, 15*(6–7), 525–542.

Loftus, J., & Andriot, A. L. (2012). "That's what makes a woman": Infertility and coping with a failed life course transition. *Sociological Spectrum, 32*(3), 226–243.

Lundin, S. (2012). "I want a baby; don't stop me from being a mother": An ethnographic study on fertility tourism and egg trade. *Cultural Politics, 8*(2), 327–344.

Maher, J., & Saugeres, L. (2007). To be or not to be a mother? Women negotiating cultural representations of mothering. *Journal of Sociology, 43*(1), 5–21.

Mamo, L. (2007). *Queering reproduction*. London: Duke University Press.

Markens, S. (2007). *Surrogate motherhood and the politics of reproduction*. London: University of California Press.

Martin, L. J. (2010). Anticipating infertility egg freezing, genetic preservation, and risk. *Gender & Society, 24*(4), 526–545.

Mertes, H., & Pennings, G. (2011). Social egg freezing: For better, not for worse. *Reproductive BioMedicine Online, 23*(7), 824–829.

Meyers, D. T. (2001). The rush to motherhood: Pronatalist discourse and women's autonomy. *Signs: Journal of Women in Culture and Society, 26*(3), 735–773.

Mladovsky, P., & Sorenson, C. (2010). Public financing of IVF: A review of policy rationales. *Health Care Analysis, 18*(2), 113–128.

NICE. (2014). *Stop restricting IVF treatment, NICE urges NHS*. Retrieved February 27, 2015, from https://www.nice.org.uk/news/press-and-media/stop-restricting-ivf-treatment-nice-urges-nhs

Nordqvist, P., & Smart, C. (2014). *Relative strangers: Family life, genes and donor conception*. Basingstoke, England: Palgrave Macmillan.

Pande, A. (2014). *Wombs in labour: Transnational commercial surrogacy in India*. New York: Columbia University Press.

Pandian, Z., Gibreel, A., & Bhattacharya, S. (2012). In vitro fertilisation for unexplained subfertility. *Cochrane Database Systematic Review, 4*, CD003357.

Peel, E. (2009). Pregnancy loss in lesbian and bisexual women: An online survey of experiences. *Human Reproduction, 25*(3), 721–727.

Ragoné, H. (1998). Incontestable motivations. In S. Franklin & H. Ragoné (Eds.), *Reproducing reproduction: Kinship, power and technological innovation*. Philadelphia, PA: University of Pennsylvania Press.

Remennick, L. (2000). Childless in the land of imperative motherhood: Stigma and coping among infertile Israeli women. *Sex Roles, 43*(11–12), 821–841.

Rich, S., Taket, A., Graham, M., & Shelley, J. (2011). 'Unnatural', 'unwomanly', 'uncreditable' and 'undervalued': The significance of being a childless woman in Australian society. *Gender Issues, 28*(4), 226–247.

Rudrappa, S. (2012). India's reproductive assembly line. *Contexts, 11*(2), 22–27.

Shaw, R., & Giles, D. (2009). Motherhood on ice? A media framing analysis of older mothers in the UK news. *Psychology & Health, 24*(2), 221–236.

Silva, S., & Machado, H. (2010). Uncertainty, risks and ethics in unsuccessful in vitro fertilization treatment cycles. *Health, Risk & Society, 12*(6), 531–545.

Sol Olafsdottir, H. S., Wikland, M., & Möller, A. (2012). Nordic couples' decision-making processes in anticipation of contacting a fertility clinic. *Journal of Reproductive and Infant Psychology, 30*(2), 180–192.

Sol Olafsdottir, H. S., Wikland, M., & Möller, A. (2013). Nordic couples' decision-making processes during assisted reproductive treatments. *Sexual and Reproductive Healthcare, 4*(2), 49–55.

Spar, D. L. (2006). *The baby business: How money, science and politics drive the commerce of conception*. Boston: Harvard Business School Press.

Teman, E. (2010). *Birthing a mother: The surrogate body and the pregnant self*. London: The University of California Press.

Thompson, C. (2005). *Making parents: An ontological choreography of reproductive technologies*. London: MIT Press.

Throsby, K. (2004). *When IVF fails: Feminism, infertility and the negotiation of normality*. Basingstoke, England: Palgrave.

Tonkin, L. (2010). Making sense of loss: The disenfranchised grief of women who are "contingently childless". *Journal of the Motherhood Initiative, 1*(2), 177–187.

Tonkin, L. (2012). Haunted by a 'present absence'. *Studies in the Maternal, 4*(1). www.mamsie.bbk.ac.uk.

van de Wiel, L. (2014). Freezing in anticipation: Eggs for later. *Women's Studies International Forum*. doi:10.1016/j.wsif.2014.10.019

Waldby, C. (2015). 'Banking time': Egg freezing and the negotiation of future fertility. *Culture, Health & Sexuality, 17*(4), 470–482.

Whiteford, L. M., & Gonzalez, L. (1995). Stigma: The hidden burden of infertility. *Social Science & Medicine, 40*(1), 27–36.

Wilson, K. J. (2014). *Not trying: Infertility, childlessness and ambivalence*. Nashville, TN: Vanderbilt University Press.

5

Idealized Pregnancy

As I outlined earlier, the idea of maternal sacrifice structures the ways in which fertility regulation is organized for women who do not fit the image of the 'good mother', who is required to prevent conception until such time (if ever) that she embodies the appropriate qualities of age and behaviour. This chapter will focus on how the presumption of maternal sacrifice within good motherhood plays out in the management of pregnancy. It will examine how the focus on the foetus means that women's status as autonomous citizens can become compromised. It will illustrate the experiences of being pregnant within a medicalized context, when every choice that a woman makes, from eating to prenatal testing, is taken as evidence of her willingness to perform idealized motherhood. In other words, whilst nominally 'choices' can be made, there is often only one 'right' option for responsible women to make. An important element within this chapter will be showing how women are expected to constrain their lives before they conceive. Moreover, given that fertility and fertility control are always uncertain, these discourses potentially constrain all heterosexually active women between puberty and menopause. Drawing on the debates around issues such as alcohol consumption, the chapter will illustrate the ways in which restrictions on women's lives can become

© The Editor(s) (if applicable) and The Author(s) 2016
P. Lowe, *Reproductive Health and Maternal Sacrifice*,
DOI 10.1057/978-1-137-47293-9_5

policy despite an acknowledged lack of evidence of harm to the foetus. This focuses negative attention on visibly pregnant women, who can be publicly castigated for failing to comply with the increasingly tight rules. Thus women can be encouraged to make specific choices through the idea of sacrifice even when there will be no significant outcomes to the welfare of the foetus.

Responsible Planning

As I discussed in Chap. 3, the responsibilization of women for fertility includes both preventing pregnancy and conceiving at appropriate times. At its heart, it is based on the notion that 'planning' a family is the only truly appropriate way to proceed. The notion of family planning has been built into the fabric of fertility decisions through organizations promoting birth control and specifically adopting the rationale of planning within their remit. Examples include the Family Planning Association (UK) and Planned Parenthood Federation of America, which both incorporated the notion of planning into the name of their organizations. Within the discourse of family planning, there is a clear division between trying to conceive and trying to prevent pregnancy, and women should be situated in one or the other position. Yet most of the evidence suggests that this divide does not reflect women's lives, and contraceptive and conception decisions might be better understood as a continuum (Bachrach and Newcomer 1999).

As Barrett and Wellings (2002) revealed, whilst health policy tends to use dichotomous terms such as planned/unplanned, intended/unintended and wanted/unwanted, these are rarely used by women. They found that even when pregnant women are asked specifically to define them, the complexity of their responses, which describe the myriad reasons and emotions that constitute the background to women becoming pregnant, means that they are not really useful terms. Griffiths et al. (2008) found that even when women had health conditions in which pregnancy was more complex, journeys to becoming pregnant were not straightforward. Moreover, even when women did 'plan' a particular pregnancy, this did not mean that they would do so on another occasion.

This means that women should not necessarily be divided into responsible and irresponsible categories on the basis of attitudes towards planning pregnancy, but rather each pregnancy is in a different position on the prevention/conception continuum.

Yet despite the evidence that planning pregnancy is a continuum rather than a dichotomy for many heterosexual women, and that, given that all contraception has a failure rate, planning is not always possible, this has not stopped health policy from having an increased emphasis on the preconceptive period. Preconceptive health is nominally predicated on the presumption that women can plan to 'optimize' the health of foetuses by ensuring that their bodies are in the best possible order before conception takes place. As Waggoner (2013) has argued, this has been a growing concept since the 1980s. Women are urged to give up unhealthy behaviours such as smoking and alcohol in order to support a developing foetus and ensure that any health conditions that they have are understood and/or under control. Yet as conception is largely unpredictable, due to both contraception failures and often unknown biological fertility status, to ensure 'optimization' these types of health behaviours would need to be practised by heterosexually active women until menopause.

Waggoner (2013) argues that the emphasis on pre conceptive care, which has largely developed without supporting evidence of significant harm reduction, is due to a strategy of maternalism within policy. Essentially maternalism is the conflation of women's health needs with maternal health needs. As I have outlined earlier, the association between women and motherhood is longstanding, and, as Waggoner (2013) has shown, pre conceptive care allows health policy to treat women as either pre-pregnant or pregnant, with similar 'rules' for health behaviours. Waggoner (2013) defines this as 'anticipatory motherhood' and argues that in the US context, supporters see it as a mechanism for expanding access to healthcare for women. However, whilst she acknowledges this might be the case, the policy does this on the basis of supporting restrictions on women's lives. Thus responsible heterosexual women should always make embodied decisions as if they are pregnant, sacrificing any desires for non-optimum health behaviour on the basis that they might conceive.

The emphasis on the pre conception period clearly illustrates how many of the different factors outlined in Chap. 2 come together to produce understandings of women's reproductive lives. It is only when motherhood and womanhood are conflated, in an era in which the welfare of a (future) foetus is prioritized, that it would seem logical to treat women as if they were always potentially pregnant. Put this together with an emphasis on risk consciousness, in which eliminating risk rather than assessing a balance of probabilities is in ascendance, and the only 'reasonable' choice for women is to restrict their lives regardless of whether or not they happen to be pregnant. The conflation between pre conception and pregnancy is deemed to be reasonable because the point of conception is usually unknowable and the notion that some risks of 'bad' behaviour occur in the earliest weeks of pregnancy, before any confirmation is possible. The risks are numerous and cover a wide range of issues including acts of consumption and women's embodied state.

Pregnancy Abstinence

A significant issue in 'optimising' foetal health is that women are expected to cease different activities and avoid contact with numerous substances that are deemed as being possibly harmful to the health of the developing foetus. These include smoking, certain foods, specific activities and alcohol. The exact list often varies internationally; for example, in 2015, the UK NHS discouraged eating liver but only recommended washing properly rather than prohibiting any uncooked vegetables. In contrast, the US Department of Health & Human Services made no mention of liver in its advice but stated that pregnant women should not eat raw or undercooked bean sprouts such as alfalfa, clover, mung bean, and radishes. The variation in the advice raises questions about the evidence base for the claims.

The relative importance of each issue is of course variable, but often the general message is that avoidance is the best strategy. For example, in the UK, the NHS gives this advice about hair dye:

> The chemicals in permanent and semi-permanent hair dyes are not highly toxic. Most research, although limited, shows that it's safe to colour your hair while pregnant. Some studies have found that very high doses of the

chemicals in hair dyes may cause harm. However, these doses are massive compared to the very low amount of chemicals a woman is exposed to when colouring her hair. (…) Many women decide to wait to dye their hair until after the first 12 weeks of pregnancy, when the risk of chemical substances harming the baby is much lower. (NHS Choices 2013)

This extract is typical of the ways in which health information is given in many Western countries. It states that there is little or no evidence of harm but goes on to suggest that a (good) choice that women could make is to avoid the activity anyway. Whilst as of yet the issue of hair dye has not led to specific health policies in the UK, that is not the case with alcohol consumption.

The democratization of the risk of alcohol, from babies born to chronic alcohol users to any women who drink alcohol during pregnancy, illustrates the extent to which maximising foetal welfare has come to dominate understandings of pregnancy. Foetal alcohol syndrome (FAS) was first documented in the 1970s when a paper was published giving details of a specific pattern of congenital anomalies in the children of alcoholic mothers (Armstrong 2003). The diagnostic criteria are uncertain as the clinical indicators are similar to other conditions, and particular facial features associated with the diagnosis can change over time (British Medical Association (BMA) 2007). There is also some international variation in the diagnostic criteria, further adding to the uncertainty of the condition (BMA 2007). Women with chronic alcohol usage often tend to have poor diets and may use other substances such as tobacco, and reliable (or any) information about the quantities of alcohol consumed may be absent, which further adds to the complications of diagnosis. If the clinical indicators for FAS are not met, but it is believed that the congenital anomalies or developmental issues are as a result of alcohol consumption during pregnancy, then a diagnosis can be given within the umbrella term of Foetal Alcohol Spectrum Disorder (FASD).

Golden (2005) has shown that in the USA the moral position of FAS shifted over time. In the beginning, children diagnosed with FAS were seen as unintended 'victims' of the disease of alcoholism. At this stage, moral judgements about women's behaviour were less accusatory. Later on, this changed into a discourse based on maternal deviance and incorporated a focus on women from poor and/or minority-ethnic communities. Hence, despite its legal status, women's use of alcohol was positioned alongside illegal substance use with an emphasis on moral disorder. The idea that FASD presents a social 'cost' to the nation has been widely repeated in other places including the UK (Lowe et al. 2010), Australia (Keane 2013) and Nordic countries (Leppo et al. 2014). The idea that there is a social 'cost' at both the individual and societal level is constructed through a wider discourse in which disability is seen as a 'burden' that should be avoided (Shakespeare 2013). Moreover, in the UK, the claim that FASD is the biggest preventable cause of foetal birth defects is based on widely repeated reports of incidence that have no evidence to support them (Lowe and Lee 2010).

As Lowe and Lee (2010) have argued in relation to the British policy on drinking whilst pregnant and before conception, the notion of risk has moved from uncertainty to danger in relation to the foetus. It is also important to note that the changed guidance towards abstinence acknowledged the lack of evidence but felt the only clear message was avoidance (Lowe and Lee 2010). In other words, because the (female) public cannot be trusted to understand the difference between light and problematic drinking, policy needs to make it certain. Abstinence also ensured the elimination of unknown risks, and the only cost is to women's lives. The policy thus attempted to convert the evidential uncertainty over the risk into certitude, and it does so by democratising the risk to any woman who drinks and who could conceive. As Lowe and Lee argue:

> uncertainty regarding risk and safety becomes the justification for the message 'avoid alcohol' and notably non-pregnant women are given the identical advice to women who are already pregnant. From a scientific perspective, this may appear confusing; the obliteration of distinctions between the effects of alcohol on a pregnant and non-pregnant body may appear hard to account for. However, from a perspective which seeks to make the uncertain certain, this approach to pre-pregnancy makes sense. The rules can be the same regardless. (2010: 308–309)

This shift from uncertainly to a need to eliminate a 'dangerous' risk is not limited to UK policy. Leppo et al. (2014) studied alcohol advice surrounding pregnancy in four Nordic countries and found they all follow a similar logic in promoting a precautionary principle. Leppo et al. (2014) argue that the policies reproduce three specific cultural images: the innocent foetus, the perfect mother who puts a (potential) child's welfare first, and the failed mother who 'takes chances' and consumes alcohol regardless of the unknown risk. Given that alcohol consumption is never a necessity, desiring pleasure rather than enhancing the health of the foetus places women into the category of the selfish and thus they become irresponsible women who are not fit to be mothers. However, it is not only leisure activities where women are subjected to the precautionary principle, and this highlights the extent to which the notion of sacrifice is built into understandings of pregnancy.

Eating for Who?

As Bell et al. (2009) have argued, there are similarities between the debates about drinking in pregnancy and the 'crisis' of childhood obesity. Both lack evidence about the extent of harm, but this has not stopped oversimplified messages from becoming part of public discourse (Bell et al. 2009). They argue that in the case of childhood obesity, it has now been associated with neglect, and (poor) mothers in particular are singled out as potential perpetrators of this form of 'child abuse.' As Jarvie (2013) has shown, whilst once having a chubby baby was seen as a sign of maternal success, now it is taken as a sign of failure. It is thus not surprising that body size during pregnancy has come to be seen as a significant issue with obese women, and along with 'excessive' pregnancy weight gain, both are seen as having specific risks to the foetus. Whilst the surveillance of the size of pregnant women is not new, the changing emphasis from concerns about under-nutrition to over-consumption during pregnancy gives further insight into the ways in which women are expected to put the foetus above any bodily desires of their own.

As Oakley (1986) documented, there has been a long-standing interest in the diets of pregnant women. She outlined how, for example, in the 1939–1945 war, when food was being rationed in the UK, pregnant women (alongside children) were given additional resources in order to avoid under-nutrition. Specific dietary interventions are always developed within their social and cultural contexts, and thus the exact nature of the food to be consumed or avoided changes over time. Moreover, it is important to situate understandings of pregnant embodiment within the broader issues of the disciplining of women's bodies. In a cultural environment in which women should be slim, pregnancy can either release women from this cultural norm or add pressure to conform, despite their growing pregnant body (Earle 2003; Nash 2015; Oakley 1980). Whilst some of the societal controls over women's food consumption might be relaxed during pregnancy, this is not absolute (Earle 2003). Three main issues currently arise during pregnancy in relation to diet: somatic effects (such as nausea, cravings and aversions), 'excessive' weight gain, and potentially hazardous food. Whilst each issue has its own impact on women, all require women to monitor their consumption and/or submit to medical surveillance.

As Gross and Pattison (2007) have summarised, the majority of women report cravings and aversions to particular foods during pregnancy. There is an ongoing debate about the biological processes for this phenomenon and the extent to which it is mediated by cultural consumption of specific food items (Gross and Pattison 2007). For some women, cravings and aversions are linked to experiences of nausea and vomiting during pregnancy (Gross and Pattison 2007). Yet regardless of their origins, it is clear that women often find these uncontrollable (Harper and Rail 2012). However, this does not always stop them from feeling guilty about acting on these somatic effects. Nash's (2015) study of Australian women's food consumption practices revealed the guilt that women experienced in consuming 'junk' food due to cravings. Yet despite this guilt, cravings did allow the consumption of food for women's pleasure rather than purely for foetal health. Moreover, as Nash (2015) points out, as concerns about obesity rise, in order to achieve good motherhood women are required to restrict pregnancy weight gain yet at the same time maximize foetal health via nutrition. This is not an easy balance to achieve (Nash 2015). The focus on the individual food practices of women largely ignores structural issues of food practices and body size.

Whilst both being underweight or overweight during pregnancy can lead to pregnancy complications, currently there is a medical preoccupation with pregnancy obesity (McNaughton 2011). This is clearly situated in wider discourses in which the fat body is constructed as deviant and associated with stupidity, selfishness and a lack of control (McNaughton 2011). As McNaughton (2011) has argued, these are not the qualities associated with good motherhood, and thus the obese mother is seen as being likely to fail at motherhood through being deficient in putting the needs of the foetus first and giving birth to a child 'predestined' for child-hood obesity. In the UK, this latter aspect has similar public discourses to those of children born with FAS. Jarvie (2013) found that in that discourse the obese baby/child is constructed as having an ongoing social cost and may be a potential burden to the state.

Jarvie's (2013) UK research with pregnant women with 'maternal diabesity' (women classified as obese or having gestational or type-two diabetes) illustrates the extent to which women feel stigmatized by the attention to their body size. She argues that many of the women, who often came from poorer backgrounds, rejected the medical predi-cations that they would have larger babies whose future health was at risk. Moreover, their complex lives within structural constraints meant that even if they had accepted medical advice, they could not necessarily follow the dietary advice given out by health professionals. Whilst they sought to eat 'healthily', they did not necessarily have access to proper cooking facilities, and limited budgets meant that only certain foods were economically affordable. The focus on weight, both of the preg-nant body and the developing foetus, cannot be separated from issues of socio-economic status (Jarvie 2013; McNaughton 2011). In general terms, women already at risk of being considered as 'irresponsible' moth-ers due to their social-economic status can be further stigmatized through the attention on 'excessive' body weight.

The final issue related to food is the extent to which it can be seen as potentially polluting. This is clearly demonstrated in the ubiquitous lists of 'banned' food that state health agencies produce. However, as Copelton (2007) and Nash (2015) have argued, there is a renewed emphasis on see-ing pregnant women as nutritionally vulnerable in terms of how the *qual-ity* of the food they consume impacts the developing foetus. Mackendrick (2014) has shown that within this discourse there is also rising attention in some social groups on the risk of pollution by synthetic chemicals.

Mackendrick (2014) argues that increasingly women are held responsible for identifying and eliminating the risk of this potential hazard as part of the normative work of mothering. This includes considering the consumption of potential 'toxic' substances during pregnancy. Just like the examples of hair-dye and alcohol, and like the RCOG's concern over plastic food containers mentioned earlier, the precautionary principle is the one that dominates, and this suggests that (good) mothers will take steps to exclude potentially polluting products from their diets. In Mackendrick's (2014) research in Canada with families with environmental concerns, the women interviewed took steps such as moving to organic products and checking food packaging for chemical additives both during pregnancy and when feeding their children. The women saw the time taken to research 'safer' products as part of the work of motherhood. The effort needed to identify and eliminate potential environmental contaminants was thus part of the unselfish role of motherhood.

As I have shown above, negotiating complex rules on food consumption during pregnancy is integral to the work of motherhood and thus it is intimately entwined with broader discourses of maternal sacrifice. Whilst the somatic impact of cravings and aversions allows some freedom for women to put their own needs first, the guilt that often arises from the consumption of 'junk' food indicates that they are aware that their own bodily needs and desires should not necessarily be prioritized. This is particularly the case now when there is excessive focus on pregnancy body weight, in which maternal diabesity is constructed as a significant problem. In an era in which obesity signals a lack of control, it is not surprising that larger women are thus deemed to be irresponsible mothers. They are seen as failing to make the required sacrifice in consumption that would signal good motherhood. Moreover, the individualization and responsibilization of larger pregnant women, which often ignores structural constraints on their lives, further illustrates the extent to which certain groups of women are often automatically deemed to be inadequate candidates for acceptable motherhood. The growing need to invest effort into the elimination of potentially polluting substances illustrates the work involved in managing pregnancy. The unselfish mother who puts the needs of (potential) children first is a common understanding and one that largely ignores that sacrifice is at the heart of this trope.

Moreover, it is now not enough to externally display the right attributes; increasingly the internal emotional state during pregnancy is also under surveillance.

Maternal Stress

Alongside the concerns about consumption during pregnancy, there is renewed concern about pregnant women's mental state. There is a long history to the idea that the thoughts and feelings of women during pregnancy could have a negative impact on the developing foetus. In earlier years, this was often called maternal impression and, as Shildrick (2000) has shown, both lay texts and medical texts illustrated this idea. For example, in the eighteenth century, it was discussed how excessive fear and too much pleasure during pregnancy could both lead to negative physical or mental effects on developing foetus. One of the examples of this belief is the case of Mary Toft.

As Selgman (1961) has documented, in 1726 stories began to circulate that Mary Toft, a poor uneducated woman living in the countryside of the UK, had given birth to rabbits. She was said to have seen a rabbit and had dreamt of rabbits throughout her pregnancy. Contrary to some of the illustrations at the time, they were not live births but were said to have been parts of rabbits. The rumours reached some eminent members of the medical profession, who attended the 'births' of some of the rabbit material. They verified her story as accurate and Selgman (1961) states that the facts of the rabbit births were presented to the current King. Shortly after this, Mary Toft was taken to London and other doctors became involved. Some of these doubted the story and eventually the episode was revealed as a fraud. Her confession stated that following a miscarriage she had been persuaded by an unnamed accomplice to insert parts of rabbits into her vagina and make the claims about the rabbits as a way of making money. She was sent to prison to await trial and was released after a short period. The doctors who believed and verified her story were vilified, as was common at the time, in songs and poems.

Clearly the most reasonable assessment today is that Mary Toft's story was going to be a fraud. However, the fact that several members of the medical profession, including those connected to the royal family, believed in the likelihood of this happening is something rooted in the notion of maternal impression. It is only when pregnant women's mental state is understood to be able to have a direct influence on foetal development that it becomes possible to believe that constant thoughts about rabbits could have altered the developing foetus into a rabbit. Today, similar stories would not be taken seriously, but the idea of a connection between women's mental state and the developing foetus remains. Whilst the biological mechanisms by which the foetus is affected have changed today, it is useful to consider the recent claims about the impact of maternal stress within this longer history.

As Lowe et al. (2015a) have shown, a claim has emerged recently in UK policy that maternal stress during pregnancy is having an adverse impact on the foetus' developing brain. These claims are situated within the broader rise of claims about neuroscience and parenting that will be explored further in Chap. 7. There are clear parallels to the policies on alcohol consumption during pregnancy; because of predicted social 'costs' arising from adverse development of foetal brains, it is justifiable to survey and intervene in pregnant women's lives. There is a wide range of issues potentially included in this, such as future unemployment and substance misuse. However, whilst they are nominally making biological claims that it is the hormonal impact of maternal stress that is the risk to the foetus, the policies are only really concerned with women already designated as potentially irresponsible mothers. They ignore the potential adverse impact of middle-class women, and instead focus almost exclusively on women from disadvantaged backgrounds, which raises questions about biological claims.

As Lowe et al. (2015a) have shown, policymakers in the UK state that new scientific evidence has been discovered about the importance of avoiding stress in pregnancy, but the evidence for the claims is often either missing or overstated. In some cases, evidence from animal studies is applied to the human population more generally without considering the specificity of the findings (Lowe et al. 2015a). The questionable use of evidence, alongside the selective application to poorer women, thus undermines biological claims (Lowe et al. 2015a). Shildrick (2000) argues that the eighteenth century ideas of maternal impression were rooted in concerns about appropriate behaviour of women. Arguably, the more recent concerns over maternal stress are still part of this broad trend. In both cases, women are expected to contain their emotions in the name of protecting the foetus. Hence, to achieve the ideal pregnancy, women need to pay attention to both their internal thoughts as well as the external elements of consumption. Moreover, the justification for intervention is often the 'social' costs associated with a less than perfect foetus. These notions can be associated with longstanding concerns about the reproduction of the 'unfit', from the eugenics movement to the underclass debate.

Prenatal Screening and Diagnosis

During the last decades of the twentieth century, as Rapp (1999) has documented, developments in medical technology led to a rapid expansion of prenatal screening and diagnostic procedures. These include ultrasound scanning, maternal serum testing and amniocentesis. Some procedures indicate a potential risk, whereas others can give definite answers. Some conditions are routinely tested for, whereas only families already deemed to be at risk may be offered screening for others. For example, in the UK women are usually offered screening for specific chromosome disorders (including Downs Syndrome) through a nuchal translucency ultrasound scan and/or blood test. The results of the test give an indication of the probability of the foetus being affected. If the test result indicates that they are high-risk, they are likely to be offered diagnostic testing of either chorionic villus sampling (CVS) or amniocentesis. Both CVS and amniocentesis carry a small risk of miscarriage, and like many other prenatal technologies, they cannot usually predict the severity of the condition. There are continuing debates over the implications and experiences of the expansion of prenatal screening and diagnosis; here I will be focusing on the issues that illustrate how they are related to constructions of motherhood and responsibility.

As Lupton (2013) amongst others has documented, the use of visualising technologies during pregnancy has been a significant factor in changing the focus from women to the foetus. Ultrasound images have blurred the division between 'foetus' and 'baby' and contributed to the idea of foetus as 'patient' within health professional understandings. Increasingly this means that social attributes such as gender and personality are attributed before birth, as the foetus is placed within the family network through visualising technologies (Taylor 2008). Depending on their access to particular scanning services, women may see the foetus on multiple occasions, and the development in the technologies over time has significantly improved the detail of the images. Whilst many of the scans that women undertake as part of prenatal care are still used purposefully to screen or diagnosis health issues, women and their families can understand the encounters in complex ways. A study by Williams et al. (2005) showed that the majority of women understand the medical implications, even if their primary motive is to see the developing foetus. Lupton (2013) argues that health professionals are also now considering the dual purpose of ultrasound as a screening technology as well as a chance to 'see' and 'bond' with the foetus (Lupton 2013). It has also led to the development of commercial 'keepsake' scanning companies who offer 'bonding' opportunities via the images. As Roberts (2012) has argued, commercial 'keepsake' scan providers have to provide sufficient medical knowledge to have credibility with potential clients, yet they offer a different experience to the routine scans provided through prenatal care.

These changes have had profound consequences for all women in places where these technologies are used, although the exact nature of the consequences will vary depending on social and cultural circumstances. For example, ultrasound scans to determine foetal sex are likely to have a very different meaning if there is potential for pressure to terminate female foetuses. The increasing importance of the foetus has led to a decline in women's position as primary patients within maternity care (Lupton 2013). As Ettorre (2009) argues, there has been a shift in emphasis and women come to be seen as producers of either 'fit' or 'unfit' babies. Indeed, it is only when a pregnant body is seen as divided in two that it is possible to have a hierarchy of needs or rights in which the foetus takes precedence. Whilst the widespread use of imaging technologies may have emphasized this divide, this is not necessarily a new trend. Young (1984) for example pointed out how the 'pregnancy as disease' orientation of medical texts in the nineteenth century overlooked women's embodied perspective of pregnancy. Yet as Schmied and Lupton's (2001a) work has revealed, pregnant women can struggle with always conceptualising the foetus as a separate individual. Their study found that whilst there was diversity in whether or not the foetus was conceptualized as separate or part of women's bodies, the majority of the women they interviewed conceptualized the foetus as part of themselves at some points during the interview. They argue that:

> It was apparent from the data in our study that seeing the foetus on ultrasound made the pregnancy 'more real' to the women, but it did not assist in the resolution of the ambiguity or uncertainty they experienced when trying to conceptualise and describe their unborn baby. (Schmied and Lupton 2001a: 37)

Thus whilst foetal imaging may individualize and blur the distinction between foetus and baby, the experiences of pregnant embodiment cannot be overlooked. As Roberts (2012) found, whilst pregnant women enjoyed the onscreen images during scans, they were not 'disembodied spectators' but active interpreters of the images within their embodied experiences.

The increase and routinization of prenatal screening and diagnostic procedures have led to substantive debates as to the extent to which women are able to make decisions about whether or not they want to have them. Whilst technically women should be giving informed consent to all aspects of prenatal care, when procedures are presented as routine, the extent to which women feel that they really have a choice is debated. Different procedures are likely to be presented differently, for example, and attending an appointment might be deemed sufficient evidence of consent for an ultrasound scan, whereas the invasiveness of amniocentesis may require a formal signature on a consent form. As Pilnick (2008) has shown, screening deemed to be 'non-invasive' can be offered in a context of presumed consent and thus women need to explicitly opt out rather than give specific consent. Moreover, as mentioned earlier, whilst women may be given some choice as to whether or not they want to participate, the existence of the technologies, and their routine presentation in prenatal care, mean that women cannot choose not to think about them (Lippman 1999).

As Donovan (2006) argues, the culture of screening forces women to see their pregnancies in terms of risk, and being compelled to make choices can be a burden for women. Heyman et al. (2006) undertook research with women deemed 'high risk' following chromosome screening tests and this also illustrated some of these dilemmas. Many of the women were referred for diagnostic testing and there could be quite a delay before the results were known. This caused distress for many of the women, and their anxiety over a high-risk pregnancy was not necessarily eliminated when they received results confirming that the test was negative. In Rothman's (1988) classic work, she suggests that the need to wait for confirmation of test results means that pregnancies are 'tentative' until women have received 'positive' news. For Rothman (1988), rather than investing in the pregnancy, women may need to maintain some distance in case something is revealed to be amiss. This idea of non-investment is built on the association between prenatal testing and abortion.

Many commentators have argued that the development of prenatal testing and the counselling that often accompanies results that reveal disabilities implicitly imply that the best course of action is termination. Parens and Asch (2000), for example, argue that in a world in which discrimination against people with disabilities is common and disability is viewed as a defect, prenatal screening can never be a neutral technology. The development and widespread existence of the technologies should be seen as part of discriminatory practices (Parens and Asch 2000). Others such as Shakespeare (2006) have argued that the position is more complex, and that it cannot be assumed that the technologies are always discriminatory or that individual pregnant women receive a simple message rather than consider the complexity of raising a disabled child. These decisions are potentially more difficult for families with inherited disorders.

Boardman (2014) revealed the complexity of prenatal screening for women in families living with genetic disease. Her study was with families with Spinal Muscular Atrophy (SMA), an inheritable condition that can lead to differing presentations and prognosis. Whilst SMA can be tested for prenatally, the severity of the condition cannot be predicted. Boardman (2014) found that within reproductive decisions the lives and experiences of family members with the condition were highly significant. Moreover, they were acutely aware of how their reproductive decisions were related to the notion of screening as disability discrimination. The emotional embedding of 'choice' in prenatal screening could not be separated from their wider lives as a family living with genetic disease. Whether or not they choose to utilize screening or other reproductive technologies such as pre-implantation genetic diagnosis (PGD), their embodied experiences shaped their attitudes to testing. Many other studies have revealed the ambivalence that women feel towards prenatal screening. Aune and Möller's (2012) study of women in Norway found that whilst in general women welcomed the information that testing provides, they did not necessarily want to be asked to make decisions on the basis of the information. Heyman et al. (2006) found that women did not always accept the medical assessment of their risk status, particularly if the 'high risk' cut-off point seemed to in fact to be a low probability to the women themselves.

Decisions made to accept or reject prenatal screening and diagnoses are made in the context of individual family life, but this is shaped by the broader framings of fit and unfit motherhood and ideas about foetal personhood. The widespread use of imaging technologies has reaffirmed and enhanced the centrality of the foetus during pregnancy. Technology is often used as the primary vehicle for pregnancy consultation, rather than the thoughts and feelings of women. The developments have contributed to improvements in maternal health. For example, maternal mortality from placenta praevia has been significantly reduced in areas where women have access to ultrasound scanning. However, the routinization of screening and testing has meant that they are not always perceived as a choice, and compliance can be seen as evidence of good motherhood. Yet the focus on the attributes of the foetus within ableist societies has also led to the expansion of selective abortion. In this instance, ideas about good motherhood are important. Whilst good mothers uncritically care for their children, they are also charged with reducing or eliminating 'suffering.' Should the selfless mother continue with the pregnancy and accept the extra care that a child with disabilities may entail? Alternatively, is it selflessness to give up a desired pregnancy due to the risk to health of a future child? Whilst the decision as to whether or not to terminate a pregnancy for foetal anomaly is complex, it is always constructed in relation to the wider discourses of motherhood that require women to make appropriate sacrifices.

Surveillance and Expert Knowledge

Oakley (1986) argues that it was during the seventeenth and eighteenth centuries that medicine began to include pregnancy within its discourse, although at this time it was seen as a 'natural' state. Medical texts were written to give advice on how to 'assist' nature with mainly lifestyle changes to manage any difficulty. Oakley (1986) dates a growing interest in pregnancy care in the UK back to 1901 with the publication of an article in the *British Medical Journal* stressing the importance of pregnancy health and suggesting that maternity hospitals could admit pregnant women for care during their pregnancy rather than just during labour. Barker (1998) argues that in the USA the routine medical monitoring of pregnancy did not really begin to develop until the after the First World War despite a significant increase in medical attendance in childbirth. She argues that medical textbooks prior to this did not discuss medical supervision of normal pregnancies. Barker (1998) identifies the government publication of a handbook called *Prenatal Care* in 1913 as the point in time in which biomedical discourses began to be applied to pregnancy in the USA. The pamphlet remained in circulation for several decades, with a revision in the 1930s. Barker (1998) argues that although the intended audience was pregnant women, it constructed pregnancy as disease-like, defined pregnant women as patients and gave authority to medical professionals. This helped to move pregnancy care into the domain of medicine and led the process by which biomedical understandings of risk and choice are used today to discipline women.

Oakley (1986) further argues that over time there was change from the understanding that pregnancy needed to be supported to seeing it as always a potential pathology, with a marked shift happening in the 1950s. Oakley (1986) argues that the redefinition of pregnancy to a state that needed high levels of surveillance was not justified in terms of clinical risks. Instead, it was a way of allowing both the medical profession and the state to control women's bodies and lifestyles. The common feature that weaves together both medical technologies and public health information is seeing pregnancy as a biological process which requires experts to survey, counsel and constrain women's lives in a variety of ways in order to 'maximize' the development of the foetus. Moreover, whilst pregnancy is increasingly a 'public' experience, in that there is growing acceptance of the pregnant body in the public sphere, this has been accompanied by an obligation for women to demonstrate that they are adhering to medicalized health advice as part of 'good motherhood' (Gatrell 2008).

As outlined in Chap. 2, Gatrell (2008) argues that this should be seen as emotional and embodied labour, which she calls reproductive work. For Gatrell (2008), the work of pregnancy involves following specific regimes of advice, organizing appointments and complying with the medicalized framework of prenatal care, all whilst frequently trying not to 'allow' their pregnant bodies to interfere with their other roles such as worker or carer. Gatrell argues that:

> The pregnancy work of the 'good mother' and the pregnancy work of 'supra-performance' within the workplace share two things in common. Both require women to put themselves at the bottom of the priority list and both have conventionally been hidden from view. (2008: 75)

Thus the reproductive work of pregnancy involves complying with regimes of public and medical surveillance, both of which are formed through biomedical discourses from experts about the appropriate level, if any, of risks that can be tolerated. Yet it also means that women should seek to minimize the impact of their pregnancy on others.

It is important to situate the medicalization of pregnancy within the broader framework of health understandings. The trends in prenatal care identified by Oakley (1986) and Barker (1998) are part of broader shifts in medical dominance. As Bradby (2012) argues, the early twentieth century saw a shift in technological innovation and therapeutic competency which meant doctors were able to successfully treat many more conditions. These successes were used to justify their status as professionals and the deployment of medical power. It was during the second half of the twentieth century that critiques of medicine as authoritarian began to emerge, and a gradual shift to the notion of partnership rather than paternalism took hold (Bradby 2012). Yet alongside this trend a new emphasis on health arose in which surveillance medicine came to dominate. Surveillance medicine is part of the broader trend of healthization in which individuals are obliged to ensure health and avoid illness through adopting specific lifestyles (Conrad 1992). Surveillance medicine blurs the distinction between health and illness and encourages compliance with medical proscriptions and self-surveillance to maximize health (Armstrong 1995). These trends illustrate the broader changes in understandings about health and medicine, but their operation is often heightened during pregnancy. The focus on the foetus as a uniquely vulnerable 'citizen' and the association between femininity and motherhood place pregnancy as a central site for the enacting of these trends.

Hird (2007) argues that maternity is an act of corporeal generosity. While her focus is on the embodied gifting of DNA and antibodies and other biological material through which a woman grows a child, I think this is also a useful way of considering the impact of the cultural imperative of maternal sacrifice during pregnancy. As Hird (2007) points out, gifts are rarely one-directional and are usually instead part of the larger framework of cultural obligations. Hence the requirement of women to accept surveillance as part of the embodied corporeal gift of pregnancy enables the reward of societal recognition of good motherhood. Yet, as Hird (2007) points out, this means that women are required to relinquish claims to autonomous embodied citizenship for the benefit of the foetus, which, arguably, is not yet a person. Yet this paradox is normatively defined as women's natural role, which disguises the role of expert discourse in producing this position.

Corporeal generosity is thus naturalized within medical surveillance and ideas about healthization, within which 'risk' has come to be the dominant narrative of pregnancy, and it operates through the pervasiveness of ideas about sacrifice. As Burton-Jeangros (2011) has shown, risk surveillance during pregnancy blurs the boundaries between medical and moral categories; hence 'good' motherhood requires compliance with medical norms. Pregnancy is now seen as a 'normal illness' in which women's unstable bodies require constant monitoring as their 'unruly bodies' pose a potential threat to the developing foetus (Ussher 2006). In addition, the disciplining of women's bodies through regimes of medicalized surveillance reaffirms the position of women as foetal carriers (Lupton 2012). Lupton (2012) highlights the paradoxical assumption that the biomedical regimes operate on the assumption that 'good mothers' will follow the disciplinary regimes if they are educated as to the potential benefits for their foetus, whilst simultaneously needing constant monitoring to ensure that they have complied.

For most women in the developed world, medical surveillance of pregnancy is usually routine and many women do not necessarily consider it a service that you can 'opt out' of. Yet whilst the majority of women are subject to surveillance, it is important to remember that exactly what is 'offered' may be linked to the social positioning of women. Women from more 'respectable' backgrounds are much more likely to be able to formally make choices than those who are deemed to be potentially deviant. Bridges' (2011) study of a New York public hospital is an example of this. The hospital predominantly served pregnant women without health insurance who qualified for free prenatal care through an assistance programme. Within the programme, it was mandated that women undertake a psychosocial assessment with a social worker as well as attend health education sessions and nutritional counselling alongside undertaking ultrasounds and other prenatal screening. These appointments were a condition of being a patient, and, as Bridges (2011) argues, related to their positioning as risky citizens. Regardless of what services they actually wanted, their structural position meant that others decided which services were appropriate for them.

Alongside variation in the regimes and levels of choice in surveillance medicine that are enacted on women during pregnancy, individual women position themselves differently as to the extent to which they welcome the interventions. Hammer and Burton-Jeangros (2013) found that understandings of risk and acceptance of surveillance technologies varied between women. They suggest that these range from full endorsement of the medical position to a critical questioning of the risk discourses. Their study found that even women who rejected many aspects of medicalized pregnancy did not fully reject medical intervention. They just objected to the inflation of risk avoidance into areas that were unnecessary. Yet wherever they were positioned, it was clear that they could not avoid understandings of pregnancy in term of risk. Whilst their participants could accept, question or reject risk assessments and aspects of prenatal care, they all had to engage with a normative pregnancy care model built around surveillance.

The pervasiveness of risk as the dominant narrative of pregnancy is built on a foundation of expert advice. It is experts who decide what is and is not an acceptable risk. Yet the advice experts give is not developed in a vacuum, and it is clearly shaped by normative social and cultural ideas. It is important to remember that the risks focused on are usually ones that only affect women, and risks that may inconvenience others or challenge ideas about family life are not usually considered in the same way. For example, pregnancy is known to be a key moment in the onset and escalation of domestic violence (WHO 2005). Whilst screening for domestic violence and offering support to those who report it may take place within prenatal care, there are no wholesale calls for women to avoid their partners during pregnancy. The comparison with the approach to alcohol consumption and other abstinence strategies is striking. Yet if the precautionary principle was applied universally across the risks of pregnancy, this is exactly what the experts would be advocating.

The comparison between domestic violence and alcohol consumption during pregnancy illustrates the extent to which expert advice is subject to wider social understandings rather than being an objective assessment of scientific evidence. Moreover, the development of health policy is often shaped by moral entrepreneurs. Becker (1963) defined a moral entrepreneur as a person who sees an 'evil' that upsets them and develops and enacts a strategy to eliminate this situation. Moral entrepreneurs set out to initiate change in social lives. Arguably, the impact of moral entrepreneurs has increased as the dominance of medicine has waned, and there is increasing involvement of 'users' in the policy-making arena. For example, in the UK, organizations such as the National Childbirth Trust are often called on to play a role in government policymaking forums. As Faircloth (2014) argues, this means that sometimes marginal ideas are given considerable space at the highest level. In the UK, the Department of Health relies on the claims of National Organisation for Foetal Alcohol Syndrome (NOFAS) for evidence of the prevalence of FASD, disregarding officially collected statistics that indicate significantly lower incidences (Lowe and Lee 2010). As Lowe and Lee (2010) argue, the move away from a balanced assessment of the evidence in relation to pregnancy risk has led to the imposition of advice as rules.

Consequently, we can see how expert discourses of risk and the enactment of surveillance medicine during pregnancy are entwined with broader cultural ideas about motherhood and the vulnerable foetus. In health policy and practice, ideas about the 'good' selfless mother pervade the framing of regimes of surveillance. Women, as foetal carriers, should comply with surveillance as a natural extension of their caring role. Moreover women positioned as less desirable mothers are less likely to be given options than those with a better claim to being good mothers. Medical surveillance during pregnancy is clearly important to many women, and they should be able to access whatever care they choose. However, currently prenatal surveillance is rarely an uninhibited choice as it is clearly situated within a framework of medical/moral discourses which stipulate that compliance is a sign of good motherhood.

Ogle et al. (2011) argue that this framework positions women as having a 'duty to be well.' They found that women had often normalized and undertook self-surveillance to optimize the health of the developing foetus. Yet the women in their study also had some feelings of ambivalence; they sensed the loss of a claim to put themselves first. Neiterman's (2012) research also found that surveillance had an impact on women's embodied experience of pregnancy, but she argued that the implications were different depending on where women were situated on the 'social ladder' of pregnancy. Neiterman (2012) found that by adhering to medical regimes, women who were potentially judged as 'bad' mothers were able to position themselves as potentially good, whereas women already meeting the judgement of 'good' were more able to reject aspects of the disciplining gaze. Neiterman (2012) also points out the importance of understanding of the role of different 'audiences' for different aspects of pregnancy behaviour. Women with cultural scripts positioned as alternatives to the dominant biomedical framework can find affirmation of their behaviour in likeminded peers, and women judged by strangers can find solace in the reassurances about their behaviour from health professionals. Hence, whilst the risk narrative within the culture of surveillance holds a dominant position, women are still able to accept or resist different aspects of this as part of the reproductive work they are undertaking. The corporeal generosity of women thus indicates a commitment to being selfless, and making all the 'right' sacrifices necessary to ensure the best outcome for the vulnerable foetus/child.

Conclusion

As this chapter has shown, throughout pregnancy women are expected to prioritize the welfare of the foetus over their own health, lives and desires. The cultural script of the foetus as vulnerable citizen and the idealization of good motherhood as selflessness produce prevailing discourses of putting the foetus first. Moreover, within the risk consciousness framework, the notion of considering the probability of harm has been rejected in favour of the precautionary principle. Pregnant women, as mothers-to-be, need to demonstrate their commitment to idealized motherhood by following biomedical regimes of advice and surveillance. They need to choose the right sacrifices to make to optimize foetal wellbeing, even if there is little evidence of harm. As the issue of alcohol consumption illustrates, increasingly the risk-adverse position taken by policymakers overlooks clear evidence of harm. Risks that were once associated with particular social groups can be democratized to the population more generally. In addition, the changing and international variation in 'rules' for eating illustrate the social construction of many of these risks. Whilst women may adhere to or reject all or any of the health advice on food or other risks, they still have to engage with the normative gaze of surveillance from both medical professionals and the public more generally. Visibly pregnant women who fail to display appropriate pregnant embodiment leave themselves open to public sanction. The resurgence of concerns about maternal stress indicates how women are now expected to 'control' their mental states in addition to any physical concerns about pregnancy. Moreover, in line with the notion of responsible planning, adherence with health advice is increasingly focused on the preconception period. Hence, ideas about maternal health have become synonymous with women's health (Waggoner 2013). In case they should conceive, (heterosexual) women should sacrifice any desire for non-optimal health behaviour, making ongoing sacrifices from pleasure to medical treatments in order to benefit the welfare of potential foetuses whether or not they are trying to conceive.

Developments in medical technologies, and in particular the rise of ultrasound scanning, have also had a significant impact on the experience of pregnancy. There is no doubt that the technologies have decreased some of the health risks of pregnancy, and many women welcome the opportunities to see their developing foetus. Yet alongside these benefits, the decentering of the attention from women to the body of the foetus and the blurring of the distinction between foetus and baby have had profound consequences. Women's embodied experience of pregnancy is no longer necessarily the central concern. The routine presentation of screening and diagnostic techniques within maternity care means that all women are supposed to engage with surveillance medicine, even if some are able to reject particular tests. Whilst nominally informed consent for medical treatment is still the principle that operates, the routinization of surveillance and responsibilization of women means that this may be practically difficult and position women as unwilling to display appropriate maternal behaviour.

The emphasis on the precautionary principle and its accompanying risk management regimes within biomedical concerns disguises the moral elements of judgement about women's behaviour during pregnancy. Wider social understandings are increasingly important when issuing health advice, rather than a balanced assessment of the evidence. The move to include moral entrepreneurs as 'stakeholders' in the policymaking process has potentially exacerbated this trend. Yet the impact of the disciplinary regimes will vary depending on how closely women align to normative positions of good motherhood. Women more closely situated to ideas of good motherhood are often in a better position to resist, and compliance with biomedical norms can assist some women in moving away from negative positioning. Certainly for women who are at risk of having their child removed, compliance with surveillance and biomedical instructions can help prove that they can be good mothers. Moreover, it is important to remember that even if alternative frameworks to the dominant biomedical position are found, this does not necessarily mean there will be a rejection of the maternal sacrifice trope. As will be explored more deeply in relation to childbirth, alternative positions often offer competing frameworks of appropriate maternal sacrifice rather than a rejection of it as a normative framework.

References

Armstrong, D. (1995). The rise of surveillance medicine. *Sociology of Health and Illness, 17*(3), 393–404.

Armstrong, E. M. (2003). *Conceiving risk, bearing responsibility: Fetal alcohol syndrome and the diagnosis of moral disorder*. London: John Hopkins University Press.

Aune, I., & Möller, A. (2012). 'I want a choice, but i don't want to decide'—A qualitative study of pregnant women's experiences regarding early ultrasound risk assessment for chromosomal anomalies. *Midwifery, 28*(1), 14–23.

Bachrach, C. A., & Newcomer, S. (1999). Intended pregnancies and unintended pregnancies: Distinct categories or opposite ends of a continuum? *Family Planning Perspectives, 31*(5), 251–252.

Barker, K. (1998). A ship upon a stormy sea: The medicalization of pregnancy. *Social Science & Medicine, 47*(8), 1067–1076.

Barrett, G., & Wellings, K. (2002). What is a 'planned' pregnancy? Empirical data from a British Study. *Social Science & Medicine, 55*(4), 545–557.

Becker, H. S. (1963). *Outsiders studies in the sociology of deviance*. New York: The Free Press.

Bell, K., McNaughton, D., & Salmon, A. (2009). Medicine, morality and mothering: Public health discourses on foetal alcohol exposure, smoking around children and childhood overnutrition. *Critical Public Health, 19*(2), 155–170.

Boardman, F. K. (2014). The expressivist objection to prenatal testing: The experiences of families living with genetic disease. *Social Science & Medicine, 107*, 18–25.

Bradby, H. (2012). *Medicine, health and society*. London: Sage.

Bridges, K. (2011). *Reproducing race: An ethnography of pregnancy as a site of racialization*. London: University of California Press.

British Medical Association. (2007). *Fetal alcohol spectrum disorders: A guide for healthcare professionals*. London: BMA.

Burton-Jeangros, C. (2011). Surveillance of risks in everyday life: The agency of pregnant women and its limitations. *Social Theory and Health, 9*(4), 419–436.

Conrad, P. (1992). Medicalization and social control. *Annual Review of Sociology, 18*, 209–232.

Copelton, D. A. (2007). "You are what you eat": Nutritional norms, maternal deviance, and neutralization of women's prenatal diets. *Deviant Behavior, 28*(5), 467–494.

Donovan, S. (2006). Inescapable burden of choice? The impact of a culture of prenatal screening on women's experiences of pregnancy. *Health Sociology Review, 15*(4), 397–405.

Earle, S. (2003). "Bumps and boobs": Fatness and women's experiences of pregnancy. *Women's Studies International Forum, 26*(3), 245–252.

Ettorre, E. (2009). Prenatal genetic technologies and the social control of pregnant women: A review of the key issues. *Marriage & Family Review, 45*(5), 448–468.

Faircloth, C. (2014). The problem of 'attachment': The detached parent. In E. Lee, J. Bristow, C. Faircloth, & J. Macvarish (Eds.), *Parenting culture studies* (pp. 1–24). Basingstoke, England: Palgrave Macmillan.

Gatrell, C. (2008). *Embodying women's work*. Maidenhead, England: Open University Press.

Golden, J. (2005). *Message in a bottle: The making of fetal alcohol syndrome*. London: Harvard University Press.

Griffiths, F., Lowe, P., Boardman, F., Ayre, C., & Gadsby, R. (2008). Becoming pregnant: Exploring the perspectives of women living with diabetes. *British Journal of General Practice, 58*(548), 184–190.

Gross, H., & Pattison, H. (2007). *Sanctioning pregnancy: A psychological perspective on the paradoxes and culture of research*. London: Routledge.

Hammer, R. P., & Burton-Jeangros, C. (2013). Tensions around risks in pregnancy: A typology of women's experiences of surveillance medicine. *Social Science & Medicine, 93*, 55–63.

Harper, E. A., & Rail, G. (2012). Gaining the right amount for my baby: Young pregnant women's discursive constructions of health. *Health Sociology Review, 21*(1), 69–81.

Heyman, B., Hundt, G., Sandall, J., Spencer, K., Williams, C., Grellier, R., et al. (2006). On being at higher risk: A qualitative study of prenatal screening for chromosomal anomalies. *Social Science & Medicine, 62*(10), 2360–2372.

Hird, M. J. (2007). The corporeal generosity of maternity. *Body & Society, 13*(1), 1–20.

Jarvie, R. (2013). Discourses pertaining to, and lived experiences of 'maternal obesity' (body mass index (BMI)≥ 30) and gestational diabetes mellitus/type two diabetes mellitus in the pregnancy and post-birth period. Unpublished PhD thesis, Plymouth University, Plymouth, England.

Keane, H. (2013). Healthy adults and maternal bodies: Reformulations of gender in Australian alcohol guidelines. *Health Sociology Review, 22*(2), 151–161.

Leppo, A., Hecksher, D., & Tryggvesson, K. (2014). 'Why take chances?' Advice on alcohol intake to pregnant and non-pregnant women in four Nordic countries. *Health, Risk & Society, 16*(6), 512–529.

Lippman, A. (1999). Choice as a risk to women's health. *Health, Risk & Society, 1*(3), 281–291.

Lowe, P., & Lee, E. (2010). Advocating alcohol abstinence to pregnant women: Some observations about British policy. *Health Risk & Society, 12*(4), 301–311.

Lowe, P., Lee, E., & Macvarish, J. (2015a). Growing better brains? Pregnancy and neuroscience discourses in English social and welfare policies. *Health, Risk & Society, 17*(1), 15–29.

Lowe, P., Lee, E., & Yardley, L. (2010). Under the influence? The construction of foetal alcohol syndrome in UK newspapers. *Sociological Research Online, 15*(4), 2.

Lupton, D. (2012). 'Precious cargo': Foetal subjects, risk and reproductive citizenship. *Critical Public Health, 22*(3), 329–340.

Lupton, D. (2013). *The social worlds of the unborn.* Basingstoke, England: Palgrave.

Mackendrick, N. (2014). More work for mother chemical body burdens as a maternal responsibility. *Gender & Society, 28*(5), 705–728.

McNaughton, D. (2011). From the womb to the tomb: Obesity and maternal responsibility. *Critical Public Health, 21*(2), 179–190.

Nash, M. (2015). Indulgence versus restraint: A discussion of embodied eating practices of pregnant Australian women. *Journal of Sociology, 51*(3), 478–491.

Neiterman, E. (2012). Doing pregnancy: Pregnant embodiment as performance. *Women's Studies International Forum, 35*(5), 372–383.

NHS Choices. (2013). *Is it safe to use hair dye when I'm pregnant or breastfeeding?* Page dated May 20, 2013, Retrieved December 28, 2014, from http://www.nhs.uk/chq/Pages/949.aspx?CategoryID=54&SubCategoryID=131#close

Oakley, A. (1980). *Women confined: Towards a sociology of childbirth.* Oxford, England: Martin Robertson.

Oakley, A. (1986). *The captured womb: A history of the medical care of pregnant women.* Oxford, England: Basil Blackwell.

Ogle, J. P., Tyner, K. E., & Schofield-Tomschin, S. (2011). Watching over baby: Expectant parenthood and the duty to be well. *Sociological Inquiry, 81*(3), 285–309.

Parens, E., & Asch, A. (2000). The disability rights critique of prenatal testing: Reflections and recommendations. In E. Parens & A. Asch (Eds.), *Prenatal testing and disability rights* (pp. 147–164). Washington, DC: Georgetown University Press.

Pilnick, A. (2008). 'It's something for you both to think about': Choice and decision making in nuchal translucency screening for Down's syndrome. *Sociology of Health & Illness, 30*(4), 511–530.

Rapp, R. (1999). *Testing women, testing the fetus: The social impact of amniocentesis in America.* London: Routledge.

Roberts, J. (2012). 'Wakey wakey baby': Narrating four-dimensional (4D) bonding scans. *Sociology of Health & Illness, 34*(2), 299–314.

Rothman, B. K. (1988). *The tentative pregnancy: How amniocentesis changes the experience of motherhood.* London: Pandora.

Schmied, V., & Lupton, D. (2001a). The externality of the inside: Body images of pregnancy. *Nursing Inquiry, 8*(1), 32–40.

Selgman, S. A. (1961). Mary Toft: The rabbit breeder. *Medical History, 5*(4), 349–360.

Shakespeare, T. (2006). *Disability rights and wrongs.* Abingdon, England: Routledge.

Shakespeare, T. (2013). *Disability rights and wrongs revisited.* Abingdon, England: Routledge.

Shildrick, M. (2000). Maternal imagination: Reconceiving first impressions. *Rethinking History, 4*(3), 243–260.

Taylor, J. S. (2008). *The public life of the fetal sonogram: Technology, consumption, and the politics of reproduction.* New Brunswick, NJ: Rutgers University Press.

Ussher, J. M. (2006). *Managing the monstrous feminine: Regulating the reproductive body.* London: Routledge.

Waggoner, M. R. (2013). Motherhood preconceived: The emergence of the preconception health and health care initiative. *Journal of Health Politics, Policy and Law, 38*(2), 345–371.

WHO. (2005). *Multicountry study on women's health and domestic violence against women: Summary report.* Geneva, Switzerland: World Health Organization.

Williams, C., Sandall, J., Lewando-Hundt, G., Heyman, B., Spencer, K., & Grellier, R. (2005). Women as moral pioneers? Experiences of first trimester antenatal screening. *Social Science & Medicine, 61*(9), 1983–1992.

Young, I. M. (1984). Pregnant embodiment: Subjectivity and alienation. *Journal of Medicine and Philosophy, 9*(1), 45–62.

6

Birth Plans

The idea of choice has long been a central issue in the debates about child-birth, and there are ongoing arguments over the 'best' way for women to labour and give birth. The idea of choice is used by different 'factions' ideologically and empirically as both an explanatory framework for their positions and as an ideal for overcoming what they see as the shortcomings of the 'opposition' position. As this chapter will illustrate, specific positions on birth, whether 'natural' or 'medical', are culturally promoted with the idea of choice and, despite their formal opposition, have similarities in the rhetoric used to promote their views about birth. What is considered as a normal birth practice will vary in different parts of the developed world, and healthcare policy and settings are a significant part of determining 'normal' practice. Yet the cultural messages about the 'right' choices that women should make often make use of ideas of good motherhood and the extent to which the foetus/baby is at risk to support their position. Thus, choices are presented to women as either 'right' or 'wrong', with claims of bad mothering associated with the wrong choice.

This chapter will examine the context of childbirth and the ways in which good motherhood and maternal sacrifice defend or contest different birthing models. It will begin with an outline of the twentieth-century

© The Editor(s) (if applicable) and The Author(s) 2016
P. Lowe, *Reproductive Health and Maternal Sacrifice*,
DOI 10.1057/978-1-137-47293-9_6

history of the debates over birth and set out how people and places (mid-wives/homes, obstetricians/hospitals) came to stand in for the extent to which women could or should exercise choice over childbirth. The rise of the idea of the birth plan, in which women are encouraged to exercise 'choices' on where and how to give birth, will illustrate how women are formally encouraged to nominally plan for an idealized version of 'birth' even within medical settings. Moreover, the critiques of unassisted home birth and the labelling of women who desired a caesarean section as 'too posh to push' clearly illustrate the limits of choice, even by those who support natural or medical birth. This chapter will also illustrate how the 'right' birth contributes to, or detracts from, a woman's identity as a good mother. Women who are unable to live up to their internalized ideal of a 'good' birth may feel that they have failed. This chapter will illustrate how both 'sides' in the debates over birth share common understandings about the need for good mothers to make sacrifices. The sacrifices that are called for may be different, yet, as I will argue, both natural and medical birth ideologies use ideas about choice, responsibility and good mother-hood in order to present their case as the best way to birth.

Battles for Birth?

As I outlined briefly earlier, the place and management of birth has been at the centre of reproductive debates for many years. There is not room here to address all issues in this debate; instead, I will sketch out the two main theoretical positions so they can be drawn on later. As many have argued, the manner of birth reflects both social and cultural positions, as well as an important individual experience, and birth has been a site of contestation and resistance. Prior to the twentieth century, most women in the developed world gave birth at home, whereas now the majority of women have a hospital birth. This move has been considered central to debates over the medicalization of childbirth and the rise of obstetric practice, which are believed to have reduced the remit of midwifery as the site of authoritative knowledge over birth (see for example, Davis-Floyd 2003; Oakley 1980; Rothman 2007). Whilst there is no doubt that childbirth can be difficult and sometimes fatal, the relationship between the medicalization of birth and reduced maternal and foetal mortality is still a matter of debate (see for example Cheyney et al. 2014). Whilst it is helpful to set out ideal types of the 'medical' and 'natural' models of childbirth, it is important to remember that in practice, the division between them is often less absolute than in the debates. Moreover, practices of obstetrics and midwifery are not universally standard and will vary according to the healthcare policy and/or institutional practices that structure the countries and workplaces where they are situated.

The medical management of birth is closely associated with hospitalized birth and obstetrics as a surgical discipline (see for example Davis-Floyd 2003; Oakley 1980). Martin (1987) amongst others argued that within this model women's bodies are seen as machines, and that the role of the health professional is to ensure efficient production. As a production process, 'normal' birth has narrow criteria and any variation from this needs intervention. Indeed, because of the constant risk of pathology and danger, 'normal' birth is only ever a retrospective label that can be applied afterwards when nothing untoward has happened (Scamell and Alaszewski 2012). Whilst the medical model is often criticized, it needs to be remembered that the medicalization of childbirth started to occur when maternal and infant morbidity was high, and thus fears about childbirth were not unreasonable. The medicalization of birth was not just the imposition of (male) doctors' preferences. As Leavitt (1980) has shown, feminist campaigners in the US during the early twentieth century were campaigning for access to pain relief during labour, a move that necessitated hospital birth. Leavitt (1980) suggests that these campaigns were as much about women being able to exercise choice over how they give birth rather than exclusively about access to pain relief. Yet having access to drugs inevitably meant accepting the medical management of labour and may have contributed to the standardization of hospital births.

Davis-Floyd (2003) sets out a typology of what medically managed birth consists of in the USA. Alongside the routinization of specific procedures such as foetal monitoring, and high rates of interventions such as induction or artificial rupture of the membranes (breaking the waters), she argues that the institutional culture of normal hospital routines disciplines women and structures birth as a technological process. The imposition of this model not only reaffirms the beliefs about childbirth as a disordered process in need of control but also increases the need for inter-vention to take place through its standard operating procedures. Within this technological model of birth, the desired product is a healthy baby, and the woman as 'birthing machine' is only a secondary consideration (Davis-Floyd 2003). Whilst elements of the model will vary between hos-pitals in the USA and in other places, overall this is consistent with medi-cal management in other places such as the UK (McCourt et al. 2011), Canada and Australia (Benoit et al. 2010).

Whilst challenges to the medical model of birth were evident in the 1930s (and in particular, with the publication of *Childbirth without Fear* by Dick-Read in 1942), the natural childbirth movement began to emerge more strongly in the 1960s (Rothman 2007). Challengers drew attention to what they felt were unnecessary and often dehumanising procedures associated with the medical management of birth, and they sought to reframe birth as a normal rather than pathological process, one that was at risk from the iatrogenic effects of intervention. Shaw argued that:

> Few Americans know what birth is like, even many who have given birth themselves. A general result of the patient's belief in the mystery and dan-ger of delivery, and her fear of the event, is that she is more willing to do what she is told. This in turn sets the stage for the central activity of a hospital delivery; the doctor as a star delivering a baby from the woman. (1974: 82)

Those in support of natural childbirth focus on childbirth as a nor-mal event for which women's bodies were made. Indeed for many, the pain and discomfort of natural childbirth is a key element through which women can show that they can exhibit the right qualities of sacrifice to qualify for motherhood (Malacrida and Boulton 2012). Phipps (2014) suggests that ideas such as this have been adopted by neoconservative ide-ologies as part of a broader essentializing discourse about women's natural state. Indeed if birth is a rite of passage to motherhood (Davis-Floyd 2003), then it is not surprising that a display of the necessary cultural signifiers of selflessness through endurance is often seen as important (Malacrida and Boulton 2012). As Malacrida and Boulton (2012) have shown, within this framing, bearing the pain of labour and having a vaginal birth are seen as important elements in the display of appropriate motherhood for many women.

However, the natural childbirth model also suggests that the medical model is inappropriate because many of the 'rules' in obstetric care make it harder for women to give birth. For example, it was argued that confining women to a bed during labour to enable constant foetal monitoring could prolonged labour, making it more painful and thus increasing the chances for foetal distress (Rothman 2007). The natural childbirth model posits that the pain of childbirth can be managed with support from caregivers rather than analgesics, particularly if women can find the best position physically for them to feel comfortable during contractions (Mansfield 2008). Indeed the role of professionals during birth is thus to offer guidance, support and encouragement to women rather than to play a more active role, unless an emergency occurs (Davis-Floyd 2003). Hence the natural childbirth model both emphasizes the importance of the embodied experience of labour pain yet simultaneously seeks to minimize this through a specific approach of support in birth.

Yet as Mansfield's (2008) examination of the term 'natural' in natural childbirth texts has shown, it is not clear how 'natural' birth is within this model. She argues that what was being advocated was not so much that birth just happens without intervention but that instead a specific set of social practices need to be in place to ensure that natural childbirth can occur. Mansfield (2008) argues that the texts suggest that women need to do a considerable amount of work to enable 'natural' childbirth to happen. This includes following specific guidance, managing the environment, identifying proper support and ensuring they have the correct frame of mind. Indeed, the emphasis placed on women educating themselves about birth as an essential part of natural childbirth suggests that it is not as instinctive a process as the term 'natural' would seem to imply (Mansfield 2008). As Mansfield points out, the texts

> suggest that natural childbirth requires hard and very conscious work, rather than passively letting nature take its course. In this view then, respecting birth as a natural process does not mean being passive; rather, respect of nature requires active and very social involvement. (2008: 1093)

For many advocates of natural childbirth, midwives came to be seen as the birth practitioners of choice and the home was usually designated as the best place for normal birth. Rothman (2007), for example, argues that in contrast to the foetal-centric care of obstetrics, midwifery is woman-centred. This emphasis on the different orientation of midwives is associated by Rothman (2007) with home birth. Yet just because care is given by midwives, the extent to which it is outside of the medical model is debatable. For example, in the UK, although midwives are routinely responsible for low-risk births within hospitals, both in midwifery-led units and consultant-led units - often called 'normal' labour - the extent to which they can deviate from institutionalized practices, particularly in the latter, is questionable (Pollard 2003). Pollard (2003) found that the medical model of care was institutionalized in NHS operating policies and thus structured conditions of employment. Moreover, these also influenced home births arranged with NHS midwives attending (Roberts 2005). As I will show later, these are important issues for many of those advocating unassisted birth.

Roberts' (2005) study in the UK found that restrictive policies and the organization of community midwifery meant that women planning a home birth often did not feel that they had necessarily escaped from what they saw as the unnecessary, intrusive or disempowering elements of obstetric care. Many of her participants desired a home birth because they felt that this would minimize the risk of inappropriate interventions. They felt that home birth should be safer because it would enable them to stay in control and that, as mothers, they were the best people to ensure the safety of their foetus. In particular, they highlighted a concern that the formulaic approach within obstetric care was a risk to their ability to build a relationship with their foetus/baby, and that birth as a rite of passage was a crucial element of this. Yet the organization of healthcare often meant that the idealized picture of midwifery/home birth was not necessarily obtained, and that the obstetric-model of care shaped their home births. This was because many of the women were unable to build trusting relationships with midwives whilst pregnant. A good relationship with a midwife who would be there during the birth was often a crucial component in their desired birth plan. Yet due to the organizational practices of maternity services, and the ongoing threat of 'unnecessary' recommendation of transfer to a hospital, this did not usually happen (Roberts 2005). Moreover, whilst the home may be idealized as a site of non-intervention, women having a home birth in the UK often have different medical equipment moved into their home (Roberts 2005). They can also have a range of interventions, including analgesics, which clearly indicates the complexity of practice and suggests that a simple divide between medical/obstetric and natural/midwifery models of care is unwarranted.

Indeed, as Fannin's (2003) study of 'homelike' birthing rooms in the USA has shown, the focus on place as a site of meaning for birth often overlooks the nuances in the ways that spaces operate. Her study illustrates how, as a result of the challenge from natural childbirth advocates, hospitals began to transform some birthing rooms into homelike spaces, sometimes hiding medical equipment behind a façade of domesticity— for example, by placing foetal monitors within 'bedside cabinets.' She points out that bringing the home into the hospital was seen to appeal to those who desired a more natural birth whilst retaining the safety net of obstetric care. In the context of the USA, this ensured consumer appeal whilst maintaining the medical control needed to avoid malpractice litigation (Fannin 2003). If the hospital mimicking domesticity is seen as potentially a hybrid place (Fannin 2003), arguably we could also understand the placing and use of medicalized equipment (such as Entonox cylinders) in the home as equally complicating the ideological divide.

The dichotomies of medical/natural, doctor/midwife and hospital/home suggest two competing ideological positions that women need to choose between. Yet as shown above, in practice, clearly the divide is not that simple. Indeed, as Annandale and Clark (1996) argued a long time ago, whilst the critiques of medical management were extremely important at highlighting poor treatment of women during birth, the preferred solution of natural childbirth was to impose a new set of beliefs that meant rejecting any of the benefits, such as pain relief, that could have been offered. Idealizing the home as the best place for normal birth also assumes that women will generally have a safe and secure place of residence in which appropriate levels of care and privacy can be achieved (Annandale and Clark 1996). Many women will not be in this position. Moreover, a clear component of the natural model seemed to rely on an essentializing discourse in which womanhood and motherhood were synonymous. Hence women who failed to give birth without intervention, as well as those who requested intervention, could be seen as failing as both women and mothers (Fannin 2003). Common to both positions are claims that suggest they are the way to achieve good motherhood, and this is articulated through their competing claims about control and safety, which are presented as choices that women should make. These are crucial to how the idea of maternal sacrifice operates to shape women's experiences.

Control, Safety and Birth Plans

At the heart of the battles over birth lie questions about control, safety and the extent to which, as informed 'consumers' of birth, women should be able to exercise choice. These choices are often encapsulated in a birth plan. This can be just thoughts and feelings, but more often women are encouraged to produce a written statement of what 'type' of birth they desire, including which interventions/procedures that they do, or do not, want to have. Originally introduced by those supporting natural childbirth as a way to help women avoid interventions, birth plans have now been institutionalized into hospital care, even where a highly medicalized birth is the norm (Lothian 2006). Indeed, in contrast to the original intention of helping women to resist interventions, birth plans can also be used to support women's request for them. Hence rather than solely being the preserve of those desiring natural childbirth, birth plans are now more of a formulaic method by which women are encouraged to make choices.

For natural childbirth supporters, the medical model's aim to regularize and control birth removes women's ability to labour and give birth the way that they would naturally do. Morris (2013) amongst others has pointed out that this is not necessarily due to just the desire of individual doctors but also to the institutionalized system in which they work. The emphasis on possible harms, which is encouraged by risk consciousness, has led to the development of guidelines for 'normal' progression of labour within institutions, and these prevent women from being able to give birth naturally. A major element of the critique is based on the

likelihood of 'cascading' interventions. This is the process by which routine practices of the medical model, such as electronic foetal monitoring,
increase the likelihood of more interventions (see for example Crossley
2007; Davis-Floyd 2003; Morris 2013). Moreover, it is argued that high
levels of surveillance can increase women's fear and anxiety during birth,
and that this may have a detrimental impact on their ability to give birth
without intervention (Davis-Floyd 2003).

The monitoring and intervention used within the medical model are
also deemed to have more of a focus on the outcomes for the foetus than
those for women, and this is built into the culture of risk consciousness surrounding birth. Morris (2013) found that in the USA this was
related to their perceived risk of liability following adverse outcomes,
with poor foetal outcomes believed to be more likely to result in court
cases than poor maternal care (also see Fannin 2003). Drawing attention
to a potential detrimental impact on women has been an essential part
of the critique developed by natural childbirth advocates, but they also
argue that this risk-adverse approach also undermines the foetus' welfare. For example, Davis-Floyd (2003) argues that childbirth analgesics
have a detrimental impact on the foetus, and Morris (2013) points out
how planned caesarean sections have higher rates of foetal mortality. In
addition, they suggest that as women's natural mothering abilities can
be compromised through medicalized birth, this will also have a detrimental impact on the newborn babies (Oakley 1980; Davis-Floyd 2003).
For example, the pain and restricted movement caused by a caesarean
section can impact women's ability to care. This position suggests that
by exerting standardized control over women during birth, the medical
model of birth actually increases rather than reduces biomedical risks.
This increases the risks to the foetus rather than actually making birth
safer. Hence most women should reject medical intervention, including
pain relief, in order to benefit their foetus. Despite this critique, as Fox
and Worts (1999) pointed out, there is much evidence to suggest that
women can be positive about the level of medical control, and they are
often quite satisfied with hospital deliveries, and, as will be explored later,
some desire a high level of intervention.

In contrast, for those who support the medical model, the emphasis on
natural childbirth, particularly home birth, underestimates the potential

for risk in childbirth, which could jeopardize the health of mother and foetus. They point out that, if an obstetric emergency did take place, the extra time it would take to get to hospital facilities could lead to worse and potentially life-threatening outcomes. The idea that birth is inherently risky and that the hospital is the safest place to give birth is often reflected in women's accounts of choosing a birthplace (Miller and Shriver 2012). Indeed even in the accounts of women who choose to give birth at home, the time it would take to get to the hospital is a factor that women consider (Roberts 2005). This assessment of risk can be highly individualized for women. One of the women in Roberts' (2005) research pointed out that proximity and time are not necessarily the same, arguing that they could be transferred to a hospital in approximately the same timeframe as it takes to prepare a theatre for surgery (Roberts 2005). Hence both medical and natural models make claims about safety and risk in promoting their model of birth, but the major source of risk, and therefore the solution, is different. Within the medical model, risk is primarily physiological, and close monitoring and timely interventions are seen as a way to reduce adverse outcomes. In contrast, in the natural model, the significant risk is often iatrogenic and thus reducing interventions makes birth safer. Importantly, regardless of which model is correct about the relative risks, what is clear is that the welfare of the foetus is emphasized on both sides and is what women need to prioritize when evaluating the competing claims.

That safety is an important consideration for almost all women can be related to the broader context of the risk society. Yet as Chadwick and Foster (2014) point out, whilst risk is a central consideration for many women, their definition of risk may go beyond the narrow biomedical interpretation often assumed. In their study of birth choices made by middle-class women in South Africa, they found that women were weighing different risks including loss of control and dignity within medicalized birth. For Chadwick and Foster:

> Women are rendered doubly risky in relation to childbirth. They are classified by biomedical discourse as bodies at risk of complication, abnormality, and death but are also positioned as vulnerable bodies at risk of exposure, loss of dignity and objectification, particularly in medical settings. (2014: 79)

Hence their study found that women had to choose between these risks, and this choice was related to the place and process of birth. The women in their study who chose home birth explained their decision by challenging the biomedical discourse and emphasizing the risks inherent in being objectified rather than treated as an individual. This is similar to the findings of Roberts (2005), who found that women in the UK who home-birthed also emphasized the importance of trying to manage levels of control during birth.

As Namey and Lyerly (2010) have shown, whilst control during child-birth has long been seen as an important issue, what the term means is often left unstated. Although many people have advocated for women to be able to assert more control, the lack of attention to what women define as control could mean that the research is not easily comparable. In their study in the USA, they found that women defined control as a complex mix of ideas which included being able to make or refuse certain choices but also issues of self-management, an understanding of child-birth, respect from healthcare providers, feeling safe, and having trust in those around them. Moreover, many of the women believed that birth is not always a controllable process and thus having a 'good' birth did not necessarily mean being able to exert control but to feel in a safe enough place in order to be able to lose it (also see Roberts 2005).

These competing opinions are situated within the broader notion of neoliberal risk societies and the idealization of the health consumer. As Zadoroznyj (2001) points out, given the competing ideological frame-works, childbirth seems to be the ideal setting for the informed health con-sumer to exercise choice, choosing between the medical and natural models of birth. In her study in Australia, there was evidence that some women were active in choosing the health professionals and maternity services that they thought would suit them. The ability to do this was clearly con-structed on social class lines, with more affluent middle-class women hav-ing financial resources and cultural capital more able to match their desired criteria for their birth from the range of medical care on offer. In contrast, the working-class women were less likely to show a consumer approach, particularly for first births, and described the process more in terms of con-straints than choice. Zadoroznyj (2001) found that women's material and social position was a key determinate of the extent to which women were able to exercise choice even when women desired to be involved in the management of maternity care. Moreover, as Fannin (2003) points out, even when consumer choice is emphasized, this does not mean that it is always meaningful. She points out how although the idea of choice is highlighted in domesticated birthing rooms in hospitals, the options are often limited to relatively superficial issues such as control of lighting and music.

Indeed as Craven (2007) has argued, whilst middle-class women in the US have used the idea of consumer choice as a strategy to widen the availability of birthing options, their structural position means that their choices will not necessarily be judged in the same way. For poorer women, who are more likely to have their parenting questioned, the choice to birth outside of the way sanctioned by the state could mean that child protection concerns would be raised, and thus potentially put their children at risk of removal (Craven 2007). Craven (2007) argues that using the neoliberal language and strategies of claiming consumer choices and rights may not necessarily serve the interests of less affluent families who have a more precarious relationship with the state and, in the USA, this could undermine strategies to ensure that high quality and low cost maternity care is available to all.

The limitations of birth planning have also been explored by Crossley (2007). As she has shown, rather than being able to exercise a genuine choice, birth plans can only express preferences. Moreover, as they cannot necessarily account for the unpredictability of birth, they can be of little use in practice. During birth, many women are unlikely to be able to argue authoritatively with the healthcare professionals who are advising them, so they are rarely in a position to challenge suggestions of necessary or even desirable interventions. As Crossley (2007) states, when women are presented with alternatives of a safe birth or a potential death, particularly during the later stages of pregnancy or whilst in labour, agreeing with health professionals is not really exercising a choice at all. Indeed Bryant et al. (2007) found that some health professionals did not differentiate between the concepts of shared decision-making and gaining informed consent, or they believed that a choice had been made once informed consent had been given. Assenting to a particular intervention when it is presented to you as the best (or even only) option is not the equivalent of choosing between a variety of different possibilities.

As Possamai-Inesedy (2006) has argued, in cultures where childbirth is deemed to be potentially risky and the elimination of potential risk is a key determinate of good motherhood, it is hardly surprising that many women choose hospital births. Moreover, within the medicalized framework of childbirth, it is health professionals who have control over the designation of high or low risk births that frames women's decision-making over place and procedures (Possamai-Inesedy 2006). Whilst the Netherlands has long been used as an illustration of the success and safety of normalizing homebirth, there is a trend of increasing levels of hospitalization and intervention (Christiaens et al. 2013). Christiaens et al. (2013) undertook a review of the evidence and suggested that while there are a number of factors that can account for this, women's choice is one of them and this may be related to broader ideas of women's responsibility for the health and wellbeing of the foetus/child. Hence, in contrast to the early ideas of those advocating for natural childbirth, expanding choice may lead to greater medicalization rather than a reduction of intervention. If the only truly 'safe' place for good mothers to give birth is culturally deemed to be the hospital, it is unlikely that many will opt for a home birth even if this is available to them (Hadjigeorgiou et al. 2012).

Representations in the media can be an important source of information for some women. Yet if representations of birth on television focus on problems and show how medical interventions lead to happy outcomes (Morris and McInerney 2010; Sears and Godderis 2011), it is not surprising that women feel that this is likely to be the most suitable way to give birth. In Sears and Godderis' study of a childbirth reality TV programmes in the USA, they found:

> Not a single negative outcome related to medical intervention, such as an epidural failing to relieve a women's experience of pain or complications encountered during a cesarean section, was ever shown. In all of the twenty-four episodes, the medicalized birthing interventions worked perfectly to produce happy and healthy birthing women and babies by the end of the birthing process. (2011: 190)

Whilst there is no straightforward relationship between media representations and public opinion, they are likely to contribute to the perception that the hospital is a safe space that good mothers will choose.

In a review of studies into women's experiences of their first labour (Eri et al. 2015), the hospital as a safe space was an important consideration. Yet this presumption was made more complex by a model of medical management that expected women to stay at home during early labour. The mismatch between the promotion of a hospital as a safe space and the frequent denial of entry to women in the early stages of labour was difficult for women to manage. The women wanted to be 'good patients' but were uncertain as to how to recognize the point at which medical surveillance should begin, and this could make them anxious. Encouraging women to stay at home, or even sending them home after they presented to the hospital during early labour, is often viewed as a way to prevent unnecessary interventions, yet as this review showed, some women would have preferred to be in the hospital (Eri et al. 2015). Indeed, it further confuses the overall message about issues of safety and choice. If hospitals are promoted as the safest place for birth, it does not necessarily make sense to deny women the choice of being there, particularly if this causes distress. As Eri et al. (2015) point out, the emphasis on safety and the elimination of risk can be undermined by the denial of maternity care during early labour. Moreover, although women are responsible for identifying the 'correct' time to seek hospital admission, the uncertainty of labour means that their ability to choose the 'right' time is difficult and causes them concern. Hence their position as (good) mothers who should know when this protection of the foetus is required comes under question.

Thus women are positioned as responsible choosers, both in terms of which birth ideology to focus on and what element within each framework they should choose. Yet within both frameworks, they need to make the 'right' choice to ensure that they are good mothers. Whilst the range of choices will vary depending on both their geographic and socio-economic position, a positioning as responsible choosers suggests that they are health consumers. This is epitomized in the idea of the birth plan, which suggests that there is an element of control. Yet the extent of this control is subject to the agreement of the healthcare policies and practice, and it is set within the framework of minimizing risks and performing good motherhood. Hence, in practice the discourses surrounding good motherhood structure the choices that can be made. In the medical model, performing good motherhood means agreeing to the biomedical framing of risk, whereas in the frames of natural childbirth it means enduring an intervention-free birth. Hence in both models, women's own preferences should be a secondary consideration, as they should sacrifice any or all of their own desires and focus on the best birth for their foetus.

The promotion of birth as natural and normal and encouraging women to make a birth plan, which does not account for the potential for obstetric complications, can lead to unrealistic expectations for some women (Crossley 2007). It also contributes to a sense of failure for women who desired but 'failed' to birth in the 'right' way (Crossley 2007; Malacrida and Boulton 2014). Malacrida and Boulton (2014) found that when their labour and birth did not meet their expectations, women often blamed themselves. This could be through failing to prepare themselves adequately, either physically or through a lack of assertion of their preferences to health professionals. They argue that far from being empowering, birth plans act to discipline women. Although they seem to offer a choice, in practice they position women as responsible for the outcomes, even when it is not what they had chosen to do. This is part of the responsibilization of women, who are charged with delivering the 'product' of pregnancy (Ruhl 1999). The contradictions inherent in being positioned as an informed birth consumer whilst simultaneously being expected to make the right choices as a good mother will be illustrated further in the discussion of two specific birth choices, both of which have come under heavy criticism: caesarean by maternal request and unassisted birth (also called freebirth).

Caesarean by Maternal Request (CMR)

In recent years, the numbers of women having caesarean sections has become one of the flashpoints of the conflicts over birth. Whilst it is clear that a caesarean can be life-saving, there have been growing concerns that some women are having them unnecessarily. The increase in the rates of caesarean sections at the end of the twentieth century and beginning of the twenty-first century did not make birth safer (Gregory et al. 2012), and this suggests that many women are having the procedure without medical justification. This raises concerns about whether this form of surgery is exposing women to unnecessary medical risks. For example, the WHO suggests that caesarean sections should account for no more than 15 % of births, yet many countries have higher rates, including Italy, Australia and the USA, which all had rates over 30 % (Gibbons et al. 2010). The reasons for the rise in caesarean sections has become a matter of debate, and many have questioned as to what extent the increasing numbers are due to maternal request.

Caesarean sections are often divided into two types. Elective caesareans are usually planned in advance of labour, whereas emergency caesareans occur when a situation arises either before or during labour that warrants immediate surgery. CMR is a subsection of the elective category, and it is usually defined as when a caesarean is planned without any clinical indicators suggesting it is necessary. However, the boundary between CMR and other elective caesareans is not well defined (Kornelsen et al. 2010; Morris 2013). Clinical indictors are not absolute but are instead a subjective decision by health professionals. Women also make assessments of their health as part of the complex mix of individual, social and cultural issues that lead them to request a caesarean (Kornelsen et al. 2010). Moreover, Kornelsen et al. (2010) found that their participants in Canada had decided on a caesarean before discussing it with a health professional. Hence if a request was made to a health professional by a woman with borderline clinical indicators, it is not clear if this would 'count' as CMR or not. Morris (2013) argues that despite frequent claims by health professionals that the increasing caesarean section rates are due to CMR, there is little evidence to support this case. She argues that it is difficult to untangle CMR from the wider structuring of birth as risky and organization structures which frame caesareans as safer. For example, if women are generally led to believe that, for them, a caesarean section would be less of a risk than a vaginal birth, it is not surprising that they would request it. Morris (2013) argues that this is particularly the case in the USA with women who have had a previous caesarean section.

In some places, CMR has been stigmatized in the media with the label 'too posh to push', which trivializes and stigmatizes women who take up this option (Weaver and Magill-Cuerden 2013). Weaver and Magill-Cuerden (2013) traced the history of the phrase 'too posh to push' in British newspapers and found the first mention was in 1999, with growing coverage since then. There were a number of different themes associated with the phrase. One of the issues reported was the claim that some women felt vaginal birth was distasteful or undignified, and the media was often critical of this position. Another significant theme was that the timing of birth was planned around important work, and this was constructed as a 'trivial' reason and thus one that good mothers would not make. This clearly fits into the notion that women's lives are less important than the developing foetus. CMR was particularly associated with high profile women or those who wanted (wrongly) to copy them. Not all the coverage was negative; some articles were challenging negative images of CMR, and many of them included details of risks of either caesarean or vaginal birth (Weaver and Magill-Cuerden 2013). Moreover, in the reports, there was often a blurring of the distinction between CMR and elective caesarean more generally, with the latter becoming implicitly incorporated. Weaver and Magill-Cuerden (2013) suggest this may contribute to a general over-estimation of the numbers of women who are having CMR.

At the heart of the idea of 'too posh to push' is the position that suggests women who undergo CMR are shallow or misguided, and that the lack of acceptance of labour (and pain) meant that they were not performing good motherhood. This clearly also ignores the physical impact of caesarean sections as a form of abdominal surgery. As Tully and Ball (2013) argue, although women who have elective caesarean sections may have an easier delivery, recovery from caesareans can be painful and difficult. Some of their US participants were keen to point out that this showed that having a caesarean was not really escaping the trials of birth, in contrast to the idea signified by the phrase 'too posh to push.' The way in which these women distanced themselves from the potentially stigmatizing position of having a caesarean, rather than a vaginal birth, can be seen to reaffirm the notion that pain and sacrifice are an essential part of the transition to (good) motherhood.

In many studies, fear of childbirth has been identified as one of the reasons that women may choose CMR. Fenwick et al.'s (2010) study in

Australia revealed that many of the women they interviewed considered vaginal birth to be difficult and unpredictable in contrast with a planned and controlled caesarean section. Chadwick and Foster's (2013) interviews with women in South Africa also revealed that women who chose CMR visualized vaginal birth as terrifying and disgusting and a practice through which women are exposed and shamed. In contrast, they felt that the control that CMR gave them meant that it was considered the safest option for them. Whilst their accounts often mentioned claims that natural childbirth was linked to good motherhood, they rejected this position and emphasized that the unpredictability of childbirth meant that vaginal birth was not necessarily in the best interests of the foetus. These findings are also similar to McAra-Couper et al.'s study in New Zealand. They suggest:

> Many women feel that they are obliged to embrace all the available technology to ensure the safety of their baby. This ascendency of technology over the skill of the health professional and the women's 'knowing' of her own body, in and of itself, is a precondition for the choices women make. (2012: 93)

This notion, that the medicalized framing of the 'dangers' of birth has become so entrenched that it is the dominant narrative, leads Bergeron (2007) to suggest that fully informed consent for CMR can never be obtained. She argues that, as medicalized birth has come to be seen as a normal process, the presentation of competing risks has limited the frames within which decisions about CMR are made. This can also implicitly be seen in Fenwick et al. in their argument that women who chose CMR fail to see vaginal birth as a 'natural, important and significant life process' (2010: 398). Beckett (2005) challenges these ideas as both resting on essentialized understandings of birth and ignoring the potential benefits of technologies. She argues that whilst it is clear that some women do find natural childbirth as empowering, this is not necessarily the case for all women. Moreover, suggesting that women can legitimately choose to reject birthing technologies but not choose to receive them is hugely problematic. Indeed Kornelsen et al. (2010) found that in Canada women felt that the right to choose CMR was seen as progress for women's reproductive rights. Their participants framed the option around ideas about consumer rights and were critical of healthcare providers that did not allow CMR. As Beckett (2005) argues, rejecting the possibility of CMR does nothing to enhance women's ability to make meaningful decisions over their lives within the social context in which they are situated. Whilst CMR is clearly shaped by the cultural frames of reference, all women's choices over birth are often contingent on imperfect information (Beckett 2005).

Ideas about women's rights to self-determination over birth are structured by women's gendered obligations to manage risk, particularly for the foetus (Bryant et al. 2007). Hence if women are uncertain about birth, choosing a caesarean section becomes a moral obligation (Bryant et al. 2007). This is clearly linked to ideas about good motherhood and the need of women to put the wellbeing of the foetus first. Far from being a misguided choice, CMR can thus be positioned as a rational choice for some women because of the ways in which they construct the 'best' journey for them within the ideals of motherhood. Whilst critiques of CMR often either implicitly or explicitly position women as 'victims' of medicalized childbirth, duped into a rejection of the vaginal birth rite of passage, both acceptance of and rejection of CMR are often reliant on the same motherhood frames of reference. Moreover, rather than defending medicalized birth, the medical defence of rising rates of caesarean sections, which relies on an assertion that this is an outcome of consumer choice, further positions women as irresponsible choosers.

Good mothers always choose the safest birth, and either the rejection of intervention or the request of CMR can be seen to be complying with this norm. Indeed, if childbirth's discomfort and pain are a rite of passage to motherhood, then the discomfort and pain that women experience following a caesarean section could rightly be understood in exactly the same way. For those who reject medicalized childbirth, CMR is the wrong 'choice.' They debate causes such as medicalization and misplaced beliefs in the safety of caesareans whilst upholding notions of the ideal birth as a rite of passage in which enduring labour pain is a natural sacrifice for women. For those who see CMR as an outcome of consumer demand (bad), women who are 'too posh to push' refuse to endure the work and pain of natural childbirth. Women who request CMR are thus selfish and failing for putting their own welfare above that of the foetus. The rejection of CMR as a legitimate choice for women, both by natural childbirth advocates and the popular press, indicates how accepting a highly medicalized childbirth can leave women in a stigmatized position. It is positioned as not enough sacrifice, as in the rejection of labour pain for trivial reasons, or too much sacrifice, as in a misguided understanding of foetal safety that leads women to accept unnecessary surgery. Yet for women who choose CMR, it is the best route to motherhood for them, and they accept the pain of surgery to ensure that the welfare of their foetus/baby is maximized. Those who reject CMR as a legitimate choice often emphasise the naturalness and safety of normal birth. Yet despite this, it does not mean that they support all natural births, as the issue of unassisted birth makes clear.

Unassisted Birth

A distinction needs to be made between planned unassisted births and births before arrival. Unassisted births occur when women have planned not to seek assistance from a healthcare professional during birth, whereas births before arrival are when women had intended to have a healthcare professional in attendance, but as a result of their particular circumstances (often timing or transport issues) they gave birth without a healthcare professional present. To date, far less research has been done on women who choose unassisted birth over other childbirth options in developed countries. The lack of engagement with maternity healthcare providers makes women having an unassisted birth a difficult group to identify, particularly in terms of numbers. Moreover, as Freeze (2008) found in the USA, some women who plan an unassisted birth may claim that it is a birth before arrival to avoid confrontation with healthcare professionals or child welfare authorities.

Unassisted birth is clearly situated within the ideology of natural child-birth. Miller's (2009) research in the USA found women were critical of the medical model and had initially thought they would like a midwife to attend them. Whilst researching childbirth options, many of them had found stories of other women who had had an unassisted birth and this began to be seen as more natural and personal than having a midwife. Miller found:

> These women do not see birth as a medical event and thus do not want the involvement of a doctor; they also see a midwife as unnecessary, because of the naturalness of birth and their confidence in their own ability to deliver without assistance. (2009: 62)

Over time, the women in Miller's (2009) study began to see midwifery as part of the medical model of care, and thus rejected that as well. In Freeze's (2008) study, some women felt the same and rejected midwifery as a possible hindrance to safe, normal birth. By contrast, others felt that midwife care did have a place. They felt that not all women wanted or were able to educate themselves sufficiently about unassisted birth to make it a good option. The importance of education here is a reminder of Mansfield's (2008) argument about how natural childbirth is a specific practice rather than an instinctive one. Indeed Freeze (2008) found that although women planning an unassisted birth put great faith in the idea of birthing-women's intuition as a site of authoritative knowledge, working out a process by which they could discern intuition from other thoughts and feelings was important to them. This involved trying to balance intuition with knowledge about the birth process as a way of double-checking what they were thinking and feeling, which adds complexity to the notion that without interference women birth naturally.

Lundgren (2010) found similar stances over a natural ability to give birth amongst women in Sweden who had desired a home birth, and some of whom had given birth unassisted. They spoke of having trust in themselves as capable of giving birth as well as an embodied ability to feel if something was not right, at which point they could seek professional help. Miller (2009) found that some women were also motivated by religious reasons, and their faith was a part of their decision to decline health professional care. Whatever the motivations of these women, most of the studies revealed a common idea that most women can give birth safely unassisted if they have the right space in which to do so. Moreover, whilst birth is held up to be an instinctive practice, within the world of unassisted birth, it still seems to require sufficient reproductive work to enable women to succeed.

Most of the studies of unassisted birth suggest that many women see interventions in the birth process as a significant risk to women, and that hospitals are not a good place to give birth. Indeed, the majority of women involved in unassisted birth understand that giving birth does involve risks, but they argue that for them unassisted birth is less of a risk than attended childbirth particularly in hospitals (Freeze 2008; Jackson et al. 2012; Miller 2009). In Australia, Jackson et al. (2012) found many women describing previous experiences of attended births that had been problematic or even traumatic for them. Miller (2009) suggests that the women believe that they are the best judges of risk and safety to the foetus and whether the medical environment was a suitable place for them. Miller's (2009) participants felt that they had no choice other than having an unassisted birth, as this was the only safe option available to them. Many of the women stated that they were not completely against medical care, and they would, and sometimes did, seek health professional care if they felt something was wrong (Freeze 2008; Miller 2009).

Despite its position within the natural childbirth ideology, unassisted birth is not widely supported even by those who support home birth. For example, Dahlen et al. (2011) suggest that unassisted childbirth is an outcome of institutional failures within Australian maternity services. They suggest that women are electing to birth outside the system because maternity services are failing to meet their needs. Dahlen et al. (2011) suggest there is a link between a highly medicalized approach to birth taken in countries such as the USA and Australia and the growing numbers of unassisted births. However, whilst Freeze (2008) found that some women turned to unassisted birth when they were unable to access the maternity care they needed, not all of the women in her study would choose professional health care even if less medicalized versions were available.

As Freeze (2008) has shown, critiques of unassisted birth often argue that the women are selfish, placing their desire for a particular birth experience above the welfare of their foetus/baby. She suggests that whilst the most vocal critics are those who support the medical model of birth, many supporters of midwifery/home birth also argue against unassisted birth. Her study showed that many of the supporters of unassisted child-birth dismiss this claim and argue that it is because they have concerns about the welfare of their foetus/baby that they have chosen this route. Freeze (2008) found two main explanations in support of this position. First, unassisted birth is likely to be more gentle and peaceful and a reduction of the trauma associated with medicalized birth will be beneficial for the foetus/baby. Second, they stress the mutual interdependence between mother and foetus/baby, and improving conditions for one will enhance the welfare of the other. Those who support midwifery/home birth also often use these reasons, and thus the key difference for those who advocate for unassisted birth is that they feel a midwife could prevent rather than facilitate these practices. Freeze states:

> UCers [unassisted birth advocates] contend that the "midwife as the expert in normal" argument espoused by natural childbirth advocates is just as flawed as the "obstetrician as the expert" view held by technomedicine. The only true experts, UCers argue, are mothers themselves. No one else, no matter how elaborate or technical their training, can know what the laboring woman knows, feels, and intuits about her own body and baby. (2008: 243)

Through arguing that women are best placed to ensure the safety of their birth, alongside a commitment to seek help if they think something is wrong, those involved in unassisted births can see themselves as responsible mothers and reject the label of selfishness. By positioning themselves as responsible choosers, women involved in unassisted birth align themselves with the ideals of good motherhood. They reject claims by others who critique this positioning. Indeed Freeze (2008) found that some women in her study were very critical of women who unquestionably accepted medical advice. This was seen as a delegation of responsibility to others regarding things that women should be responsible for themselves, and thus incompatible with good motherhood. The women accepted full responsibility for both good and bad outcomes of unassisted birth, and in doing so argued that they, and they alone, were the best people to promote their foetus/baby's welfare (Freeze 2008). In doing so they sacrificed the ability to 'blame' others for any poor birth outcomes as part of the responsibilization of good motherhood.

Conclusion

From its traditional position as the transition between womanhood and motherhood, childbirth is an important element in the construction and reproduction of ideas about (good) motherhood and maternal sacrifice. It is also one of the few areas in which reproductive work is at least nominally recognized though the designation of birthing as labour. For the majority of women in the developed world, fear of their own death is no longer associated with childbirth. This is a significant progression that women elsewhere may not share. Despite this, perceptions of risk still significantly influence the competing ideologies of birth. Moreover, regardless of the birthing ideology, ideas about good motherhood are central to the promotion or denigration of particular positions. Good mothers either work with medical professionals and prioritize the safety of the foetus through the medical model or they give birth naturally to avoid the detrimental impact that interventions have on the health of their foetus and their ability to mother. Whilst the competing ideologies prioritize different birth processes, they are remarkably consistent on ideas about the importance of idealized motherhood and the need for women to make appropriate sacrifices to achieve this.

The debates over control, safety and risk in birth play out in the oppositions of natural/medical, midwife/obstetrician and home/hospital. The ideologies nominally position women as health consumers who can exercise choice, either between the competing spaces, or over elements within them. Yet they simultaneously suggest that responsible choosers will make the 'right' choice. For the advocates of medicalized birth, accepting surveillance and interventions positions women as good mothers who prioritize the health of the foetus/baby, as a 'normal' birth can only be seen in retrospect when nothing adverse happened. Hence, women should sacrifice any desire for a particular birthing experience and follow medical advice. For those who support natural childbirth, avoiding the risks of inappropriate intervention is paramount, and enduring the pain of childbirth is an important rite of passage that minimizes the risk to the foetus/baby. Here good mothers sacrifice interventions, such as pain relief, in order to prove themselves as good mothers. The birth plan can become the site of these contestations, and 'failing' to follow it can leave women feeling that they have failed a motherhood 'trial.'

The two exemplar positions covered here, CMR and unassisted birth, have been used to illustrate the ways in which birth choices, risk, safety and responsible motherhood are intertwined. For those who support natural childbirth, CMR is an outcome of the over-medicalization of birth which has 'duped' women into false claims of safety. In the popular press, it is seen as a failure of women to accept the pain and work of labour, a picture that omits acknowledgment of the impact of surgery on women. Hence CMR results from either the wrong kind of birth or inadequate sacrifice, and women who choose this option can be stigmatized. Yet those who choose CMR reject this positioning by staking claim to the belief that, for them, CMR was the safest option. Women who choose unassisted birth are also seen potentially as 'bad' mothers, with many health professionals arguing that this is either a failure of healthcare systems or a 'false' belief held by women about risk and safety that is putting their foetus/baby at serious risk. This label is clearly rejected by women choosing unassisted birth, who instead argue that women as mothers instinctively are the best guardians of their foetus/baby's welfare. Thus both women who choose CMR and those who undergo unassisted birth reject claims of selfishness and position themselves as good mothers who are making responsible choices and who are prepared to make appropriate sacrifices to ensure that their births are the best way for the foetus/child to enter the world.

References

Annandale, E., & Clark, J. (1996). What is gender? Feminist theory and the sociology of human reproduction. *Sociology of Health & Illness, 18*(1), 17–44.

Beckett, K. (2005). Choosing cesarean feminism and the politics of childbirth in the United States. *Feminist Theory, 6*(3), 251–275.

Benoit, C., Zadoroznyj, M., Hallgrimsdottir, H., Treloar, A., & Taylor, K. (2010). Medical dominance and neoliberalisation in maternal care provision: The evidence from Canada and Australia. *Social Science & Medicine, 71*(3), 475–481.

Bergeron, V. (2007). The ethics of cesarean section on maternal request: A feminist critique of the American College of Obstetricians and Gynecologists' position on patient choice surgery. *Bioethics, 21*(9), 478–487.

Bryant, J., Porter, M., Tracy, S. K., & Sullivan, E. A. (2007). Caesarean birth: Consumption, safety, order, and good mothering. *Social Science & Medicine, 65*(6), 1192–1201.

Chadwick, R. J., & Foster, D. (2013). Technologies of gender and childbirth choices: Home birth, elective caesarean and white femininities in South Africa. *Feminism & Psychology, 23*(3), 317–338.

Chadwick, R. J., & Foster, D. (2014). Negotiating risky bodies: childbirth and constructions of risk. *Health, risk & society, 16*(1), 68–83.

Cheyney, M., Burcher, P., & Vedam, S. (2014). A crusade against home birth. *Birth, 41*(1), 1–4.

Christiaens, W., Nieuwenhuijze, M. J., & De Vries, R. (2013). Trends in the medicalisation of childbirth in Flanders and the Netherlands. *Midwifery, 29*(1), e1–e8.

Craven, C. (2007). A "consumer's right" to choose a midwife: Shifting meanings for reproductive rights under neoliberalism. *American Anthropologist, 109*(4), 701–712.

Crossley, M. L. (2007). Childbirth, complications and the illusion of choice: A case study. *Feminism & Psychology, 17*(4), 543–563.

Dahlen, H. G., Jackson, M., & Stevens, J. (2011). Homebirth, freebirth and doulas: Casualty and consequences of a broken maternity system. *Women and Birth, 24*(1), 47–50.

Davis-Floyd, R. E. (2003). *Birth as an American rite of passage* (2nd ed.). London: University of California Press.

Eri, T. S., Bondas, T., Gross, M. M., Janssen, P., & Green, J. M. (2015). A balancing act in an unknown territory: A metasynthesis of first-time mothers' experiences in early labour. *Midwifery, 31*(3), e58–e67.

Fannin, M. (2003). Domesticating birth in the hospital: "Family-centered" birth and the emergence of "homelike" birthing rooms. *Antipode, 35*(3), 513–535.

Fenwick, J., Staff, L., Gamble, J., Creedy, D. K., & Bayes, S. (2010). Why do women request caesarean section in a normal, healthy first pregnancy? *Midwifery, 26*(4), 394–400.

Fox, B., & Worts, D. (1999). Revisiting the critique of medicalized childbirth: A contribution to the sociology of birth. *Gender & Society, 13*(3), 326–346.

Freeze, R. A. S. (2008). *Born free: Unassisted childbirth in North America.* Unpublished PhD thesis, Graduate College of the University of Iowa, Iowa City, IA.

Gibbons, L., Belizán, J. M., Lauer, J. A., Betrán, A. P., Merialdi, M., & Althabe, F. (2010). The global numbers and costs of additionally needed and unnecessary caesarean sections performed per year: Overuse as a barrier to universal coverage. *World Health Report, 30*, 1–31.

Gregory, K. D., Jackson, S., Korst, L., & Fridman, M. (2012). Cesarean versus vaginal delivery: Whose risks? Whose benefits? *American Journal of Perinatology, 29*(1), 7–18.

Hadjigeorgiou, E., Kouta, C., Papastavrou, E., Papadopoulos, I., & Mårtensson, L. B. (2012). Women's perceptions of their right to choose the place of child-birth: An integrative review. *Midwifery, 28*(3), 380–390.

Jackson, M., Dahlen, H., & Schmied, V. (2012). Birthing outside the system: Perceptions of risk amongst Australian women who have freebirths and high risk homebirths. *Midwifery, 28*(5), 561–567.

Kornelsen, J., Hutton, E., & Munro, S. (2010). Influences on decision making among primiparous women choosing elective caesarean section in the absence of medical indications: Findings from a qualitative investigation. *Journal of Obstetrics and Gynaecology Canada, 32*(10), 962–969.

Leavitt, J. W. (1980). Birthing and anesthesia: The debate over twilight sleep. *Signs: Journal of Women in Culture and Society, 6*(1), 147–164.

Lothian, J. (2006). Birth plans: The good, the bad, and the future. *Journal of Obstetric, Gynecologic, & Neonatal Nursing, 35*(2), 295–303.

Lundgren, I. (2010). Women's experiences of giving birth and making deci-sions whether to give birth at home when professional care at home is not an option in public health care. *Sexual & Reproductive Healthcare, 1*(2), 61–66.

Malacrida, C., & Boulton, T. (2012). Women's perceptions of childbirth "choices" competing discourses of motherhood, sexuality, and selflessness. *Gender & Society, 26*(5), 748–772.

Malacrida, C., & Boulton, T. (2014). The best laid plans? Women's choices, expectations and experiences in childbirth. *Health: An Interdisciplinary Journal for the Social Study of Health, Illness and Medicine, 18*(1), 41–59.

Mansfield, B. (2008). The social nature of natural childbirth. *Social Science & Medicine, 66*(5), 1084–1094.

Martin, E. (1987). *The woman in the body*. Buckingham, England: Open University Press.

McAra-Couper, J., Jones, M., & Smythe, E. (2012). Caesarean-section, my body, my choice: The construction of 'informed choice' in relation to inter-vention in childbirth. *Feminism & Psychology, 22*(1), 81–97.

McCourt, C., Rance, S., Rayment, J., & Sandall, J. (2011). *Birthplace qualita-tive organisational case studies: How maternity care systems may affect the provi-sion of care in different birth settings. Birthplace in England Research Programme.* Final report part 6. NIHR Service Delivery and Organisation programme.

Miller, A. C. (2009). "Midwife to myself": Birth narratives among women choosing unassisted homebirth. *Sociological Inquiry, 79*(1), 51–74.

Miller, A. C., & Shriver, T. E. (2012). Women's childbirth preferences and practices in the United States. *Social Science & Medicine, 75*(4), 709–716.

Morris, T. (2013). *Cut it out: The C-section epidemic in America.* London: New York Press.

Morris, T., & McInerney, K. (2010). Media representations of pregnancy and childbirth: An analysis of reality television programs in the United States. *Birth, 37*(2), 134–140.

Namey, E. E., & Lyerly, A. D. (2010). The meaning of "control" for childbearing women in the US. *Social Science & Medicine, 71*(4), 769–776.

Oakley, A. (1980). *Women confined: Towards a sociology of childbirth.* Oxford, England: Martin Robertson.

Phipps, A. (2014). *The politics of the body.* Cambridge, England: Polity Press.

Pollard, K. (2003). Searching for autonomy. *Midwifery, 19*(2), 113–124.

Possamai-Inesedy, A. (2006). Confining risk: Choice and responsibility in childbirth in a risk society. *Health Sociology Review, 15*(4), 406–414.

Roberts, N. (2005). *Birthing autonomy: Women's experiences of planning home births.* Abingdon, England: Routledge.

Rothman, B. K. (2007). Labouring then: The political history of maternity care in the United States. In W. Simonds, B. K. Rothman, & B. M. Norman (Eds.), *Laboring on: Birth in transition in the United States* (pp. 3–28). Abingdon, England: Taylor & Francis.

Ruhl, L. (1999). Liberal governance and prenatal care: Risk and regulation in pregnancy. *Economy and Society, 28*(1), 95–117.

Scamell, M., & Alaszewski, A. (2012). Fateful moments and the categorisation of risk: Midwifery practice and the ever-narrowing window of normality during childbirth. *Health, Risk & Society, 14*(2), 207–221.

Sears, C. A., & Godderis, R. (2011). Roar like a tiger on TV? Constructions of women and childbirth in reality TV. *Feminist Media Studies, 11*(2), 181–195.

Shaw, N. S. (1974). *Forced labor: Maternity care in the United States.* Oxford, England: Pergamon Press.

Tully, K. P., & Ball, H. L. (2013). Misrecognition of need: Women's experiences of and explanations for undergoing cesarean delivery. *Social Science & Medicine, 85*, 103–111.

Weaver, J., & Magill-Cuerden, J. (2013). "Too posh to push": The rise and rise of a catchphrase. *Birth, 40*(4), 264–271.

Zadoroznyj, M. (2001). Birth and the 'reflexive consumer': Trust, risk and medical dominance in obstetric encounters. *Journal of Sociology, 37*(2), 117–139.

7

Raising Babies

In the stages before birth women are judged in relation to motherhood, yet they do not fully meet the nominal essential criterion of motherhood, caring for children. Yet after birth, rather than necessarily an increase or change in ideas about the role of women as mothers, in the main there is just a continuation to the existing framing. Part of the way that this is achieved is through an erosion of the pre-pregnancy, pregnancy and post-natal periods. The trend for women to be considered as always potentially pregnant was discussed in Chap. 5, and here I will look at the blurring of the pregnancy and postnatal periods, with a particular focus on infant feeding and early-years parenting policy. The chapter will also highlight the trend of the scientization of parenting, in which expert knowledge is marshalled to produce a normalized account of what good mothers do and what sacrifices they should make.

The chapter will begin by examining the ways in which feeding babies are far from an individual choice. The current promotion of breastfeeding as the only 'right' choice, regardless of the implications for women's lives, is part of a longer trend of expert pronouncements on infant feeding in which moral judgements about women as mothers are central. I will show how global campaigns that originate in areas where women

© The Editor(s) (if applicable) and The Author(s) 2016
P. Lowe, *Reproductive Health and Maternal Sacrifice*,
DOI 10.1057/978-1-137-47293-9_7

do not have access to clean water or safe formula milk are deployed to promote the benefits of breastfeeding to women in developed countries. Women who choose not to breastfeed or cannot breastfeed thus appear as failing to make the 'right' choice, and their position as good mothers becomes 'doubtful.' The chapter will then consider the ways in which specific forms of maternal sacrifice are advocated within parenting policy. Debates around early-years care and child development, whilst nominally directed at parents, usually impact women more, as they predominantly retain responsibility for raising children. In particular, the focus on emotional bonding as a key determinate for children's future lives acts to constrain women's choices over their work and social lives. Hence, whilst parenting could be gender neutral, ideas of maternal sacrifice as normative structure how and who should bring up children.

The Problem of Infant Feeding

There has always been a need to feed babies in ways other than through breastfeeding by their mothers. This could be due to a mother's embodied inability to produce milk or a need, or desire, to leave the child with another carer. Socio-economic conditions may present requirements or opportunities for women to be separated from their babies. Despite now living at a time when alternatives to breastfeeding are highly developed and physically safe, and when equal parenting is seen as important, women in the developed world are increasingly castigated for not breastfeeding. To understand how and why we came to this position, it is useful to consider the development of bottle-feeding and how the discourse shifted to position women as either cultural dupes and/or bad mothers.

Historically there were two main options for babies who were not breastfed by their mothers: feeding with artificial substances that were often not nutritionally sound, or finding another woman to breastfeed the baby. Cross-feeding, individual arrangements for women to breastfeed the babies of family and friends, is believed to have been a common practice, although due to its informal nature specific records of its prevalence are few (Thorley 2008). An alternative to cross-feeding is wet-nursing, the employment of women to breastfeed as well as sometimes care for a baby. As Golden's (1996) history of wet nursing in the USA has shown, whilst some welcomed wet nursing as a profession, many others had deep reservations about the practice due to unease about allowing a usually poor woman to potentially 'contaminate' the home. It also had implications for the positions of both mothers and wet nurses in relation to changing ideas about good motherhood. As part of the changes of industrialization and urbanization in the nineteenth century, there was growing separation between the poor and wealthier families, and the poor came to be seen as 'medically threatening and morally lax' (Golden 1996: 39). This meant that increased supervision of servants was required, especially those employed to wet nurse. Before the advent of safe artificial foods, a wet nurse could be the difference between life and death for an infant, yet their 'suspect' nature posed a risk of the transmission of 'immoral' values, as it was believed that the temperament of children was linked to the quality of breast milk (Golden 1996). As I will show later, this idea that breast milk can pass an emotional state between a woman and baby still has resonances today. Moreover, as many of the women available for wet nursing were women who had given birth outside marriage and had left their own babies in the care of others to undertake paid employment, their moral status was in question from the beginning.

However, it was not just the women employed to wet-nurse who were seen as problematic. As Golden (1996) points out, the women who employed them could be seen as potentially failing at motherhood. Women were exhorted to breastfeed themselves, with particular condemnation for those who were deemed to be prioritising non-mothering activities due to selfishness rather than focusing on their children's welfare. As motherhood began to be defined as women's vocation during the nineteenth century, women unwilling to feed their children could be seen as failing (Golden 1996). However, alongside this ran the notion that middle and upper class women were biologically different from poor women and could lack the embodied means to breastfeed. She argues:

> Whereas popular writers championed mothers who overcame all varieties of pain and suffering to breast-fed their babies and popular medical guides similarly exalted maternal sacrifice, the [*medical*] textbook authors paid homage to ideal mothers, but also enumerated the conditions that prevented women from nursing. (1996: 53)

Alongside moral and physical concerns, the employment of wet-nurses could never fully address the need for alternative foods for infants. This is especially true for wet-nurses themselves, who often had to leave their own babies behind when they sought employment. Both Golden (1996) and Wolf (2001) have argued that the commercial development of artificial baby foods emerged from concerns over the high mortality rates of babies not fed by their mothers and was encouraged by new understandings of science, bacteriology and nutrition. As new formulas emerged that were safe, convenient and effective, women increased their use of them (Apple 1987; Wolf 2001). This was part of the development of scientific motherhood: the idea that science could enhance childraising through the professionalization of motherhood (Apple 1987; Golden 1996). Moreover, as Wolf (2001) argues, despite over a century of public health campaigns exhorting the health benefits of breastfeeding, women still often opt for formula for some or all of the time. Yet rather than seeing formula milk as beneficial for women and allowing children to be safely cared for in their mothers' absence, some have demonized it, and mothers who cannot or will not breastfeed are positioned as potentially failing in a key site of motherhood (Wolf 2011).

The Moral Construction of Lactation

As Lee (2011) has shown, breastfeeding advocacy has continued to be promoted by policymakers who seek to both increase the numbers of women breastfeeding and the duration of the length of breastfeeding over time. A significant part of this is the Baby Friendly Initiative (BFI) developed and maintained by the WHO and United Nations Children's Fund (UNICEF) (Lee 2011). For example, the UNICEF UK website states:

> The UNICEF UK Baby Friendly Initiative provides a framework for the implementation of best practice by NHS trusts, other health care facilities and higher education institutions, with the aim of ensuring that all parents make informed decisions about feeding their babies and are supported in their chosen feeding method. (…) Implementing Baby Friendly standards is a proven way of increasing breastfeeding rates. (UNICEF UK undated)

This statement is worth considering further. Whilst it suggests that the purpose of the BFI is to support parents in making informed decisions, the outcome of their deliberations should be an increase in breastfeeding. The assumption is that breastfeeding is best for babies and women need support in making this specific choice. That women might have different needs and priorities and could make an informed choice *not* to breastfeed is not considered seriously. As the name 'baby friendly' implies, women's position is assumed to be synonymous with what experts deem to be 'best' for their baby. That it might not be in women's interest to breast-feed is not something that is considered seriously.

Jansson (2009) traced the emergence of breastfeeding as an international health concern. She has shown how one of the earliest mentions of breastfeeding was in the *Maternity Protection Convention* adopted by the International Labor Organization (ILO) in 1919. As she argues, at this point in time, the rights of workers generally were not well established, and women were not equal citizens. The document argued for a number of maternity rights, including the right to breastfeed during working hours, which reaffirmed the prevailing idea that women were not equal workers. Over the course of the twentieth century, there have been many changes in women's employment and employment rights. By the 1970s, Jansson (2009) argues that international concern over the decline in breastfeeding focused on two particular issues. The first was change in the employment patterns of women, and the second was concern about the marketing of formula milk in the developing world, where there were high rates of infant mortality, particularly in the case of unsafe water supplies. In order to add to the legitimacy of the campaigns against the promotion of formula in the developing world, breastfeeding was defined as universally good, and the 'protection' of mothers from the marketing of formula milk extended worldwide (Jansson 2009). Moreover, as Jansson (2009) has shown, the right to breastfeed and access to facilities to express milk have become more established in employment law, and this has happened by stressing the right of the child to breast milk. This can have advantages for women; for example, it can support arguments that call for longer maternity leave. However, it also has a negative effect, as positioning women as predominantly mothers rather than workers reaffirms traditional gendered ideologies over who should care for children.

The BFI emerged as part of these global trends. The underlying assumption behind BFI, and many other breastfeeding campaigns, is that women who decline breastfeeding only do so through ignorance or as the dupes of formula marketing campaigns. Palmer (2009) is typical of this position. She suggests that infant feeding companies as well as ill-informed experts have contributed to a loss of faith in breastfeeding. For Palmer (2009), whilst women should have a choice, they should all be informed that formula milk is significantly detrimental to their baby's health. This is hardly a neutral position and is not necessarily based on the evidence. As Wolf (2011) has shown, the evidence that underpins the health claims of breastfeeding is not as solid as many breastfeeding advocates claim. Many of the studies that purport to show breastfeeding is advantageous are poorly designed and can often only measure association rather than causation (Wolf 2011). Wolf (2011) found that the standard position that breastfeeding is beneficial is often stated in academic publications that have found no benefit in the particular health issue that was under investigation. Moreover, in most cases, there is simply no causal explanation as to why breastfeeding might influence later health outcomes; it is just presumed that it does. Wolf (2011) suggests breastfeeding does convey limited health benefits, notably a reduction in gastrointestinal (GI) conditions. However, whether or not these limited health advantages outweigh other issues, especially the impact on women, is rarely discussed within breastfeeding advocacy literature.

As Carter's (1995) study in the UK outlined many years ago, infant feeding decisions are made in the broader context of women's lives. Whilst health issues can be important, exclusive breastfeeding involves a significant commitment from women leaving them feeling exhausted and in discomfort as well as placing significant restrictions on their lives. Carter (1995) suggested that the promoters of breastfeeding rarely consider this social context. In the USA, Blum (1999) argued that breastfeeding is a form of embodied politics in which it can represent both freedom and/ or social control depending on the individual bodies in question. Both Carter (1995) and Blum (1999) illustrated how breastfeeding cannot be separated from issues of socio-economic position and the wider discourses of good mothering. The issues highlighted in these analyses are still prevalent today, although they are now positioned within heightened anxieties about risk and the vulnerability of the child.

Hence it could be argued that the promotion of breastfeeding relies on scientific authority rather than scientific evidence (Lee 2011). By making claims to science, the moral obligation of women to breastfeed can be hidden, yet today it is clearly rooted in the ideologies of intensive motherhood and risk consciousness within the individualized agenda of new public health (Faircloth 2013; Knaak 2010; Lee 2011). Breastfeeding is promoted as the 'natural' and 'best' choice for feeding babies, regardless of the significant impact that it has on women. The promotion of breastfeeding thus goes beyond a discussion about infant nutrition and has come to be positioned as a measure of motherhood itself (Faircloth 2013; Knaak 2010; Lee 2008; Murphy 1999). As Lee sums up:

> 'Breast is best' communicates a broader message than about nutrition. The imperative to breastfeed also reflects the ideology of intensive mothering, which in turn includes ideas about the need for mothers to manage risk by heeding expert warnings and advice (…) While the pro-breastfeeding message often appears as neutral, making reference to the health benefits of breastfeeding (…) 'healthiness' provides the idiom in which a particular approach to mothering is expressed. (2008: 476)

This moral imperative to breastfeed has a considerable impact on the identity of women as mothers, regardless of how they feed their babies. Good mothers may need to sacrifice any desire for an independent life in order to provide for infants, regardless of safe alternatives.

Feeding Work and Identities

The construction of breastfeeding as the 'natural' way to feed babies has implications for the way that it is experienced. Like 'natural' childbirth, 'natural' breastfeeding is a specific social practice that involves considerable effort. Breastfeeding on demand is a form of embodied labour that can be painful and tiring, and it means that women have to be available to their babies at all times. Even if women express breast milk in order to be able to leave them for longer, this takes considerable effort and often needs equipment to pump and store the milk. Stearns (2009) suggests that the time and work intensiveness of breastfeeding, which is exclusively the work of mothers, has rarely been fully considered as a form of embodied labour. She argues that breastfeeding is a unique form of mother-work which involves a range of practices including the need to dress appropriately, control the substances they consume, accept negative aspects of breastfeeding (such as tiredness) and manage wider societal expectations (which can include avoiding public exposure of their breasts). This work places restrictions on breastfeeding women's lives and appears to be in contrast to ideas about wider equality in terms of both employment and parenting. The work of breastfeeding is an important consideration when assessing the impact of the breastfeeding messages on women's identity.

As Andrews and Knaak's (2013) study of breastfeeding mothers in Canada and Norway found, the emotional and physical toll of breastfeeding can have a significant impact on women. Whilst nominally a 'choice', the rhetoric of breastfeeding meant that for many of their participants this was the only real option to take. In Canada, the women described the 'choice' to breastfeed as something that others might not do, but not one that they had considered, although they had been asked by healthcare professionals. The normalization of breastfeeding was even stronger in Norway, with none of the women recalling being asked about their intentions. Thus for Norwegian mothers, breastfeeding is the only option, at least at the beginning. All of the women described breastfeeding as exerting emotional and physical difficulties for some or all of the time, and they felt under tremendous pressure either directly or indirectly to persevere regardless of the problems that they encountered. Similar stories emerge in other parts of the world including Australia (Schmied and Lupton 2001b), Denmark (Larsen and Kronborg 2013) and the UK (Williamson et al. 2012). Moreover as Williamson et al. (2012) point out, the emphasis on the 'naturalness' of breastfeeding often leaves women unprepared for pain or other negative issues.

The message that breastfeeding is 'natural' and the 'best' way to feed babies has significant implications for women who find it difficult or do not breastfeed their children. Rather than being able to exercise a choice over feeding, they are placed in a position of potential moral jeopardy as their identity as good mothers comes under threat (Murphy 1999). In Denmark, Larsen and Kronborg (2013) found that women who were experiencing problems breastfeeding blamed themselves for failing to be adequate mothers. Women experiencing difficulties breastfeeding felt they were failing to meet their baby's basic needs for food and comfort. This challenged their identity as (good) mothers. Changing to formula feeding was reported as beneficial for the women and their babies, yet it left them in a position of having to enact moral work to 'prove' their position as good mothers to others. Lee (2007) found in the UK that as breastfeeding has become synonymous with good motherhood, 'failing' to breastfeed can leave women feeling guilty and/or having to prove their (good) motherhood identity. Ludlow et al. (2012) found similar issues in Canada. In this case, their participants reworked the concept of 'best' away from a narrow interpretation of health towards a notion of 'best for the family' that enabled them to position the benefits of formula-feeding (less time-consuming, more equitable) as more suitable in their particular circumstances.

Indeed as writers such as Murphy (1999) and Lee (2007) have argued, even when formula-feeding is a majority practice, such as in the UK, women may still feel the need to defend their decision to others. Lee (2007) found that women were often questioned over their decision to use formula milk and this was intrusive. Yet as their confidence grew, they rejected the idea that formula milk was 'second best', using the health and development of their children as a way to show that they were good mothers. Williams et al. (2013) found a similar trend in Australia; even when women are adamant that they have nothing to feel guilty about, they nevertheless still do feel some guilt at formula-feeding. This study, like others, found that the construction of breastfeeding as 'natural' was significant to their participants. If breastfeeding is a natural part of motherhood, then those who cannot or do not want to breastfeed are thus 'unnatural.' The 'unnatural' mother is not one that is usually associated with good motherhood, and this necessitates the need for women to justify their decisions in order to reassert their position as good mothers.

The moral positioning of breastfeeding as a 'natural' part of good motherhood also has implications for women who do exclusively breastfeed. Faircloth (2013) has explored this in relation to women who choose to breastfeed long-term (beyond babyhood) as part of attachment parenting. (Attachment parenting is a specific mothering style which prioritizes a 'nurturing connection' through specific mothering practices.) Faircloth (2013) found that her participants used the concept of 'natural' to make claims about human biology/history in which breast milk is the only suitable food. They also evoked the idea of natural in the sense that it was the only course of action. Yet whilst the idea that breastfeeding is 'natural' or 'best' is accepted, long-term breastfeeding is often positioned as problematic. Hence a decision to breastfeed beyond babyhood is often seen as a deviant act (Faircloth 2013). To justify this, the women used science to legitimate their decision. Their reading of science 'proved' that their 'natural' decision to breastfeed long-term was justified within the wider framework of attachment parenting that they were committed to (Faircloth 2013). Alongside long-term breastfeeding, maternal-child proximity is another key element within attachment parenting to facilitate bonding, which has come to be seen as a foundational issue for a child's future health.

Food for Love?

The emphasis on breastfeeding can thus be seen to go further than any nutritional benefits of breast milk over formula milk. It is a measure of (proper) maternal devotion and, potentially, a way to ensure the production of 'better' future adults. This is constructed and reproduced through the idea of bonding. Eyer (1992) found that the notion that bonding at or near birth developed rapidly in the 1970s, although she argues it built on earlier ideas such as attachment theory. Attachment theory was developed in the 1950s and 1960s by Bowlby and Ainsworth and at its heart is the belief that the relationship between the mother and child is central to infant development and all future relationships that the child will have (Eyer 1992; Kanieski 2010). Eyer (1992) argues that bonding was accepted and promoted at a time when women were challenging the idea of their 'natural' place in the home, and it required them to have appropriate feelings alongside compliance with recommended practices. She argues that:

> The requirement to give active love to their babies right after birth is a standard many women find impossible to meet. Locking women into such practices and then blaming them for failing to conform constitute an emotional drain not only on women but the entire family. (1992: 13)

Wall (2001) argues that some of the reluctance to recognize the problems that many women experience whilst trying to breastfeed comes from its association with the idea of bonding. Bonding is also seen as a natural process, providing that nothing (or nobody) interferes. As Wall (2001) points out, breastfeeding is often promoted as a continuing relationship, reuniting mother and child as one, as if they were still in pregnancy. If women are the eco-system charged with ensuring the 'best' environment for the developing foetus, breastfeeding is a way to continue this relationship, reaffirming women's role as primary caregiver (Wall 2001). Whilst it is clear that some women do experience this form of bond through breastfeeding (Faircloth 2013; Schmied and Lupton 2001b), not all will do so. Moreover, the ideas of bonding and breastfeeding have echoes with earlier concerns about wet nursing. The concern in that case was with the potential transmission of 'immorality', whereas today the emphasis is on the emotional benefits that breastfeeding may bring. It also continues the emphasis on maternal mental health beginning in pregnancy.

Schmied and Lupton (2001b) described how, for some women in Australia, breastfeeding was not just overwhelming in terms of the time and effort it took but also led to a loss of a sense of self. Their lives were not their own, and their sense of agency was restricted as they needed to be constantly available for feeding. The sense of embodied alienation was heightened when they had difficulties such as pain or an unsated baby (Schmied and Lupton 2001b). Larsen and Kronborg (2013) found that many of the Danish mothers they interviewed felt that it was only when they had stopped trying to breastfeed and changed to bottle-feeding that they felt they were able to begin forming a close relationship with their baby. All of the mothers felt that this had benefited their baby and, as they no longer had concerns about failing to meet their child's basic needs, they were in a better position to care for them (Larsen and Kronborg 2013). In these cases, the mothers did not reject the necessity of bonding but they challenged the need to breastfeed to achieve this. Infant feeding is not the only way that women are charged with ensuring the development of future citizens. Alongside and intertwined with the ideas of breastfeeding and bonding and attachment lay concerns that women's mental health may adversely impact the babies' developing brains.

The Rise of Neuroparenting

At the end of the twentieth century, the brain came to be seen as a central concern in childraising discourse. As Wall (2010) documented in Canada, it was during the 1990s that brain capacity started to be noticeable in discussions about childrearing. Bonding was transformed from a way of optimising emotional and psychological health to being seen as a crucial element in how the physical architecture of the brain was built. Moreover, as the brain is seen as singularly important for everyone, a 'risk' to the brain signifies potential ongoing hazard in the lives of children. Indeed as Macvarish (2014) highlights, the idea of brain development was used both to encourage optimization and as an area of concern. In the former, loving and stimulating babies in particular ways is seen as enhancing their development, whereas in the latter, policy interventions to discipline particular groups of 'failing' mothers were promoted or adopted in order to prevent the transmission of harm. In the UK, what emerged was a specific understanding of early intervention in child welfare policies built around a reductionist argument of brain development (Lowe et al. 2015b). The central premise is that normal development will be disrupted unless the correct 'environmental influences' ensure proper neural development during the early years of a child's life (Lowe et al. 2015b). Crucially the environmental influences that they are concerned about are women's bodies and behaviour.

Bruer (1999) has shown how this understanding of children's brain development arises from three specific ideas: developmental synaptogenesis, sensitive periods, and enriched environments. Developmental synaptogenesis (rapid increase in synapse density) does take place in the early years, but as Bruer (1999) argues this is not the only time it occurs. Moreover, importantly, it has not yet been established that denser synapses mean additional brain functionality, and thus this change may not have any impact on children's capacity to develop. Bruer (1999) further argues that the majority of skills and behaviours are learnt throughout life rather than being dependent on exposure in the early years. The small number of time-sensitive skills that are important are in areas that it would be extremely rare for a child not to encounter. For example, animal experiments have shown that depriving the young of sound and vision does affect their development, but even neglected children are unlikely (thankfully) to be in a similar position. As Bruer (1999) points out, whilst Hubel and Wiesel (1970) demonstrated that if you sewed newborn kitten's eyes shut, it had a long-term impact on their vision, yet even in significantly adverse circumstances children are still likely to be exposed to the different forms of light needed for their sight development.

The final issue highlighted by Bruer (1999) is the issue of what is sufficient as an environment for child development. Altered brain development may be an outcome of very extreme neglect, but there is little evidence that enriched environments will develop better brains. The studies of children who were subjected to extreme neglect in Romanian orphanages are often used in this area. For example, Behan et al. (2008) found impairment in specific cognitive domains in 46% of children who had experienced early severe deprivation through spending their early lives in Romanian institutions that, under the Ceauşescu regime, had large numbers of children in each room with little or no stimulation or interaction with adults. Rutter et al. (2010) have made an ongoing study of the outcomes of some of these children. They found that even after early extreme neglect there could be good recovery and they argue that a key factor was that the children were living in an institution. Thus whilst child neglect is a serious issue, there is little evidence to date that it leads to deficits in brain development (Bruer 1999; Wastell and White 2012). This lack of evidence has not stopped the claims that the early years are crucial to developing a child's brain to capacity. For example, O'Connor et al. (2012) found issues such as sexual orientation and the risk of psychiatric disorders being linked to early brain development.

In Australia, Lawless et al. (2014) argue that the language of brain development is being used in a similar way to the language of attachment theory. As detailed assessments cannot be made about the state of a baby's mental health, Lawless et al. (2014) argue it is the mother's behaviour that has become monitored. Crucially, as during pregnancy, the mother's emotional state is now again seen as a potential risk to the child. Moreover, as maximising your child's development is a crucial part of intensive motherhood, mothers must monitor their own emotions for potential deviation from a state that would maximize development. This is part of the framework of individualized risk, and Lawless et al. (2014) found that it dominated professional understandings of infant mental health and minimized attention on structural issues such as poverty. They argue that:

> Threads from discourses of brain science, attachment theory, critical periods, children's needs, mothering and maternalism have woven together to shape thinking and practices around infant mental health in often invisible ways. (Lawless et al. 2014)

This particular understanding of brain development as deterministic of life chances has had a profound impact on recent policy development in the area of child welfare. As Edwards et al. (2015) have shown, in the UK the concerns over maternal stress having a detrimental impact on the developing foetus/child focus on relationships rather than social deprivation. The practitioners they interviewed strongly believed in the neuroscientific claims and used a variety of means to convince the young parents that they were working with of their validity. The underlying message is, as Edwards et al. (2015) argue, that the poor are responsible for the faulty brain wiring that leads to their poverty, through the levels of maternal stress and lack of 'appropriate' emotional investment in their children. In other words, mothers are positioned as the architects of their children's disadvantage through a failure to control their emotions.

Medicalized interventions that intervene in family life to try to 'cure' the problems have come to dominate policy thinking in the UK (Macvarish et al. 2015; Edwards et al. 2015; Wastell and White 2012). Moreover,

Featherstone et al. (2013) have shown how this has led to a specific form of child protection in which quick removal of children is seen as a better option than family support. These studies highlight how brain development arguments are dominating ideas about deficits in family life and the designation of a 'child at risk'. As Lowe et al. (2015b) argue, these ideas also undermine the notion that children are autonomous individuals who are active agents in their own lives. Moreover policy claims that (poor) brain development is a causal factor in issues such as long-term unemployment, drug use and crime suggest that women's (unnatural) behaviour is responsible for a significant number of social problems. Just like anxieties over the 'immoral' wet nurses, biological transmission of 'degeneracy' remains a policy concern. Indeed a key element in the UK policy is the idea of intergenerational transmission; if your brain was not developed properly as a child, then this leads to your failure later as a parent (Lowe et al. 2015b). This clearly has resonances with the concerns mentioned in Chap. 3 that some women should be prevented from conceiving because of the risks of undesired traits developing in their children.

This trend has coalesced into the idea of 1000 critical days, a notion that the period from conception to age two is a crucial determinant of all future lives. It is important to remember that the idea of 1000 days is being used differently in different parts of the world, and it can support interventions (such as access to nutrition) that can be important to women and children's health. Nevertheless, the focus on this period of time is of critical importance to women, as it merges pregnancy and the post natal period together as if there were no significant difference between them. As a study in the UK found, this is not uncommon in policy documents surrounding early child development (Lowe et al. 2015b). Hence although policies may speak of parents and parenting, the erosion of the distinction of birth firmly places the responsibility on women.

Performing 'Good' Motherhood

The transition to motherhood has always been a significant time in women's lives, and it can be experienced both positively and negatively. During the course of the twentieth century, it could be argued that women's increased rights in the public sphere made it more acceptable for women to reject or redefine their identities so that motherhood was not necessarily seen as central. Yet as outlined above, the erosion of a significant difference between pregnancy and the post natal period (and the distinction between pre-pregnancy and pregnancy outlined earlier), which uses biological claims to underpin the connections, has had profound consequences for women. If breast milk and maternal bonding biologically determine a child's future life and are also seen to prevent a range of social problems (such as drug use and crime), the responsibilization of women within intensive motherhood is set to continue. This impacts how women feel themselves as well as how they are judged by others.

As discussed in Chap. 2, the ideals of good motherhood set out particular ways of being and behaving. Lupton (2000) found that, in Australia, women described the ideals of motherhood as including the adoption of particular personality traits such as patience, calmness and selfless devotion alongside protecting and meeting the needs of their babies. At the heart of this is the idea that the child's welfare takes precedence over everything else. Sevón (2007) describes this as a moral maternal agency in which women develop a maternal ethic of care that stresses a strong sense of intuitiveness in learning to meet their babies' needs. Alongside this runs maternal vulnerability in which, as Sevón (2007) argues, there is a risk of, or instances of, being unable to meet these expectations. The association between good motherhood and womanhood means that it is hard to admit when the transition to motherhood is not fully meeting the expectations of the role (Miller 2005; Sevón 2007). As Lawler (2000) argues, children have needs that mothers should meet, whilst mothers are deemed to have only wants, not needs.

The changes in attitudes towards mothers can be further illustrated in Wall's (2013) study of a motherhood magazine in Canada. She showed how understandings of mother's employment and daycare have changed over time. She compared articles in the 1980s with ones from 2007 to 2010. She found that in the latter period there was much more emphasis on children's needs; they were seen as far more vulnerable, and there was a significant shift to an emphasis on mother's responsibility to ensure sufficient cognitive stimulation to enable 'good' brain development. This was matched by a decrease in consideration of any need for mothers to have a life beyond their children. Whilst women are increasingly working outside of the home, the idea that this provides necessary fulfilment for women was no longer discussed in any detail. Whilst this could just signal general acceptance on this point, it was coupled with an emphasis on a child's increasing need for cognitive investment, so Wall (2013) argues that the message was not that simple. Moreover the recent period also stressed the need for women to consider and mitigate any 'risks' associated with using daycare. This could include seriously considering their options *before* they become pregnant, including perhaps changing employers. This suggests that (potential) good mothers may need to sacrifice their careers for future children. This is not necessarily surprising given the emphasis on women considering themselves as constantly pre-pregnant in other areas of their lives. Wall (2013) argues that despite an increase in the numbers of mothers of small children working, the 'risks' and 'responsibilities' on women have grown. Smyth (2014) found a similar emphasis on ensuring 'proper' education in her study of an Australian website for parents of preschool children. She showed how the expectation is that mothers will turn every opportunity into a learning one. Smyth (2014) argues that by suggesting that learning opportunities are built into all domestic routines, the advice seeks not just to regulate mother-child interaction but also suggests that boosting brain capacity is a central part of the work of mothering.

The understanding of the work of motherhood as 'natural' can be problematic for women. Miller (2005) argues that whilst the biological act of giving birth is a physical marker of transition between pregnancy and motherhood, this does not necessarily coincide with a shift in the way that women feel about themselves. Her study of women in the UK found that it took time after the birth for women to develop an identity as mothers. This period was often experienced by women as being difficult and they lacked control over their lives. The ideals of motherhood as natural and instinctive did not match what they were experiencing. Whilst they were usually able to perform the work of motherhood, this was distinct from being a mother. Read et al. (2012) found in Canada that some of the women they interviewed described new motherhood as a 'horrible shock.' Whilst they understood in theory that babies need a lot of care, they were unprepared for the relentlessness of it. They felt that unrealistic images of motherhood were common and did not convey how difficult it could be. This study found that the pressures to prioritize their children before themselves put women off having any more children.

Alongside women's own feelings, their competence to mother is often under scrutiny from others. Miller (2005) found that some new mothers were worried about being outside of the home as they were uncertain whether their performance would meet the criteria of a 'good' mother under public scrutiny. It took time before they felt confident in their own abilities and developed their identities to include motherhood. Developing a sense of themselves as experts, as Miller (2005) argues, allows them to ignore or challenge professional advice and be confident in their performance as good mothers. Indeed, Smyth's (2012) study of women in Northern Ireland and the USA found that health professionals considered mothers as experts to be a potential problem. One of her participants described how the extensive research on her son's medical condition was treated with suspicion by health professionals treating him. As Smyth (2012) points out, over-performance of motherhood can produce similar critiques to under-performance. The critique of extended breastfeeding mentioned earlier is another example of deviant over-performance. Getting the balance right between under- and over-performing motherhood can be a difficult path for women to achieve.

Women often want and need to regain a sense of their old identity, a sense of themselves that is beyond being just a mother, yet this can make them feel guilty. Women who return to paid employment worry that this could be seen as detrimental to their child, and women who stay at home have concerns that 'just' being a mother is not really sufficient for being an adult in society (Miller 2005). For Miller's participants, the prevailing cultural scripts devalued both positions. Lupton and Schmied (2002) found similar dilemmas amongst first-time Australian mothers. Women who returned to work often felt guilty and worried about their children's welfare, yet at the same time they felt it was necessary in order to preserve or regain a sense of themselves. They justified their absence by stressing that it would not be possible for them to be good mothers without having an independent life. Hence for them, going to work was justified as it ensured that they were able to perform motherhood properly when they were with their children. Yet they recognized that others might not validate this position.

Clearly, women will have different degrees of investment in motherhood as an identity. Faircloth (2013) found that many of the women who adopted attachment parenting chose to stay with their children and spoke of full-time motherhood as both a vocation and a political act. It was not just the need to be close to their children and attentive at all times that usually precluded paid employment; they also often rejected the idea that others could properly care for their children. Similarly, Smyth (2012) found some women in her study who adopted mothering as a primary identity and sought fulfilment through an idealized notion of motherhood. Yet even though the women felt that this was a natural position, some struggled to achieve this in practice. In contrast, Maher (2005) found that, for many women in Australia, mothering was predominately an activity rather than an identity, and thus having a role as a worker did not necessarily conflict with that of a mother. However, what is in common in these accounts is the way in which the women positioned themselves as good mothers who made the right choices and appropriate sacrifices.

Being or performing motherhood is not a static or singular identity, and the demands of good motherhood can be accepted or rejected to different degrees. Nevertheless, the choices and roles that women take on are understood by and through wider societal understandings, and thus normative ideas of good motherhood impact those who wish to conform and those who redefine or reject them. Moreover, whilst what good mothers actually do can be culturally and historically specific, certain principles can be seen to be at the root of them. These include the idea that mothering is 'natural' for women and that 'good' mothers sacrifice their own desires and put their children first. These ideas are played out in different ways depending on the social and economic position of women.

Motherhood in Context

The prevailing norms of motherhood, and the extent to which women feel obliged to conform to them, depend on a complex range of factors. These include, but are not limited to, issues of social class, ethnicity, sexuality and disability, as well as the geographic area in which they are situated. Whilst some women may need to 'prove' they are good mothers in different ways to others, it is still clear that they are all underpinned by the idea of maternal sacrifice. In this section, I clearly cannot cover all the potential variations, but I will use some specific examples to illustrate how the idea of maternal sacrifice is embedded into the different ways in which groups of women are encouraged, disciplined or sanctioned for failing to perform motherhood in the right way. Clearly not all women will engage with the discourses in the same way; some may adopt them willingly, some may feel they have little choice but to comply with all or some of the ideas, and others may resist. Nevertheless, the normative frames do send out particular messages that women need to interact with, both in terms of mothering work and mothering as an identity.

As I outlined briefly in Chap. 2, Hays' (1996) concept of intensive motherhood has come to be seen as a dominant narrative in women's lives. Hays (1996) outlined the ways in which women's unselfish nurturing of the sacred child came to dominate ideas of good mothering. Hays states that:

> Just as it is the child's innocence that makes childhood sacred, it is the mother's unselfish and nurturing qualities that make motherhood sacred. Giving of oneself and one's resources freely is the appropriate code of maternal behaviour. (1996: 125)

Hence regardless of any wider changes there had been during the twentieth century to women's formal rights in the political or employment spheres, the ideology of intensive motherhood ensured that women's responsibility for children remained unchallenged. Moreover, as Lareau (2003) found, the work involved within intensive motherhood can lead to differential practices. For the middle classes in particular, it often included a commitment to ensure their children would maximize skills and talents through concerted cultivation in order to secure their future classed position.

Perrier's (2013) study of middle-class mothers in the UK revealed that many of the women sought to maintain a difficult balance between ensuring they were child-focused and not 'spoiling' their children. She argues that they sought to achieve a balance between the two through the quality of the time that they spent with their children. Part of the demarcation of the different positions was in the activities and toys that they provided for them. The mothers reported things like limiting the time their children watched television, and doing crafts together rather than buying them plastic toys. This need for appropriate activities could be rooted in the prevailing ideas about cognitive development. Whilst the ability to provide their children with appropriate educational activities was important, they often emphasized informal learning activities rather than formal ones. Ensuring the balance was thus an important part of the work of motherhood, and in order to achieve a 'good mother' identity the women needed to position themselves apart from both the 'irresponsible or consumerist' mother who provided toys (rather than time) and the 'pushy' mother who attempted to hothouse her child (Perrier 2013: 666). The over- and under-performance of motherhood is clearly illustrated in these images.

In this study, in order to maintain their position as good mothers, women needed to make themselves available to spend time with their children and provide appropriate activities to achieve the label of 'quality time.' Perrier (2013) argues that rather than being secure in a classed position, this is a mothering identity marked by ambivalence. Whilst they clearly wanted to ensure appropriate educational development of their children, they also needed to guard against excess. 'Quality time' is marked by mother-child interaction, such as discussion or the sharing of play or tasks. Women needed to ensure that they devoted sufficient time to their activities, and balancing this with other areas of their lives could be an issue of concern. Using time as a measure of the quality of childhood clearly indicates that good mothers should sacrifice other areas of their lives in order to achieve this. Whilst time spent at work can provide sufficient material resources, providing time and not toys is the marker of a good mother for these women.

In Edin and Kefalas' (2007) study of poor women in the USA, there are different challenges and sacrifices needed. For the women in their study, choosing to keep and raise their children in difficult circumstances is not just a sign of good motherhood but also the source of a sense of responsibility and purpose. Edin and Kefalas (2007) found that providing love and basic care often required considerable effort due to their material circumstances, and thus not abandoning or losing their children to the care system is the way in which the women proved successful motherhood. The women defined good motherhood in terms of commitment and the devotion to try to raise children 'right' in difficult environments (Edin and Kefalas 2007). Whilst they may not have the same ability to provide appropriate learning activities that wealthier mothers have, they make other sacrifices such as spending any surplus money on things for their children. Indeed, women who had better clothes than their children could be criticized for failing to make sufficient sacrifices (Edin and Kefalas 2007). It is not that they thought that branded clothes and toys were enough, but these provided a tangible sign for the external audience that they were good mothers. Unlike what was found amongst the women in Perrier's (2013) study, the level of material resources in the home was much more uncertain, and thus making sacrifices in order to be a good provider was very important.

Often embedded in classed understandings of motherhood is age, with younger mothers more likely to come from poorer backgrounds. Romagnoli and Wall's (2012) study of young mothers in Canada illustrates the difficulties in achieving a balance between a need to invest 'quality time' for cognitive development and a need to provide material resources to their children. Moreover, as Romagnoli and Wall (2012) point out in their study, for the poor young mothers, the risks of not providing sufficient quality motherhood are very different from the risks faced by middle-class women. Failure to perform mothering adequately was not just a threat to identity, as they could have their children removed through child protection processes, similar to the women in Edin and Kefalas' (2007) study. Thus, ensuring that they displayed the appropriate sacrifices demanded of mothers was a requirement for their continuing ability to be mothers. Romagnoli and Wall (2012) found that the young women were aware of their devalued position yet they rejected the idea that they could not be good mothers. Like the women in Edin and Kefalas' (2007) study, they took pride in ensuring that their children were safe and healthy, as well as being able to source affordable activities for their children. Whilst they were aware of parenting advice about children's early learning and brain development, they did not necessarily accept it. However, due to the general perception that young women cannot be good mothers, they often had to perform intensive motherhood in public to avoid any risk of social services intervention. Hence in this instance, the women may need to sacrifice time and resources and their belief in the best way to raise their children in order to maintain their position as good mothers.

Whilst intensive motherhood often involves significant caring work on a day-to-day basis, the ideology can also impact the lives of women who are living apart from their children. Granja et al. (2015) undertook interviews with mothers in prison in Portugal and found that many of the women were active in finding spaces to perform good motherhood despite their very limited ability to enact caring practices. Many of the children were being cared for by friends or relatives, and the women were active in try-ing to negotiate what forms of care would be provided. Some described being actively involved in things like school choices and sending what little money they earned in prison to their children outside. They did not deny that any poor behaviour exhibited by their child could be a result of their mothering behaviour and felt guilty about the impact that they might have had on their children. Yet at the same time they stressed the importance of, and tried to maintain, emotional connections in order to help their children develop. The idea within intensive mothering of emotion being an essential element clearly resonated with the ideas of bonding and brain development, even if in this case the women were at a distance. Granja et al. (2015) show that the need to perform good mothering in prison was important and required women to sacrifice the very limited resources that they had. Whether or not this was successful at maintaining an emotional connection was contingent on both the prison regime and the carers that their children were living with. In this case, the work of motherhood was reduced to very little, but the emotional investment was significant. Even at a distance, maternal love is seen as central to the performance of good motherhood, and women's identities as mothers could be seen through the sacrifices that they made for their children.

Conclusion

This chapter has illustrated the different ways in which women continue to be positioned as responsible for children even though nominally gen-der equality is formally supported. Policies often used the terms parent and parenting yet the responsibility largely falls on women. This process is embodied from the beginning due to the erosion of the distinction of birth in demarking a boundary between a woman and the foetus/baby. As we have seen in previous chapters, women should consider and act as if they were mothers prior to pregnancy, during pregnancy and after birth. Should they fail to act in accordance with the prevailing norms of motherhood they may feel guilty, be sanctioned or even risk losing their children to the care of the state. The behaviour that constitutes good motherhood is situational; it may be different depending on the social and economic situation of the women themselves. The level of sanction will also vary; white middle-class heterosexual married women are likely to be able to choose a mothering 'style' at odds with the prevailing norms with much less concern for adverse outcomes than mothers already positioned as 'others.'

That babies need food and love to survive is clearly not in doubt. However, claims that this food and love needs to come exclusively from women can be questioned. The promotion of breastfeeding as 'natural' and 'best' reproduces the idea of women as normative caregivers. Breastfeeding can be difficult and time-consuming work and it requires women to put the needs of the babies above their desires until they are weaned. Whether this is through constant proximity or through expressing milk, women's lives are constrained. Women who fail to make the required sacrifices are positioned as potentially deviant and may feel guilty about choosing to use formula milk, even though in the developed world this is a safe and effective way to feed babies. The emphasis on the transmission of 'character' through breastfeeding is also important. Today the ideas about bonding through breastfeeding suggest it is important emotionally and psychologically and has physical implications for the construction of the brain. This has echoes of the past, when concerns were raised about the implications of employing 'immoral' characters as wet-nurses, which might lead to contamination of the moral worth of children. Hence breastfeeding is not just physical work that is time-consuming and sometimes difficult - it also ideally encompasses emotional work. Women need to feel the right emotions in order for their child to develop their potential.

The emphasis on the need to ensure appropriate cognitive development encompasses both the physical architecture of the brain and the transformation of children's lives into ongoing learning opportunities. Judgements about the mental state of young children are made through the bodies and behaviour of their mothers. The life chances of future generations, and their potential cost to society, are often considered to be both physically and psychologically transmitted through the action of mothers. The language of brains may be recent but the concept of inter-generational transmission of undesirability is clearly not. This has been a central organising idea in the development of birth control policies: the least desirable should be prevented from reproducing.

The transition to motherhood can be a difficult time for women. Many feel that general perceptions of motherhood overlook the difficulties that being a new mother encompasses. The emphasis on the naturalness of it all disguises the often overwhelming onslaught of work, emotions and pressure to conform to idealized images of good motherhood. It takes time for women to feel confident in themselves and the care that they are providing, and to regain a sense of their own identity, a 'self' beyond just that of a mother. The under-performance of (good) motherhood is positioned as failing your child, but the over-performance of mother-hood is also potentially deviant. Women need to justify their position, to show that this is the 'best' for their child regardless of which path they follow in their mothering identity or wider lives. What 'good' mothers do is variable - it changes over time and between places - but nevertheless it is underpinned by the necessity of putting your child's welfare first. Depending on the extent to which a range of choices are available, this can be operationalized in different ways.

Hence the underpinning idea within the changes over time, and between people and places, is that women should make sacrifices to ensure that their child's best interests are prioritized. Whilst this could be seen as a normal or natural thing for parents to do, the concept itself is used to support prevailing ideas of best interests of the child whether or not there is any empirical basis to those claims. As I have outlined above, and will develop further in the next chapter, just as good motherhood always requires maternal sacrifice, maternal sacrifice can be seen to define good motherhood. Women, along with their supporters or critics and wider discourses in society, can operationalize this idea to justify how and why they reproduce and/or raise their children. It is the central organising concept from which all others flow.

References

Andrews, T., & Knaak, S. (2013). Medicalized mothering: Experiences with breastfeeding in Canada and Norway. *The Sociological Review, 61*(1), 88–110.

Apple, R. D. (1987). *Mothers and medicine: A social history of infant feeding, 1890–1950*. London: University of Wisconsin Press.

Behan, M. E., Helder, E., Rothermel, R., Solomon, K., & Chugani, H. T. (2008). Incidence of specific absolute neurocognitive impairment in globally intact children with histories of early severe deprivation. *Child Neuropsychology, 14*(5), 453–469.

Blum, L. M. (1999). *At the breast: Ideologies of breastfeeding and motherhood in the contemporary United States*. Boston: Beacon Press.

Bruer, J. (1999). *The myth of the first three years: A new understanding of early brain development*. New York: The Free Press.

Carter, P. (1995). *Feminism, breast and breastfeeding*. Basingstoke, England: Macmillan Press.

Edin, K., & Kefalas, M. (2007). *Promises I can keep: Why poor women put motherhood before marriage*. London: University of California Press.

Edwards, R., Gillies, V., & Horsley, N. (2015). Brain science and early years policy: Hopeful ethos or 'cruel optimism'? *Critical Social Policy, 35*(2), 167–187.

Eyer, D. E. (1992). *Mother-infant bonding: A scientific fiction*. London: Yale.

Faircloth, C. (2013). *Militant lactivism: Attachment parenting and intensive motherhood in the UK and France*. New York: Berghahn.

Featherstone, B., Morris, K., & White, S. (2013). A marriage made in hell: Early intervention meets child protection. *British Journal of Social Work, 44*(7), 1735–1749.

Golden, J. (1996). *A social history of wet nursing in America: From breast to bottle*. Cambridge, England: Cambridge University Press.

Granja, R., da Cunha, M. I. P., & Machado, H. (2015). Mothering from prison and ideologies of intensive parenting enacting vulnerable resistance. *Journal of Family Issues, 36*(9), 1212–1232.

Hays, S. (1996). *The cultural contradictions of motherhood*. New Haven, CT: Yale University Press.

Hubel, D. H., & Wiesel, T. N. (1970). The period of susceptibility to the physiological effects of unilaternal eye closure in kittens. *Journal of Physiology, 206,* 419–436.

Jansson, M. (2009). Feeding children and protecting women: The emergence of breastfeeding as an international concern. *Women's Studies International Forum, 32*(3), 240–248.

Kanieski, M. A. (2010). Securing attachment: The shifting medicalisation of attachment and attachment disorders. *Health, Risk & Society, 12*(4), 335–344.

Knaak, S. J. (2010). Contextualising risk, constructing choice: Breastfeeding and good mothering in risk society. *Health, Risk & Society, 12*(4), 345–355.

Lareau, A. (2003). *Unequal childhoods: Class, race, and family life.* London: University of California Press.

Larsen, J. S., & Kronborg, H. (2013). When breastfeeding is unsuccessful— Mothers' experiences after giving up breastfeeding. *Scandinavian Journal of Caring Sciences, 27*(4), 848–856.

Lawler, S. (2000). *Mothering the self: Mothers, daughters, subjects.* Abingdon, England: Routledge.

Lawless, A., Coveney, J., & MacDougall, C. (2014). Infant mental health promotion and the discourse of risk. *Sociology of Health and Illness, 36*(3), 416–431.

Lee, E. (2007). Health, morality, and infant feeding: British mothers' experiences of formula milk use in the early weeks. *Sociology of Health & Illness, 29*(7), 1075–1090.

Lee, E. (2008). Living with risk in the age of 'intensive motherhood': Maternal identity and infant feeding. *Health, Risk & Society, 10*(5), 467–477.

Lee, E. (2011). Breast-feeding advocacy, risk society and health moralism: A decade's scholarship. *Sociology Compass, 5*(12), 1058–1069.

Lowe, P., Lee, E., & Macvarish, J. (2015b). Biologising parenting: Neuroscience discourse, English social and public health policy and understandings of the child. *Sociology of Health & Illness, 37*(2), 198–211.

Ludlow, V., Newhook, L. A., Newhook, J. T., Bonia, K., Goodridge, J. M., & Twells, L. (2012). How formula feeding mothers balance risks and define themselves as 'good mothers'. *Health, Risk & Society, 14*(3), 291–306.

Lupton, D. (2000). 'A love/hate relationship': The ideals and experiences of first-time mothers. *Journal of Sociology, 36*(1), 50–63.

Lupton, D., & Schmied, V. (2002). "The right way of doing it all": First-time Australian mothers' decisions about paid employment. *Women's Studies International Forum, 25*(1), 97–107.

Macvarish, J. (2014). 'Babies' brains and parenting policy: The insensitive mother. In E. Lee, J. Bristow, C. Faircloth, & J. Macvarish (Eds.), *Parenting culture studies* (pp. 165–183). Basingstoke, England: Palgrave Macmillan.

Macvarish, J., Lee, E., & Lowe, P. (2015). Neuroscience and family policy: What becomes of the parent? *Critical Social Policy, 35*(2), 248–269.

Maher, J. (2005). A mother by trade: Australian women reflecting mothering as activity, not identity. *Australian Feminist Studies, 20*(46), 17–29.

Miller, T. (2005). *Making sense of motherhood: A narrative approach*. Cambridge, England: Cambridge University Press.

Murphy, E. (1999). 'Breast is best': Infant feeding decisions and maternal deviance. *Sociology of Health & Illness, 21*(2), 187–208.

O'Connor, C., Rees, G., & Joffe, H. (2012). Neuroscience in the public sphere. *Neuron, 74*(2), 220–226.

Palmer, G. (2009). *The politics of breastfeeding: When breasts are bad for business.* London: Pinter & Martin.

Perrier, M. (2013). Middle-class mothers' moralities and 'concerted cultivation': Class others, ambivalence and excess. *Sociology, 47*(4), 655–670.

Read, D. M., Crockett, J., & Mason, R. (2012). "It was a horrible shock": The experience of motherhood and women's family size preferences. *Women's Studies International Forum, 35*(1), 12–21.

Romagnoli, A., & Wall, G. (2012). 'I know I'm a good mom': Young, low-income mothers' experiences with risk perception, intensive parenting ideology and parenting education programmes. *Health, Risk & Society, 14*(3), 273–289.

Rutter, M., Sonuga-Barke, E. J., Beckett, C., Castle, J., Kreppner, J., Kumsta, R., et al. (2010). Deprivation-specific psychological patterns: Effects of institutional deprivation. *Monographs of the Society for Research in Child Development, 75*(1), 1–252.

Schmied, V., & Lupton, D. (2001b). Blurring the boundaries: Breastfeeding and maternal subjectivity. *Sociology of Health & Illness, 23*(2), 234–250.

Sevón, E. (2007). Narrating ambivalence of maternal responsibility. *Sociological Research Online, 12*(2). Retrieved from http://www.socresonline.org.uk/12/2/sevon.html

Smyth, L. (2012). *The demands of motherhood: Agents roles and recognition.* Basingstoke, England: Palgrave.

Smyth, C. (2014). Boost your preschooler's brain power! An analysis of advice to parents from an Australian government-funded website. *Women's Studies International Forum, 45*, 10–18.

Stearns, C. A. (2009). The work of breastfeeding. *Women's Studies Quarterly, 37*(2), 63–80.

Thorley, V. (2008). Breasts for hire and shared breastfeeding: Wet nursing and cross feeding in Australia, 1900–2000. *Health and History, 10*(1), 88–109.

UNICEF UK. (n.d.). *What is the baby friendly initiative?* Retrieved June 27, 2015, from http://www.unicef.org.uk/BabyFriendly/About-Baby-Friendly/What-is-the-Baby-Friendly-Initiative/

Wall, G. (2001). Moral constructions of motherhood in breastfeeding discourse. *Gender & Society, 15*(4), 592–610.

Wall, G. (2010). Mother's experiences with intensive parenting and brain development discourse. *Women's Studies International Forum, 33*(3), 253–263.

Wall, G. (2013). 'Putting family first': Shifting discourses of motherhood and childhood in representations of mothers' employment and child care. *Women's Studies International Forum, 40*, 162–171.

Wastell, D., & White, S. (2012). Blinded by neuroscience: Social policy, the family and the infant brain. *Families, Relationships and Societies, 1*(3), 397–414.

Williams, K., Donaghue, N., & Kurz, T. (2013). "Giving guilt the flick"? An investigation of mothers' talk about guilt in relation to infant feeding. *Psychology of Women Quarterly, 37*(1), 97–112.

Williamson, I., Leeming, D., Lyttle, S., & Johnson, S. (2012). 'It should be the most natural thing in the world': Exploring first-time mothers' breastfeeding difficulties in the UK using audio-diaries and interviews. *Maternal & Child Nutrition, 8*(4), 434–447.

Wolf, J. H. (2001). *Don't kill your baby: Public health and the decline of breastfeeding in the nineteenth and twentieth centuries.* Columbus, OH: Ohio State University Press.

Wolf, J. B. (2011). *Is breast best: Taking on the breastfeeding experts and the new high stakes of motherhood.* London: New York University Press.

8

Maternal Sacrifice and Choice

Throughout the book, I have illustrated how ideas about women's roles as bearers and carers who naturally put their children first are used to justify a range of different ideological frameworks, policies and practices in the area of reproductive health. Whilst women are often offered a choice, the idea of maternal sacrifice is deployed to make it clear which option is the 'right' choice. This is not to suggest that women always accept or comply with these norms; however, the framing is important as it shapes the way that rejection and acceptance can be articulated and practised. Whilst the sacrifices that women should make will vary depending on factors such as social class, ethnicity, sexuality, disability and age, the fact that they should make sacrifices is a uniting factor. The concepts of 'intensive motherhood' (Hays 1996) and 'total motherhood' (Wolf 2011) have usefully outlined the expectations on women in relation to motherhood. These concepts clearly illustrate the idea that motherhood is supposed to be all-consuming with a distinct hierarchy in which the normative expectation is that women should be the ones to change their lives, even if these changes have an adverse impact. This book has built on these concepts to illustrate how the idea of maternal sacrifice is a powerful tool in disciplining women across fertility and

© The Editor(s) (if applicable) and The Author(s) 2016
P. Lowe, *Reproductive Health and Maternal Sacrifice*,
DOI 10.1057/978-1-137-47293-9_8

motherhood issues, and how it can support diverse and ever-changing expectations of child welfare.

This chapter will illustrate the ways in which maternal sacrifice is a significant feature of the symbolic order. Women's reproductive bodies are situated, constrained and/or controlled through the appropriation of understandings about natural care for the young. This is why the rhetoric of choice in reproductive health is not on its own a sign of autonomy. Gendered social norms shape understandings of what actions and outcomes are 'best', and responsibility and risk become embodied obligations that can be difficult to challenge. The different areas of reproductive health are interwoven and we cannot fully understand perceptions and experiences of contraception without linking them right through to the valorisation of breastfeeding within child welfare policies. Moreover, it is the gendered understanding rooted in ideas about women's bodies, biologies and roles in society that underpins the wider impact on women, regardless of whether or not they are mothers. Maternal sacrifice can discipline women's bodies and behaviour in a way that it is not always easy to see or challenge through the production of norms and values. As an exercise of power, it can be subtle and often unchallenged despite the fact that the surveillance over women's lives is often explicit. This chapter will also consider how the 'norms' of reproduction, which blur pre-pregnancy, pregnancy and the time after birth, allow inequality to persist by treating women as if they were always pregnant. The majority of women care deeply about their children and will offer appropriate care and support for any children they might conceive or raise. However, as I will argue, the appropriation of this desire can unnecessarily restrict women's lives, and this takes place whether or not they are mothers.

Problematizing Choice

As I outlined earlier, Chambers (2008) has shown that having a choice is often presented within liberal thought as evidence of autonomy. If people are able to exercise choice in adopting or rejecting specific actions, then even if this should result in disadvantage, it is not unjust, as they could have chosen differently. Hence, whilst it is often important in liberalism to remove unfair discrimination, if people choose something that disadvantages them, this is unproblematic, as they did not have to make that choice. This position, as Chambers (2008) makes clear, largely ignores the social construction of norms. If we accept that that gendered norms and understandings are constructed socially rather than as the outcome of biological functions, then we need to accept that there is no *a priori* behaviour that is not shaped by the social context. Chambers (2008) uses the term 'influence' to describe the impact that gendered norms have on understandings in society. This is developed partially from Foucauldian understandings of the panopticon, in which people's behaviour is a result of the disciplinary effects of social norms. Influence does not mean that norms, such as gendered behaviour, are immutable or are not interrelated with other social processes, but it does shape the context in which some 'choices' are either generally unthinkable or not really a choice, or even why people might opt for a choice that is harmful to them. As Chambers' argues:

> A perfectly rational, freely choosing individual is constrained by the fact that she must choose from the options available to her, that are cast as appropriate for her. These options themselves may be limited; or they may violate an individual's well-being or her equality, since in order to access some benefit, the individual may be required to harm herself, and she may be required to harm herself when no such requirement is placed on other types of individuals seeking to access the benefit. (2008: 263)

For Chambers (2008), influence can be seen when individuals are under pressure to make a choice to harm themselves in order to comply with or benefit from a social norm. Harm here can be defined as anything from disadvantage to actual bodily injury. Chambers' (2008) concept of influence seeks to draw attention to the ways in which choices can be scripted and thus making a choice on its own is not enough to ascertain autonomy; we need to explain the social context.

This position can be usefully explained using the example of breastfeeding already outlined in Chap. 7. If women are expected to breastfeed, and it is suggested that this is what good mothers do, then women may choose breastfeeding even if it is not in their best interests to do this.

Breastfeeding can lead to both physical harm to women (from pain to breast abscesses) and lead to disadvantage (for example, in the restriction of movements). It can also be detrimental to babies if women are undernourished (for example, see Wagner et al. 2008 on vitamin D deficiency). Moreover rather than presenting the options of formula-feeding and breastfeeding neutrally, information is often presented to women as a moral decision rather than practical one. Either you want the 'best' for your baby and you are a 'good mother' or you are not. For first-time mothers in particular, there is clearly a 'right' answer to this question, and whilst it is possible for women to reject breastfeeding, it cannot be presumed that all women who initiate breastfeeding after childbirth have made an autonomous choice. Breastfeeding is often the first act of care after birth that a first-time mother will perform, which is likely to make it particularly difficult to refuse. Women who exercise choice in subsequently changing to bottle-feeding could be seen as being able to take autonomous action. Yet their need to defend that position indicates that this action is not completely free of the role of influence even though they have been able to action a particular choice.

Chambers (2008) argues that influence can create injustice; social norms mean that people are choosing things that are harmful. This is a structural disadvantage even when it is freely chosen. Hence to understand autonomy we need to consider not just the ability to choose but also the conditions in which the choice is offered. She points out that it may be the case that one choice does confer some benefits, but in different circumstances people would not have to make that specific choice. Choosing to breastfeed just after childbirth, for example, conveys the benefit of being positioned as a good mother, but if other options are given which convey the same status, women may not elect to breastfeed. Indeed, women who opt for or change to formula-feeding may do so because they have other options for displaying or performing the disciplinary position of good motherhood.

It is this latter argument that draws us back to the difficulties of the pervasiveness of gendered norms. Whilst it is clearly important to ensure that choices are as free of disadvantage and influence as possible, it is clearly not easy to do this given the myriad of ways in which women are subjected to disciplinary practices around motherhood. Whilst action could be taken to ensure that a particular view on feeding is not promoted, on its own it would not be sufficient to challenge the broader narrative, especially because of the ways in which motherhood is an embodied identity position. Moreover, given the hierarchy of foetus/child first and the conflation of womanhood and motherhood, the gendered norms of motherhood have a significant impact on women's lives that go beyond reasonable care for the young and place unnecessary restrictions on women's lives.

For Showden (2011), agency is a more useful concept of exploring the ways in which embodied identity positions are constrained and enabled. In a similar way to Chambers (2008), she sees traditional understandings of autonomy as too limiting to explain the ways in which structures and norms determine the capacity for action. Showden (2011) argues that whilst autonomy can be seen as self-governance, agency encompasses the social construction of the individual and group identity as well as the forces that shape their capacity to choose. For Showden (2011), identities are not fixed or singular categories but are multiple, interactive, and shaped by different times and spaces; they are always grounded by embodiment. The cultural meanings that arise through and develop from bodies, and are read and interpreted by others, are the context in which individuals can act. As she argues:

> Although biology is not destiny, it is nonetheless a relatively stable and common (shared) social construction. Embodiment provides the general framework for our interaction with the world around us, shaping our experiences and our sense of the real and the possible. (2011: 23–24)

Understanding the centrality of embodied identity in exploring the ways in which giving choices is not sufficient to ensure freedom from influence is an important addition to Chambers' (2008) argument. Showden (2011) clearly shows how the capacity to act is shaped by and through identity, which in turn is an embodied position. Showden (2011) also reminds us that there is a difference between public and private identity; they are entwined but not the same. In public, bodily markers such as ethnicity and social class position us in groups, and they can also be an important space for displaying appropriate positioning. Our private sense of self intertwines with this public positioning, but it is not identical to the way we are positioned publically.

This difference between public and private can be illustrated in an understanding of the difference between performing and being a good mother. As I outlined in Chap. 5, pregnant women are positioned as a potential risk to the foetus and, when in public, are judged on their behaviour in relation to notions of good motherhood. Drinking alcohol whilst visibly pregnant thus risks public sanction and contravenes the norms surrounding good motherhood. The pregnant body positions women as mothers who are socially required to put the foetus first, and the social norm requires a particular performance. Although women may reject that abstinence is a necessary action for good mothers, and may drink alcohol at home, they may not wish to challenge this position by drinking alcohol in public. Similarly in Chap. 7, I outlined how new mothers may be reticent to leave the house until they can be sure that they can adequately perform good motherhood. Once they feel able to give an adequate performance, they may venture out more, even if they still have not fully incorporated motherhood into their understanding of themselves.

Showden (2011) argues that, in relation to infertility, in order to increase women's agency it is necessary for a number of things to happen. First, the norm of (good) motherhood for women needs to be challenged politically. Infertility is not a personal failing and non-motherhood should not be positioned as a potentially dubious choice. Second, there needs to be more emphasis on the causes and prevention of infertility rather than the 'solution' of fertility treatments. Finally, access to fertility treatments should be distributed more equally to ensure wider access. Treatment should not be reserved just for those who are wealthy enough to pay and/or socially positioned closer to the norm of white, middle-class, heterosexual motherhood. Showden (2011) argues that it is only when all of these issues change that reproductive freedom could be achieved. However, whilst all these things are important, I am not sure they go far enough in addressing the deep-seated requirement of sacrifice that is part of the embodied identity of motherhood. Without a challenge to the way that this shapes the capacity to act, new 'norms' of motherhood requiring sacrifice will arise even if these other issues are dealt with.

The Requirement of Sacrifice

Without women's bearing of children, our families, groups and communities cease to exist. The norms and controls over women's behaviour arise from their ability to reproduce and a need to control the boundaries of this reproduction (Yuval-Davis 1980, 1997). The idea of maternal sacrifice, an often embodied requirement that appears to arise from a natural instinct to protect the young, has an important symbolic function in ensuring these social relationships are maintained. Maternal sacrifice as a symbol is used to both reassert gendered relationships and to promote a broader sense of community order. The good mother is always positioned in opposition to the other/bad/nominal mother who is a danger to the reproduction of the community. Women who fail to feel the right emotions endanger not just their developing foetus but also the moral order. Historically, maternal impression potentially led to 'monstrous' births, such as the rabbits of Mary Toft discussed earlier. Today, women's inadequacy is said to lead to a risk of antisocial families, such as the failure for proper brain development detailed in Chap. 7.

The majority of women (and men) care for children and wish to support them to grow and develop into successful adulthood. What counts as success is culturally varied, and here I am not advocating a particular process but simply claiming that it is the usual course of action for adults to support children as they develop. Although this everyday care is the work of motherhood, this does not necessarily require that it be performed by the birth mother (or even necessarily women at all) nor that the interests of any child or children be automatically positioned as the most significant factor in the relationship. The everyday practice of growing and caring for children would almost certainly persist even if maternal sacrifice as a symbolic position were eroded or eliminated. Hence the disciplining of women to act selflessly; potentially harming themselves to promote the welfare of actual or future children has come to be seen as having an important function beyond that of everyday care of the young.

Maternal sacrifice thus is both a symbolic and practical requirement of suffering and/or selflessness in which individual women 'naturally' put the needs and welfare of any existing or potential children first.

As a symbolic position it relates to the gendered position of women as 'natural' nurturers who have primary responsibility for children. In this context, it is easy to explain the slippage between pre-pregnant, pregnant and post natal states. Maternal sacrifice as a symbolic requirement helps erode consideration of the different embodied states, and it disciplines women to consider themselves as always needing to make decisions as if they were growing and/or caring for a child. It is not necessary for women to actually be pregnant or to be caring for a child to both impose and enact particular behavioural norms in which selflessness for (imagined or actual) children takes priority.

Alongside the symbolic operation, maternal sacrifice is also a demand made by others in order to further their particular concerns. Operationalizing the symbolic position is a way of trying to ensure that specific social, political or policy aims can be met. The concept of maternal sacrifice as an embodied obligation of women can thus be used to underpin positions that have very little bearing on foetal or child health. It is used to promote both abstinence and LARCs through the idea that young women should sacrifice any desire to have children until the time when they meet the current normative standards of age. As I mentioned in Chap. 3, these calls go far beyond concerns with younger teenagers becoming sexually active, with some campaigns now denigrating pregnancy in the early twenties as well. That early childbearing is more common in disadvantaged groups is clearly important here. As the norm for later childbearing in wealthier families increases, this pressure is likely to increase. Yet it is often poverty rather than the age of motherhood that restricts the lives of children and young people, and given the limited opportunities available to those living in disadvantage, the extent to which delaying childbearing would make a substantial difference is debatable (see for example SmithBattle 2012). Yet rather than recognising structural factors, some emphasize the idea of motherhood as an embodied and naturalized position. Hence a rejection of sacrifice is not just potentially deviant but also potentially undermining towards women's position more generally in the intertwining of womanhood and motherhood. In other words, women are responsible for making appropriate sacrifices in the name of motherhood, regardless of whether or not they are or intend to be mothers.

Risk, Responsibility and the Vulnerable/Foetus Child

The responsibilization of women through the operation of risk consciousness has heightened the need for women to make sacrifices. As I outlined in Chap. 2, Lee (2014) sets out four intertwined elements of risk consciousness that shape understandings of reproductive health. I would argue that maternal sacrifice is a mechanism through which each of these can operate. As the definition of harm has changed and the precautionary principle has become stronger, women are charged with making the sacrifices necessary to ensure that they maximize the welfare of the vulnerable foetus/child. This can of course be seen most strongly in the 'rules' for pregnant women, in that they are expected to abstain from various different substances and/or activities. Whilst many of these are contested, they are at least relatively straightforward to either adopt or reject. In other areas, such as childbirth, the sacrifices in the name of foetal safety are more complex to negotiate. When both medical and natural childbirth, caesarean and unassisted birth, use the prevention of harm to promote their birth ideology, it can be harder for women to understand the 'right' sacrifice that should be made. Will sacrificing a desire for a pain-free medicalized birth be better than sacrificing an aspiration for natural childbirth and accepting a caesarean? Both can be recommended in the name of protecting the vulnerable foetus/child, and it is always impossible to know if other choices would have had better outcomes. Moreover, the emphasis on birth plans, which suggests that women are health consumers who can be savvy choosers, reinforces this idea that a (good) birth is the outcome of women making the right sacrificial decisions.

The responsibilization of women means that those who choose badly, or 'fail' in the choices that they have made, have not demonstrated the appropriate responsibility to be seen as good mothers. Hence the risk is individualized in the specific decisions women make. This position also has implications for women who experience reproductive loss. If women are generally positioned as responsible and supposed to make the right sacrifices in their lives to ensure the maximization of foetal welfare, then the cultural message is that pregnancy loss is a female failure (Layne 2003).

The emphasis on women's ability to control their bodies and behaviour, with little consideration of women's own welfare, socio-economic considerations, or the uncertainty of the biological reproductive process, means that any adverse outcome can be understood as a failure of women rather than an unforeseen or uncontrollable event. Alongside this individualization, the risks are also generalized, so all women need to act in accordance to perceived health risks regardless of any adverse outcome on their own lives. This justifies the calls by some public health campaigners to have vaccination style programmes to fit LARCs in young women, even if they are not heterosexually active at the time, regardless of the side effects that they may have to endure.

Within an era of risk consciousness, failure to make the right choices over risks can also be seen as a moral failing rather than just a reproductive one. Women who do not make the required sacrifices cannot be good mothers, as good mothers will always put the welfare of the vulnerable foetus/child first. This position can be used to justify increased surveillance over women's lives, particularly those from disadvantaged backgrounds. The rise of concerns over maternal stress in both pregnancy and early-year childcare, with its focus on the minds of women, is illustrative of this point. As I outlined in Chap. 7, maternal stress is often surveyed and measured, and women are castigated for putting their children's development at risk (Edwards et al. 2015). As Edwards et al. (2015) have shown, professionals that ignore the material deprivation causes of stress and focus instead on relationships position women as the architects of their children's future poverty. The poor outcomes of these children are positioned as having nothing to do with disadvantage. Instead their mothers did not make the right sacrifices, in this instance by failing to control their emotions.

The future of the vulnerable foetus/child is thus positioned as the outcome of women's decision-making, and women are always potentially a risk to their futures. This conceptualization of maternal/foetal conflict justifies the surveillance of (disadvantaged) women and reduces attention on the more likely causes of harm, such as poverty and the role of professionals in deciding acceptable behaviour. It supports policies of putative treatment of women who are currently pregnant or may become pregnant in the future. The sterilization of drug-using women or incarceration of suicidal pregnant women can be called for because these women are not seen as capable of making the right sacrifices in the name of the foetus/child. Action should be taken not because these are vulnerable adults but because of the presumed risk they pose to any future children. This hierarchy, in which women's welfare is usually presumed as secondary to that of any foetus/child, is central to the idea of maternal sacrifice.

Whose Body?

This emphasis on women's lives being secondary can also be used to explain the justification for the blurring of the boundaries between pre-pregnancy, pregnancy and the post natal period. Understanding a woman and the foetus/child as a single unit rather than a dyad is clearly rooted in essentialist ideas such as those supported by neoconservatism (Phipps 2014). Women are often required to consider themselves as always potentially pregnant or mothering and to make bodily decisions on that basis. This is also aligned with a presumption of heterosexuality; clearly women are only 'at risk' of pregnancy if they are sexually active with men. It is from this position that current concerns about women's bodies and behaviour can move beyond the immediate issue under discussion. Once alcohol is deemed to be problematic in pregnancy, it should be avoided throughout women's fertile lives. Prior to pregnancy, this argument is supported by the risk of unplanned conception. After birth, tentative questions about the impact on breast milk can be mooted, but more generally, the underlying concern is about whether or not alcohol consumption is compatible with good motherhood. In the UK, the Department for Health clearly suggests that it is not, suggesting that abstinence, or at least very low consumption, is preferable beyond the breastfeeding period (Lowe et al. 2010).

Whilst the argument that a woman and the foetus/child can be positioned as a single unit is compelling, this does not really explain the extent to which women's bodies are overlooked in the discourses surrounding reproductive health. Increasingly the issue is not that they are a single unit but that women's position is subsumed and the only body that counts is that of the foetus. This can be clearly seen in the elevated position of the foetus in the anti-abortion debates and also in the positioning of the foetus as patient during pregnancy. As I discussed earlier, the free-floating foetus has become an iconic image, a patient whose welfare should be promoted, even at a cost to women. Constructing the foetus as potentially at risk from its mother's body or behaviour justifies intervention and is explained through ideas of maternal/foetal conflict. This conceals other interpretations, such as a conflicts between women and health professionals over appropriate behaviour for women, particularly about medical intervention during pregnancy and birth.

The rise of imaging technologies and the public foetus have recently played an important role in refocusing attention away from women. Images of pregnancy often use images of the free-floating foetus or focus on the pregnancy bump of a headless woman. This decentering of women from being central to pregnancy also takes place in medical discourse. Even the speciality name, foetal surgery, illustrates the extent to which pregnant women may be a secondary consideration. The discursive privileging of the foetus, which hides the position of women as central to the procedures, suggests again that there is a hierarchy of bodies in place. This also aligns with the anti-abortion rhetoric which downplays the considerable embodied impact of pregnancy by suggesting that adoption is always a viable alternative.

The emphasis on women's reproductive bodies, with the priority on foetal welfare, is clearly in line with traditional discriminatory ideas of gender. This fits with neoconservative views of gender and family life. Whilst family policy often refers to parents and parenting, the gender-neutral language merely disguises the embodied responsibilities of women. Parents cannot breastfeed: only women can perform this embodied work, even if they are expressing milk so it can be given later via a bottle. The current emphasis on breastfeeding, despite the widespread availability of safe alternatives in the developed world, thus reasserts women's primary role as bearers and carers. If women wish to breastfeed then they should be able to access any support they need to facilitate this, and they should be able to feed babies in public spaces. However this should equally apply to formula-feeding, and women should be allowed to make decisions over feeding, considering their own welfare and family circumstances, without being made to feel the need to explain or justify their decision.

Reproductive Work

The reproductive work of women is extensive and can be seen when they are avoiding conception, trying to conceive, pregnant, or raising children. Although reproductive work is often considered private and rooted in ideas about family life, the positioning of women as reproducers of the collective means that there is always a wider interest in their bodies. Understanding reproductive health as women's work in which they are both producers and consumers helps to reveal the different ways in which women's lives are disciplined. The mother-worker positioning of women who are pregnant in surrogacy arrangements (Pande 2014) and accounts of women trying to balance their lives in the workplace (Gatrell 2008) both illustrate how reproductive labour and paid work intersect in complex ways and how women are expected to be both good workers and good mothers for the benefit of others. These requirements may include having to perform emotional work on themselves rather than just performing the specific roles needed. Good mother-workers will feel the right emotions rather than just physically undertaking the reproductive work required of them.

The metaphors of work and economics used to explain the 'production' of children are not a new phenomenon. Martin (1987) illustrated how machine explanations for the body, with the doctor as the technician who fixes it, were common in medical textbooks. Alongside this were explanations of menstruation as 'failed' production. She argues that any 'lack' of production is seen as problematic within capitalist societies, as it signals a breakdown from efficiency. Moreover, as the female reproductive cycle usually produces only a single egg, in contrast to the more active male production of sperm, this suggests women's position as potentially unproductive. Martin (1987) argues that the cultural metaphors used to explain science and medicine are important, as this helps to construct understandings and practice. The positioning of women's bodies as unproductive and/or machines in need of assistance justifies interventions to improve the productivity of the mother-worker.

Women as producers are thus charged with ensuring the best outcome of pregnancy. They should discipline their minds and bodies to ensure the best outcome for the foetus/child. The work expected of women includes accepting the responsibility for the prevention of pregnancy if they are not deemed to be suitable candidates. It may also encompass paying for fertility treatments should conception not happen when it is desired. A key part of reproductive labour is ensuring that steps are taken to eliminate risks. Moreover, the risks that are highlighted are clearly in line with broader gender norms. Thus refusing alcohol or travelling in new cars is a risk that women need to consider seriously, whereas banning a non-violent male partner from the house, as pregnancy is a risk period for the onset of domestic violence, is not. The latter of course is an unwarranted extreme action, and it is unlikely that anyone would seriously suggest that we should consider this. However, the fact that the zero-tolerance approach to risk is only advocated when the risk requires female reproductive work is not insignificant.

The positioning of women as mother-workers encompasses both neoliberal and neoconservative ideologies. Within neoliberalism, the individualized mother-worker needs to be a flexible, savvy consumer making the right choices for the care of her foetus/child. Her individualized responsibility for ensuring the effective 'production' of pregnancy involves managing the optimization of the prevention, conception, birth and development of the new generation of workers. Ideally these will need the minimum of state intervention, which is why women need to be disciplined to prevent the biological transmission of any undesired traits. The mechanisms by which women can be disciplined into efficient production are through a neoconservative emphasis on women's natural role as good mothers who make sacrifices for their children. Hence the disciplining of women through discourses of maternal sacrifice draws on both ideological frameworks.

Good Motherhood and Maternal Sacrifice

Many writers have identified the importance of the idea of good motherhood, and this includes ideas about selflessness and sacrifice. Good motherhood clearly works as a practice that can be adapted to fit different ideological positions and changing social, cultural and policy frameworks. In other words, whilst it continues to be important for women to be good mothers, the actual performance required to attain this position is not fixed. The shifts and turns in the varying requirements for good motherhood have been captured previously. As I outlined earlier, Hays (1996) documented the shift towards intensive motherhood and Wolf (2011) argues that total motherhood is a more useful category to explain the more recent norms of motherhood performance. This book has sought to build on this but has attempted to highlight one particularly important area, which is the bedrock on which the different interpretations of good motherhood are built. The symbolic position of maternal sacrifice is constant, even when other norms and issues change.

It is important to understanding the connections between the different areas of reproductive health as it sheds new light on how the ideas of responsibility and choice are used to discipline women into making the right sacrifices. As I outlined in Chap. 3, throughout the history of birth control, there has always been an emphasis on concerns about 'unrespectable' women, and a debate as to whether birth control encouraged sexual activity or prevented an undesirable conception. Women's behaviour and concerns about inappropriate motherhood have framed these debates since the early nineteenth century and are now played out in the different positions of abstinence and LARCs. Both agree on the undesirability of young women becoming mothers and require women to make sacrifices to ensure appropriate conception. The choices being promoted are either to accept sexual abstinence or to delay motherhood by using LARCs regardless of any embodied impact. Both positions use the rhetoric of choice, the responsibilization of women, and the need for women to consider the welfare of any future foetus. The sacrifice called for is to postpone motherhood until the required social position arrives, whether this is marriage, age or economic security. In the case of LARCs, this can include accepting any harmful consequences or side-effects in order to be positioned as a responsible chooser of contraception willing to make the required sacrifices for the benefit of future generations.

The positioning of some women as 'undesirable' mothers whose responsibility it is to avoid conception is embedded in medical discourses, although ironically, as Fairhurst et al. (2005) found, this can mean that women are judged to be so chaotic that they are not to be trusted with advanced supplies of EHC. The positioning of women as responsible for birth control, and any contraceptive failures, is linked to wider gender norms. This shapes both the choices that women feel that they should make and how they are positioned by others, such as health professionals. Unplanned pregnancies are often deemed to be women's failure, particularly in women who are positioned as undesirable mothers. Women who continue pregnancies in adverse circumstances may be positioned as irresponsible by others, but unplanned or difficult pregnancies can also strengthen women's embodied identity position as good mothers who will do their utmost to ensure that they puts the needs of their children first.

Linked to these ideas about birth control are the different frames of abortion. The three positions of health, women's reproductive rights, and foetal rights all draw on ideas of women's responsibility and a requirement of sacrifice. In the health frame, the medicalization of abortion positions women as incapable of taking responsibility. Doctors, or healthcare regulations, are required to protect women from harm. Women, by failing to prevent pregnancy, are positioned as irresponsible choosers who cannot be trusted, so others need to make the decisions in their best interests. The promotion of LARCs to women presenting for abortion, and the push for TRAP laws to restrict abortion, are examples of this trend and illustrate how both anti-abortion and abortion rights advocates often draw on the same cultural ideas about motherhood.

Whilst nominally the reproductive rights framing of abortion supports women's autonomous decisions, the emphasis on abortion as a regrettable, if necessary decision shows that this frame is also drawing on ideas of women as responsible mothers. Here women are able to freely choose abortion but do so in the context of the women making the 'right choices.' Hence although this does allow women to exercise agency, positioning abortion as necessary but promoting it as desirable only in 'rare' circumstances reinforces the notions of 'good' and 'bad' abortions. Women seeking the former may be making the right sacrifice whereas women who have 'bad' abortions have failed to be responsible. The sacrifice demanded in the foetal rights frame is that women should continue with their pregnancy regardless of the impact on themselves. Pregnancy is thus a penance for either illicit sexual activity and/or a failure to prevent conception. If women are deemed unfit to parent, then the sacrifice they should make is to give up their child for adoption.

The complex intertwining of motherhood and womanhood continues for those who may experience trouble conceiving. The pronatalist stance of many communities and nations can be the influence by which women without children can be considered to have failed to perform proper womanhood. Positioning women without children as selfish is also a reminder of the gender norms of reproduction. Women should be prepared to make any sacrifice to conceive, providing obviously that they have the potential to be good mothers. The metaphor of the biological clock ticking down the time for conception, and the portrayal of women who ignore it as gambling with their fertility, further support the responsibilization of women. Women who are positioned as choosing to delay childbirth for 'selfish' reasons are thus held responsible for any biological failures. Individual women may never see (future) motherhood as part of their identity, yet regardless of their intention to avoid or become mothers, the idea that women need to be selflessly devoted to their children can be seen in the narratives of both those who desire or do not want children.

Undergoing fertility treatment can be experienced not necessarily as a choice but as a necessary, arduous quest in which the right sacrifices for motherhood can be demonstrated. The different descriptions of treatment amongst those who seek to conceive themselves and those who are contracted to provide eggs or wombs further illustrate the powerful narratives. Although the emphasis on biological connectedness remains important, the shifts between gametes, gestation and intention as markers of 'true' motherhood illustrate the flexibility of identity in practice, even if it is not necessarily seen like this in wider discourses. Yet in all areas sacrifice remains an important element. Women seeking motherhood can be measured through the hardships of time, effort and money devoted to ensuring conception, whereas those offering eggs or womb need to enact enough care that this is not positioned as baby-selling yet not so much concern that they usurp the position of the commissioning mother. This reproductive labour can include body mapping, in which the temporary-carer status of women acting as surrogates displaces their pregnant bellies from their own identities. This sacrifice both confirms their position as good women and reaffirms the status of the real mother. Moreover, the accounts of women who have experienced reproductive loss reinforce the notion that it is social desire and investment rather the biological experiences that construct understandings of conception, relinquishment and loss. Within the social positioning to be or become a good mother, self-discipline and selfishness are required as the border between pre-pregnancy and pregnancy is blurred.

The emphasis on planning pregnancy is important both to ensure that potential 'bad' mothers do not have children and to enable women to maximize foetal welfare by restricting their lives before they become pregnant. As Waggoner (2013) argues, 'anticipatory motherhood' can lead to significant restrictions on women's lives, but these can be justified through the idea of maternal sacrifice. The only 'reasonable' choice that can be made is to conform to pregnancy rules, as to deviate from this undermines women's position as good mothers. This is particularly true for visibly pregnant women whose behaviour is often surveyed in public spaces. The growing lists of restrictions are often presented as a choice, but the choice is presented as 'taking a risk' or being a good mother and protecting your foetus. The lack of evidence needed to promote something as potentially harmful reinforces women's position as both less important than the developing foetus and having responsibility for any adverse outcome. The individualization and responsibilization of pregnant women for the health and welfare of the developing foetus ignore both structural issues, such as poverty, and the idea that women have independent lives. It is not just pleasures such as alcohol that women need to relinquish; they should consider eliminating anything designated as a risk regardless of the impact on their lives. The emphasis on the dangers of maternal stress also means that women are required to monitor and feel the right emotions alongside other reproductive work.

The emphasis on the foetus as primary patient has been heightened by the use of imaging technologies that have decentered women as the primary concern of health professionals during pregnancy. Whilst presented as a choice, the routinization of prenatal screening and diagnostic procedures has fundamentally changed women's experiences. Whilst women can and do understand the technological encounters in different ways, the emphasis is no longer on the thoughts, feelings and experiences of women. Good mothers are expected to maximize foetal wellbeing and be selflessly devoted to their children, but they are also charged with reducing or eliminating 'suffering.' The potential clash between these frames in relation to the diagnosis of foetal anomalies can put women in a difficult position. Whilst a sacrifice is always called for, this could be either to care for a child with disabilities or to relinquish a wanted pregnancy.

The responsibilization of women to make the 'right' choice is also seen in the area of birth. Here competing positions both utilize ideas of good motherhood in calling for women to make the right sacrifice. Both those who advocate for medicalized birth and those who support natural childbirth argue that their position is the right choice for women to maximize the welfare of their foetus/child. The focus on safety, in an era of risk consciousness, frames women as responsible for adverse outcomes in a similar way to how the precautionary principle is applied to pregnancy. The focus on the birth plan as a way for women to exercise choice simultaneously underestimates the level of control that women are able to exercise and makes them responsible for failing to do so. Even those who advocate unassisted birth, which at one level could be seen as being free from structural constraints, use ideas of maternal sacrifice to justify their position. They reject the claims of selfishness and instead see themselves as responsible choosers who seek to protect their foetus/child from the iatrogenic impact of medicine. Regardless of which ideology of birth women subscribe to, what is important is that women make the right choices, be responsible for outcomes, and sacrifice their own preferences in order to ensure that the birth is the best that could be achieved. Again, whilst women may accept or reject specific birth ideologies, the way they use the same frame to justify their positions illustrates its symbolic importance.

The erosion of the separation between the pregnancy and postnatal periods ensures that women's gendered position as bearers and carers does not come into question. The moral imperative to breastfeed, despite safe alternatives, is a good example of the way that choices are shaped and promoted in specific ways. Breastfeeding information, like pregnancy advice, is presented so that women either have to opt to breastfeed or defend their reasons for bottle-feeding in order to maintain their identity position as good mothers. Disguised in the rhetoric of informed choice, education programmes such as the BFI are clear about the only 'good' option to choose. The fact that breastfeeding requires significant amounts of women's work can be ignored, as it is presented as a necessary sacrifice. The new emphasis on babies' brains also links the pregnancy and postnatal periods with its emphasis on the bodies and behaviour of women. Women are physically and emotionally required to perform good motherhood, working on themselves to ensure that they maximize their child's development. The endless and selfless devotion required of women within intensive motherhood often goes beyond what is necessary to ensure the welfare of children. In other words, it is maternal sacrifice that is the key component of good motherhood, and the need for sacrifice remains. What women need to do to be good mothers changes over time, but the need for them to make sacrifices is a constant feature.

Maternal sacrifice provides the normative framework within which women's reproductive behaviour is situated. At its heart is the notion that nothing is more important than maximising the wellbeing of children. The idea is symbolic in that it idealizes the selflessness and suffering of women beyond what is necessary to ensure foetal/child welfare. It is also transformative in that it reaffirms women's position in the social order and the position of their children's place within specific social hierarchies. In today's neoliberal and neoconservative ideologies, the sacrifices that are called for are often presented as choices, but autonomy is limited by the influence of the maternal sacrifice framing. This means that women may be pressurized into making choices that are harmful or justifying their rejection of a particular decision. The disciplinary influence of sacrifice embedded in understandings of good motherhood has an impact on women's embodied identity position. The performance of sacrifice can transform women from a potentially 'othered' position to that of a good mother, and any lack of sacrifice can suggest moral transgression or a need for vindication in women otherwise positioned as respectable. Despite the formal pronouncements of choice, women's reproductive lives are still bound by idealized notions of responsibility, and the ideological use of maternal sacrifice is used to justify positions that undermine women's autonomy.

References

Chambers, C. (2008). *Sex, culture, and justice: The limits of choice.* University Park, PA: Pennsylvania State University Press.

Edwards, R., Gillies, V., & Horsley, N. (2015). Brain science and early years policy: Hopeful ethos or 'cruel optimism'? *Critical Social Policy, 35*(2), 167–187.

Fairhurst, K., Wyke, S., Ziebland, S., Seaman, P., & Glasier, A. (2005). "Not that sort of practice": The views and behaviour of primary care practitioners in a study of advance provision of emergency contraception. *Family Practice, 22*(3), 280–286.

Gatrell, C. (2008). *Embodying women's work.* Maidenhead, England: Open University Press.

Hays, S. (1996). *The cultural contradictions of motherhood.* New Haven, CT: Yale University Press.

Layne, L. L. (2003). *Motherhood lost: A feminist account of pregnancy loss in America.* London: Routledge.

Lee, E. (2014). Introduction. In E. Lee, J. Bristow, C. Faircloth, & J. Macvarish (Eds.), *Parenting culture studies* (pp. 1–24). Basingstoke, England: Palgrave Macmillan.

Lowe, P., Lee, E., & Yardley, L. (2010). Under the influence? The construction of foetal alcohol syndrome in UK newspapers. *Sociological Research Online, 15*(4), 2.

Martin, E. (1987). *The woman in the body.* Buckingham, England: Open University Press.

Pande, A. (2014). *Wombs in labour: Transnational commercial surrogacy in India.* New York: Columbia University Press.

Phipps, A. (2014). *The politics of the body.* Cambridge, England: Polity Press.

Showden, C. R. (2011). *Choices women make: Agency in domestic violence, assisted reproduction, and sex work.* London: University of Minnesota Press.

SmithBattle, L. (2012). Moving policies upstream to mitigate the social determinants of early childbearing. *Public Health Nursing, 29*(5), 444–454.

Waggoner, M. R. (2013). Motherhood preconceived: The emergence of the preconception health and health care initiative. *Journal of Health Politics, Policy and Law, 38*(2), 345–371.

Wagner, C. L., Taylor, S. N., & Hollis, B. W. (2008). Does vitamin D make the world go 'round'? *Breastfeeding Medicine, 3*(4), 239–250.

Wolf, J. B. (2011). *Is breast best: Taking on the breastfeeding experts and the new high stakes of motherhood.* London: New York University Press.

Yuval-Davis, N. (1980). The bearers of the collective: Women and religious legislation in Israel. *Feminist Review, 4*(1), 15–27.

Yuval-Davis, N. (1997). *Gender and nation.* London: Sage.

Index

Printed by Printforce, the Netherlands